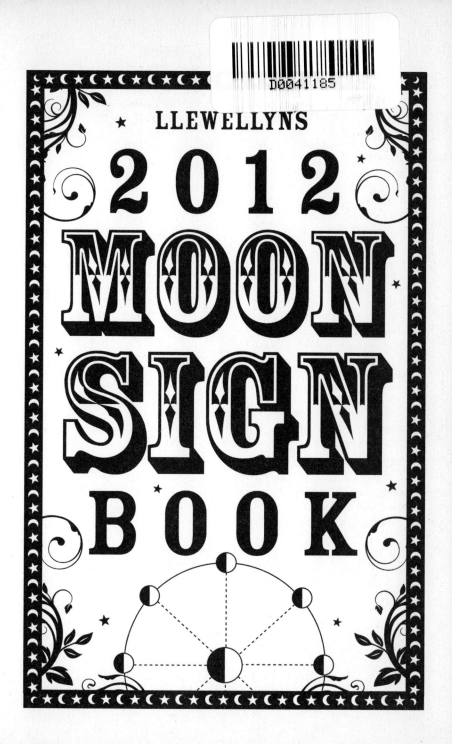

LLEWELLYNS

2012
MOON
SIGN
BOOK

Llewellyn's 2012 Moon Sign Book®

ISBN 978-0-7387-1208-6

Cover Design: Kevin R. Brown
Cover Illustrations: Floral elements: iStockphoto.com/Heidi Kristensen;
  Moon: iStockphoto.com/Magnilion
Editor: Nicole Edman
Designer: Sharon Leah
Stock photography models used for illustrative purposes only and may not endorse or represent the book's subject.

Any Internet references contained in this work are current at publication time, but the publisher cannot guarantee that a specific location will continue to be maintained.

Astrological data compiled and programmed by Rique Pottenger. Based on the earlier work of Neil F. Michelsen.

You can order Llewellyn annuals and books from *New Worlds*, Llewellyn's catalog. To request a free copy of the catalog, call toll-free 1-877-NEW-WRLD, or visit our Web site at www.llewellyn.com.

Llewellyn Worldwide Ltd.
2143 Wooddale Drive
Woodbury, MN 55125-3989
www.llewellyn.com

Table of Contents

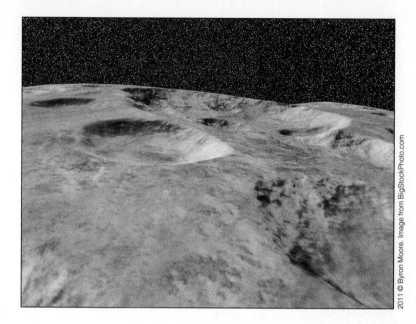

What's Different About the Moon Sign Book?

R eaders have asked why *Llewellyn's Moon Sign Book* says that the
Moon is in Taurus when some almanacs indicate that the Moon
is in the previous sign of Aries on the same date. It's because there are
two different zodiac systems in use today: the tropical and the sidereal. *Llewellyn's Moon Sign Book* is based on the tropical zodiac.

The tropical zodiac takes 0 degrees of Aries to be the Spring Equinox in the Northern Hemisphere. This is the time and date when the
Sun is directly overhead at noon along the equator, usually about
March 20–21. The rest of the signs are positioned at 30-degree inter-
vals from this point.

The sidereal zodiac, which is based on the location of fixed stars,
uses the positions of the fixed stars to determine the starting point of

0 degrees of Aries. In the sidereal system, 0 degrees of Aries always begins at the same point. This does create a problem though, because the positions of the fixed stars, as seen from Earth, have changed since the constellations were named. The term "precession of the equinoxes" is used to describe the change.

Precession of the equinoxes describes an astronomical phenomenon brought about by the Earth's wobble as it rotates and orbits the Sun. The Earth's axis is inclined toward the Sun at an angle of about 23½ degrees, which creates our seasonal weather changes. Although the change is slight, because one complete circle of the Earth's axis takes 25,800 years to complete, we can actually see that the positions of the fixed stars seem to shift. The result is that each year, in the tropical system, the Spring Equinox occurs at a slightly different time.

Does Precession Matter?

There is an accumulative difference of about 23 degrees between the Spring Equinox (0 degrees Aries in the tropical zodiac and 0 degrees Aries in the sidereal zodiac) so that 0 degrees Aries at Spring Equinox in the tropical zodiac actually occurs at about 7 degrees Pisces in the sidereal zodiac system. You can readily see that those who use the other almanacs may be planting seeds (in the garden and in their individual lives) based on the belief that it is occurring in a fruitful sign, such as Taurus, when in fact it would be occurring in Gemini, one of the most barren signs of the zodiac. So, if you wish to plant and plan activities by the Moon, it is helpful to follow *Llewellyn's Moon Sign Book*. Before we go on, there are important things to understand about the Moon, her cycles, and their correlation with everyday living. For more information about gardening by the Moon, see page 61.

Weekly Almanac

Your Guide to Lunar Gardening & Good Timing for Activities

Grow what you love. The love will keep it growing.
~Emilie Barnes

January

January 1–7

We first make our habits, and then our habits make us.

~JOHN DRYDEN

Date	Qtr.	Sign	Activity
Jan 2, 5:16 pm– Jan 5, 5:44 am	2nd	Taurus	Plant annuals for hardiness. Trim to increase growth.
Jan 7, 4:05 pm– Jan 9, 2:30 am	2nd	Cancer	Plant grains, leafy annuals. Fertilize (chemical). Graft or bud plants. Irrigate. Trim to increase growth.

Save your poinsettia plants by placing them in a sunny window in a cooler area of your home and reduce watering until spring. The leaves from a pointsettia are not poisonous, but they are toxic and should be kept away from small children and pets. In April or May, cut the plants back to about 6 inches and repot in slightly larger pots. New shoots will develop soon after you resume watering.

January 1
1:15 am EST

JANUARY

S	M	T	W	T	F	S
1	2	3	4	5	6	7
8	9	10	11	12	13	14
15	16	17	18	19	20	21
22	23	24	25	26	27	28
29	30	31				

January 8–14 ♑

I think a life in music is a life beautifully spent and this is what I have devoted my life to.

~Luciano Pavaratti

Date	Qtr.	Sign	Activity
Jan 7, 4:05 pm– Jan 9, 2:30 am	2nd	Cancer	Plant grains, leafy annuals. Fertilize (chemical). Graft or bud plants. Irrigate. Trim to increase growth.
Jan 9, 2:30 am– Jan 9, 11:35 pm	3rd	Cancer	Plant biennials, perennials, bulbs and roots. Prune. Irrigate. Fertilize (organic).
Jan 9, 11:35 pm– Jan 12, 4:44 am	3rd	Leo	Cultivate. Destroy weeds and pests. Harvest fruits and root crops for food. Trim to retard growth.
Jan 12, 4:44 am– Jan 14, 8:28 am	3rd	Virgo	Cultivate, especially medicinal plants. Destroy weeds and pests. Trim to retard growth.

Fend off January's cold weather and give your immune system a boost with a ginger-apple-thyme herbal tea infusion. Place slices of apple and ginger along with a sprig of fresh thyme in a French press and add hot water. Steep 10 minutes and press down the strainer. Pour the tea into your favorite cup and enjoy! This aromatic beverage will be a hit with guests, too.

2011 © Dana Bartekoske. Image from BigStockPhoto.com

○

January 9
2:30 am EST

JANUARY

S	M	T	W	T	F	S
1	2	3	4	5	6	7
8	9	10	11	12	13	14
15	16	17	18	19	20	21
22	23	24	25	26	27	28
29	30	31				

♑ January 15–21

Life isn't about finding yourself, it's about creating yourself.

~George Bernard Shaw

Date	Qtr.	Sign	Activity
Jan 16, 11:33 am– Jan 18, 2:29 pm	4th	Scorpio	Plant biennials, perennials, bulbs and roots. Prune. Irrigate. Fertilize (organic).
Jan 18, 2:29 pm– Jan 20, 5:40 pm	4th	Sagittarius	Cultivate. Destroy weeds and pests. Harvest fruits and root crops for food. Trim to retard growth.
Jan 20, 5:40 pm– Jan 22, 9:53 pm	4th	Capricorn	Plant potatoes and tubers. Trim to retard growth.

Here's a surprise tip for cold-climate gardeners: There are several types of banana trees, including the Musa Basjoo, that are hardy to -20°F. Order the banana tree plant from a reliable nursery in the spring. When it's warm enough outside, choose a sunny spot that has well-drained soil and plant according to directions. Once a banana tree is established, it is a tough, hardy plant that can survive in four seasons of weather.

_____

_____

_____

_____

◑
January 16
4:08 am EST

January

S	M	T	W	T	F	S
1	2	3	4	5	6	7
8	9	10	11	12	13	14
15	16	17	18	19	20	21
22	23	24	25	26	27	28
29	30	31				

2011 © John Reinhard. Image from BigStockPhoto.com

January 22–28 〜〜〜

A room without books is like a body without a soul.

~Cicero

Date	Qtr.	Sign	Activity
Jan 20, 5:40 pm– Jan 22, 9:53 pm	4th	Capricorn	Plant potatoes and tubers. Trim to retard growth.
Jan 22, 9:53 pm– Jan 23, 2:39 am	4th	Aquarius	Cultivate. Destroy weeds and pests. Harvest fruits and root crops for food. Trim to retard growth.
Jan 25, 4:11 am– Jan 27, 1:28 pm	1st	Pisces	Plant grains, leafy annuals. Fertilize (chemical). Graft or bud plants. Irrigate. Trim to increase growth.

B anana trees are actually large perennial herbs. If you want this plant to thrive in your yard, some planning will ensure better results. Choose a variety that is suitable for the zone where you live and plant in a location that gets lots of sunlight. Twelve hours of sunshine a day is optimal. Unless you buy a dwarf variety, these plants have the potential to become quite tall, so consider using them to provide structure and form to your garden area.

2011 © Aravind Teki. Image from BigStockPhoto.com

●

January 23
2:39 am EST

		JANUARY				
S	M	T	W	T	F	S
1	2	3	4	5	6	7
8	9	10	11	12	13	14
15	16	17	18	19	20	21
22	23	24	25	26	27	28
29	30	31				

〰〰 February

January 29–February 4

Life is a banquet, and most poor suckers are starving to death.

～Auntie Mame

Date	Qtr.	Sign	Activity
Jan 30, 1:28 am– Jan 30, 11:10 pm	1st	Taurus	Plant annuals for hardiness. Trim to increase growth.
Jan 30, 11:10 pm– Feb 1, 2:14 pm	2nd	Taurus	Plant annuals for hardiness. Trim to increase growth.
Feb 4, 1:04 am– Feb 6, 8:24 am	2nd	Cancer	Plant grains, leafy annuals. Fertilize (chemical). Graft or bud plants. Irrigate. Trim to increase growth.

Plan now the garden work you will do in the spring. Make a note of areas where water collects in your garden and make changes by adding drainage or amending soil when the weather warms. Sketch an outline of your garden, select plants to fill in empty spots, and order them. Seed pansies and geraniums for planting in April and May.

◑

January 30
11:10 pm EST

FEBRUARY

S	M	T	W	T	F	S
				1	2	3	4
5	6	7	8	9	10	11
12	13	14	15	16	17	18
19	20	21	22	23	24	25
26	27	28	29			

February 5–11 〰

Beauty rubs off. You cannot stand face-to-face with a
Rembrandt and walk away the same person.

~VICTORIA MORAN

Date	Qtr.	Sign	Activity
Feb 4, 1:04 am–Feb 6, 8:24 am	2nd	Cancer	Plant grains, leafy annuals. Fertilize (chemical). Graft or bud plants. Irrigate. Trim to increase growth.
Feb 7, 4:54 pm–Feb 8, 12:32 pm	3rd	Leo	Cultivate. Destroy weeds and pests. Harvest fruits and root crops for food. Trim to retard growth.
Feb 8, 12:32 pm–Feb 10, 2:54	3rd	Virgo	Cultivate, especially medicinal plants. Destroy weeds and pests. Trim to retard growth.

When you plant a crop, mark its expected maturity date in the *Moon Sign Book*. The actual date something matures can vary, depending on weather conditions, but having this little reminder can help you plan ahead and manage your workload when it's time to harvest.

○
February 7
4:54 pm EST

FEBRUARY

S	M	T	W	T	F	S
			1	2	3	4
5	6	7	8	9	10	11
12	13	14	15	16	17	18
19	20	21	22	23	24	25
26	27	28	29			

〰〰 February 12–18

Regard the moon / La lune ne garde aucune rancune.
"The moon does not keep any resentment."

~George Eliot

Date	Qtr.	Sign	Activity
Feb 12, 5:01 pm– Feb 14, 12:04 pm	3rd	Scorpio	Plant biennials, perennials, bulbs and roots. Prune. Irrigate. Fertilize (organic).
Feb 14, 12:04 pm– Feb 14, 7:56 pm	4th	Scorpio	Plant biennials, perennials, bulbs and roots. Prune. Irrigate. Fertilize (organic).
Feb 14, 7:56 pm– Feb 17, 12:03 am	4th	Sagittarius	Cultivate. Destroy weeds and pests. Harvest fruits and root crops for food. Trim to retard growth.
Feb 17, 12:03 am– Feb 19, 5:28 am	4th	Capricorn	Plant potatoes and tubers. Trim to retard growth.

When your houseplants begin to show signs of new growth, it's time to start feeding them again. While using an organic fertilizer is recommended, synthetic fertilizers are often the best choice for indoor plants. If you do decide to use an organic product, fish emulsion, which is a complete fertilizer, is recommended. If mold appears on the soil's surface, it is harmless to the plant.

◑
February 14
12:04 pm EST

February

S	M	T	W	T	F	S
			1	2	3	4
5	6	7	8	9	10	11
12	13	14	15	16	17	18
19	20	21	22	23	24	25
26	27	28	29			

2011 © Vasiliy Yakobchuk. Image from BigStockPhoto.com

February 19–25 🦋

*Labour to keep alive in your breast that little spark of
celestial fire, called conscience.*

~GEORGE WASHINGTON

Date	Qtr.	Sign	Activity
Feb 17, 12:03 am– Feb 19, 5:28 am	4th	Capricorn	Plant potatoes and tubers. Trim to retard growth.
Feb 19, 5:28 am– Feb 21, 12:31 pm	4th	Aquarius	Cultivate. Destroy weeds and pests. Harvest fruits and root crops for food. Trim to retard growth.
Feb 21, 12:31 pm– Feb 21, 5:35 pm	4th	Pisces	Plant biennials, perennials, bulbs and roots. Prune. Irrigate. Fertilize (organic).
Feb 21, 5:35 pm– Feb 23, 9:48 pm	1st	Pisces	Plant grains, leafy annuals. Fertilize (chemical). Graft or bud plants. Irrigate. Trim to increase growth.

If it is warm enough where you live to work in the garden now, woody canes can be removed from roses and healthy canes can be cut back by about one-third. Do this early in the week. Fertilize around lilacs and strawberries before the New Moon. Dispose of old chemicals after consulting with local authorities about proper disposal.

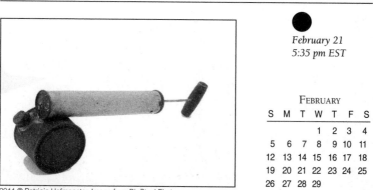

⚫

February 21
5:35 pm EST

FEBRUARY

S	M	T	W	T	F	S
			1	2	3	4
5	6	7	8	9	10	11
12	13	14	15	16	17	18
19	20	21	22	23	24	25
26	27	28	29			

March

February 26–March 3

Hold fast to dreams, for if dreams die, life is a broken winged bird that cannot fly.   ~LANGSTON HUGHES

Date	Qtr.	Sign	Activity
Feb 26, 9:29 am–Feb 28, 10:27 pm	1st	Taurus	Plant annuals for hardiness. Trim to increase growth.
Mar 2, 10:08 am–Mar 4, 6:17 pm	2nd	Cancer	Plant grains, leafy annuals. Fertilize (chemical). Graft or bud plants. Irrigate. Trim to increase growth.

A hummingbird uses nectar to fuel its fast metabolism and relies on insects for food. These birds don't migrate in flocks. They are, instead, solitary birds that travel alone and may appear in your area at any time. If you do feed them, use a mixture of one part white cane sugar to four parts water. It is not necessary to boil the water, and do NOT use honey, fruit, Jello, brown sugar, or red food coloring. These things will ferment in the water and can kill hummingbirds. Unused syrup can be stored for up to two weeks in the refrigerator.

February 29
8:21 pm EST

S	M	T	W	T	F	S
				1	2	3
4	5	6	7	8	9	10
11	12	13	14	15	16	17
18	19	20	21	22	23	24
25	26	27	28	29	30	31

MARCH

2011 © Steve Byland. Image from BigStockPhoto.com

March 4–10 ✿

The winter is like a guest who lingers—Having said goodbye for days, She squeezes our hands with icy fingers, Then sits down and stays and stays and stays.

~ANITA McLEAN WASHINGTON

Date	Qtr.	Sign	Activity
Mar 2, 10:08 am–Mar 4, 6:17 pm	2nd	Cancer	Plant grains, leafy annuals. Fertilize (chemical). Graft or bud plants. Irrigate. Trim to increase growth.
Mar 8, 4:39 am–Mar 8, 11:50 pm	3rd	Virgo	Cultivate, especially medicinal plants. Destroy weeds and pests. Trim to retard growth.

When you buy houseplants, avoid those that have roots coming out of drainage holes in the pots. Also avoid large plants that are in small pots, because their root systems may be inadequate. When buying pots for your new houseplants, some rules of thumb are:

• Use simple pots with decorative plants.

• A plant shouldn't be more than twice as high and one and a half times as wide as its pot.

2011 © Olga van de Veer. Image from BigStockPhoto.com

○
March 8
4:39 am EST

MARCH

S	M	T	W	T	F	S
				1	2	3
4	5	6	7	8	9	10
11	12	13	14	15	16	17
18	19	20	21	22	23	24
25	26	27	28	29	30	31

March 11–17

You were born with wings. Why prefer to crawl through life?

~Jalal al-Din Muhammad Rumi

Date	Qtr.	Sign	Activity
Mar 11, 12:24 am– Mar 13, 2:54 am	3rd	Scorpio	Plant biennials, perennials, bulbs and roots. Prune. Irrigate. Fertilize (organic).
Mar 13, 2:54 am– Mar 14, 9:25 pm	3rd	Sagittarius	Cultivate. Destroy weeds and pests. Harvest fruits and root crops for food. Trim to retard growth.
Mar 14, 9:25 pm– Mar 15, 6:24 am	4th	Sagittarius	Cultivate. Destroy weeds and pests. Harvest fruits and root crops for food. Trim to retard growth.
Mar 15, 6:24 am– Mar 17, 12:11 pm	4th	Capricorn	Plant potatoes and tubers. Trim to retard growth.
Mar 17, 12:11 pm– Mar 19, 8:05 pm	4th	Aquarius	Cultivate. Destroy weeds and pests. Harvest fruits and root crops for food. Trim to retard growth.

Some insects rely on their sense of smell to find a food source. Others use color to target their food source. Aphids, whiteflies, cucumber beetles, cabbage-root flies, and cabbage worms are attracted to yellowish colors, for example. You can fool insects by choosing an off-color variety of their favorite food. With good care and regular watering, you can also encourage your plants to be healthy and resistant to insect attacks.

◐

March 14
9:25 pm EDT
Daylight Saving Time begins
March 11, 2:00 am

MARCH

S	M	T	W	T	F	S
				1	2	3
4	5	6	7	8	9	10
11	12	13	14	15	16	17
18	19	20	21	22	23	24
25	26	27	28	29	30	31

March 18–24 ✄

Knowledge comes, but wisdom lingers.

~ALFRED, LORD TENNYSON

Date	Qtr.	Sign	Activity
Mar 17, 12:11 pm– Mar 19, 8:05 pm	4th	Aquarius	Cultivate. Destroy weeds and pests. Harvest fruits and root crops for food. Trim to retard growth.
Mar 19, 8:05 pm– Mar 22, 5:57 am	4th	Pisces	Plant biennials, perennials, bulbs and roots. Prune. Irrigate. Fertilize (organic).
Mar 22, 5:57 am– Mar 22, 10:37 am	4th	Aries	Cultivate. Destroy weeds and pests. Harvest fruits and root crops for food. Trim to retard growth.
Mar 24, 5:43 pm– Mar 27, 6:43 am	1st	Taurus	Plant annuals for hardiness. Trim to increase growth.

I t's time to trim away storm- and winter-damaged tree branches. Cut them off as close as possible to the main branch. Trim dormant deciduous trees before leaf buds swell. Feed the deciduous trees with a complete fertilizer (one with nitrogen, phosphorus, and potassium). Watch fruit trees for signs of aphids that like new spring growth.

_____

_____

_____

_____

●

March 22
10:37 am EDT

MARCH

S	M	T	W	T	F	S
				1	2	3
4	5	6	7	8	9	10
11	12	13	14	15	16	17
18	19	20	21	22	23	24
25	26	27	28	29	30	31

♈ March 25–31

I find that a great part of the information I have was acquired by looking up something and finding something else on the way.

~Franklin Pierce Adams

Date	Qtr.	Sign	Activity
Mar 24, 5:43 pm– Mar 27, 6:43 am	1st	Taurus	Plant annuals for hardiness. Trim to increase growth.
Mar 29, 7:07 pm– Mar 30, 3:41 pm	1st	Cancer	Plant grains, leafy annuals. Fertilize (chemical). Graft or bud plants. Irrigate. Trim to increase growth.
Mar 30, 3:41 pm– Apr 1, 4:35 am	2nd	Cancer	Plant grains, leafy annuals. Fertilize (chemical). Graft or bud plants. Irrigate. Trim to increase growth.

Fresh rosemary and thyme mixed with coarse salt and fresh-ground black pepper, garlic, and lemon zest makes a wonderful, aromatic rub for pork tenderloin. Place the leaves from two sprigs of rosemary and two sprigs of thyme, seasoning, zest, and garlic in a food processor. Blend. Add ¼ cup olive oil. Spread this paste on all sides of the pork tenderloin. Roast at 475°F in a baking dish for about 20 minutes, or until interior temperature of the roast is 145°F. Let the meat rest until the temperature is 155°F.

March 30
3:41 pm EDT

MARCH

S	M	T	W	T	F	S
				1	2	3
4	5	6	7	8	9	10
11	12	13	14	15	16	17
18	19	20	21	22	23	24
25	26	27	28	29	30	31

April ♈

April 1–7

Since 'tis Nature's law to change, constancy alone is strange.

~JOHN WILMOT, EARL OF ROCHESTER

Date	Qtr.	Sign	Activity
Mar 30, 3:41 pm–Apr 1, 4:35 am	2nd	Cancer	Plant grains, leafy annuals. Fertilize (chemical). Graft or bud plants. Irrigate. Trim to increase growth.
Apr 5, 11:32 am–Apr 6, 3:19 pm	2nd	Libra	Plant annuals for fragrance and beauty. Trim to increase growth.
Apr 7, 11:18 am–Apr 9, 11:12 am	3rd	Scorpio	Plant biennials, perennials, bulbs and roots. Prune. Irrigate. Fertilize (organic).

If you still have canned or dried fruit to use up at winter's end, make some compote. Fruit compote is a low-calorie dessert that has good nutritional value and the added benefit of being gluten-free. Made from fresh, canned, or dried fruits, spices, and light syrup, compote is often served with Passover meals. It also goes well with plain yogurt, hot cereal, goat cheese, mascarpone, ice cream, and some meats.

2011 © Jörg Beuge. Image from BigStockPhoto.com

○

April 6
3:19 pm EDT

APRIL

S	M	T	W	T	F	S
1	2	3	4	5	6	7
8	9	10	11	12	13	14
15	16	17	18	19	20	21
22	23	24	25	26	27	28
29	30					

♈ April 8–14

It is not only a matter of not caring who knows—it is also a matter of knowing who cares.   ∼IDRIES SHAH

Date	Qtr.	Sign	Activity
Apr 7, 11:18 am– Apr 9, 11:12 am	3rd	Scorpio	Plant biennials, perennials, bulbs and roots. Prune. Irrigate. Fertilize (organic).
Apr 9, 11:12 am– Apr 11, 1:02 pm	3rd	Sagittarius	Cultivate. Destroy weeds and pests. Harvest fruits and root crops for food. Trim to retard growth.
Apr 11, 1:02 pm– Apr 13, 6:50 am	3rd	Capricorn	Plant potatoes and tubers. Trim to retard growth.
Apr 13, 6:50 am– Apr 13, 5:48 pm	4th	Capricorn	Plant potatoes and tubers. Trim to retard growth.
Apr 13, 5:48 pm– Apr 16, 1:38 am	4th	Aquarius	Cultivate. Destroy weeds and pests. Harvest fruits and root crops for food. Trim to retard growth.

Place sprigs of twigs gathered from trees and shrubs in vases filled with water. When the new green leaves emerge, it's a signal that spring is near. Water early-blooming shrubs regularly. And put a small birdhouse near or in your garden. If a bird moves in, it will take care of a lot of bugs.

_____

_____

_____

◑
April 13
6:50 am EDT

APRIL

S	M	T	W	T	F	S
1	2	3	4	5	6	7
8	9	10	11	12	13	14
15	16	17	18	19	20	21
22	23	24	25	26	27	28
29	30					

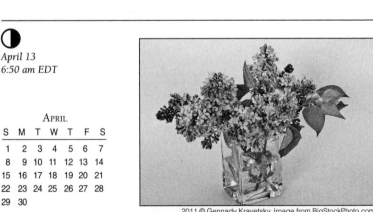

2011 © Gennady Kravetsky. Image from BigStockPhoto.com

April 15–21 ♈

It is impossible to enjoy idling thoroughly unless one has
plenty of work to do.   ∽Jerome K. Jerome

Date	Qtr.	Sign	Activity
Apr 13, 5:48 pm– Apr 16, 1:38 am	4th	Aquarius	Cultivate. Destroy weeds and pests. Harvest fruits and root crops for food. Trim to retard growth.
Apr 16, 1:38 am– Apr 18, 11:59 am	4th	Pisces	Plant biennials, perennials, bulbs and roots. Prune. Irrigate. Fertilize (organic).
Apr 18, 11:59 am– Apr 21, 12:05 am	4th	Aries	Cultivate. Destroy weeds and pests. Harvest fruits and root crops for food. Trim to retard growth.
Apr 21, 12:05 am– Apr 21, 3:18 am	4th	Taurus	Plant potatoes and tubers. Trim to retard growth.
Apr 21, 3:18 am– Apr 23, 1:05 pm	1st	Taurus	Plant annuals for hardiness. Trim to increase growth.

What has more vitamin A than carrots and twice as much as spinach? Dandelion leaves! One of the best ways to use dandelions is to chop them into small pieces and mix with other salad greens. Doing this will minimize the bitterness that offends most people who try them. Cooking the leaves and stems with bacon will also dilute the bitterness and enhance their flavor.

●

April 21
3:18 am EDT

APRIL

S	M	T	W	T	F	S
	1	2	3	4	5	6
7	8	9	10	11	12	13
14	15	16	17	18	19	20
21	22	23	24	25	26	27
28	29	30				

April 22–28

Uncovering what is wrong must always precede the discovery of what is right.

~Guy Finley, *The Secret of Letting Go*

Date	Qtr.	Sign	Activity
Apr 21, 3:18 am– Apr 23, 1:05 pm	1st	Taurus	Plant annuals for hardiness. Trim to increase growth.
Apr 26, 1:42 am– Apr 28, 12:10 pm	1st	Cancer	Plant grains, leafy annuals. Fertilize (chemical). Graft or bud plants. Irrigate. Trim to increase growth.

Not much disappoints gardeners more than seeing tomatoes develop blossom end rot, which is caused by a lack of calcium in the soil. Adding Epsom salts to the soil before you plant will prevent blossom end rot. Use 1 pound of Epsom salts in a 4x6-foot raised-bed garden. If you didn't pre-treat the soil in your garden and you see blossom end rot starting, pick and discard the affected fruit. Then begin watering the tomato plants with a mixture of ½ cup Epsom salts dissolved in 1 gallon of water. Do this a couple of times throughout the growing season. Use 1 gallon of the mixture for each plant, pouring it around the base of the plant.

APRIL

S	M	T	W	T	F	S
1	2	3	4	5	6	7
8	9	10	11	12	13	14
15	16	17	18	19	20	21
22	23	24	25	26	27	28
29	30					

2011 © Stephanie Frey. Image from BigStockPhoto.com

May

April 29–May 5

When fishes leap in silver stream ... And the forest bees are humming near, And cowslips in boys' hats appear ... We then may say the May is come.

~John Clare, "May"

Date	Qtr.	Sign	Activity
May 2, 10:04 pm–May 4, 10:20 pm	2nd	Libra	Plant annuals for fragrance and beauty. Trim to increase growth.
May 4, 10:20 pm–May 5, 11:35 pm	2nd	Scorpio	Plant grains, leafy annuals. Fertilize (chemical). Graft or bud plants. Irrigate. Trim to increase growth.
May 5, 11:35 pm–May 6, 9:39 pm	3rd	Scorpio	Plant biennials, perennials, bulbs and roots. Prune. Irrigate. Fertilize (organic).

Daffodils don't need much water when they're blooming but should be watered in the weeks after they bloom (unless your area receives a lot of rain) to encourage rooting and help the bulbs store nutrients for the next year. Remove spent flower heads immediately, but do not remove plant foliage; let it die back naturally and then remove it.

2011 © Tanya McConnell. Image from BigStockPhoto.com

● *April 29*
5:57 am EDT

○ *May 5*
11:35 pm EDT

May

S	M	T	W	T	F	S
		1	2	3	4	5
6	7	8	9	10	11	12
13	14	15	16	17	18	19
20	21	22	23	24	25	26
27	28	29	30	31		

 **May 6–12**

Every path has its puddle.   ~ENGLISH PROVERB

Date	Qtr.	Sign	Activity
May 5, 11:35 pm– May 6, 9:39 pm	3rd	Scorpio	Plant biennials, perennials, bulbs and roots. Prune. Irrigate. Fertilize (organic).
May 6, 9:39 pm– May 8, 10:00 pm	3rd	Sagittarius	Cultivate. Destroy weeds and pests. Harvest fruits and root crops for food. Trim to retard growth.
May 8, 10:00 pm– May 11, 1:03 am	3rd	Capricorn	Plant potatoes and tubers. Trim to retard growth.
May 11, 1:03 am– May 12, 5:47 pm	3rd	Aquarius	Cultivate. Destroy weeds and pests. Harvest fruits and root crops for food. Trim to retard growth.
May 12, 5:47 pm– May 13, 7:42 am	4th	Aquarius	Cultivate. Destroy weeds and pests. Harvest fruits and root crops for food. Trim to retard growth.

Companion planting—planting two plants for a particular purpose—can help you control garden pests, provide shelter for beneficial insects, create diversity, and enrich the soil. A key part of combining plants is a plant's natural ability to attract or repel bugs. Dill and yarrow attract bees that will help pollinate other plants. Sage, spinach, and borage love tomato plants. Read more about companion planting on pages 73–74.

May 12
5:47 pm EDT

MAY

S	M	T	W	T	F	S
		1	2	3	4	5
6	7	8	9	10	11	12
13	14	15	16	17	18	19
20	21	22	23	24	25	26
27	28	29	30	31		

May 13–19 ☿

*Civilization exists by geological consent, subject to change
without notice.*   ~WILL DURANT

Date	Qtr.	Sign	Activity
May 12, 5:47 pm– May 13, 7:42 am	4th	Aquarius	Cultivate. Destroy weeds and pests. Harvest fruits and root crops for food. Trim to retard growth.
May 13, 7:42 am– May 15, 5:45 pm	4th	Pisces	Plant biennials, perennials, bulbs and roots. Prune. Irrigate. Fertilize (organic).
May 15, 5:45 pm– May 18, 6:03 am	4th	Aries	Cultivate. Destroy weeds and pests. Harvest fruits and root crops for food. Trim to retard growth.
May 18, 6:03 am– May 20, 7:05 pm	4th	Taurus	Plant potatoes and tubers. Trim to retard growth.

Some plants don't like each other, and some can actually release harmful chemicals into the air or soil to stop other plants from crowding them. This is called allelopathy, and it helps plants prevent other plants from competing for nutrients, moisture, and rooting space. Broccoli, cabbage, young corn, fennel, and sunflowers are among the allelopathics, so be careful what you plant near them in your garden. In fact, keep sunflower seed hulls away from planting areas to reduce the chance of crop damage.

2011 © Hamiza Bakirci. Image from BigStockPhoto.com

MAY

S	M	T	W	T	F	S
		1	2	3	4	5
6	7	8	9	10	11	12
13	14	15	16	17	18	19
20	21	22	23	24	25	26
27	28	29	30	31		

♊ May 20–26

I look upon the pleasure we take in a garden as one of the most innocent delights in human life.   ∼CICERO

Date	Qtr.	Sign	Activity
May 18, 6:03 am– May 20, 7:05 pm	4th	Taurus	Plant potatoes and tubers. Trim to retard growth.
May 20, 7:05 pm– May 20, 7:47 pm	4th	Gemini	Cultivate. Destroy weeds and pests. Harvest fruits and root crops for food. Trim to retard growth.
May 23, 7:31 am– May 25, 6:11 pm	1st	Cancer	Plant grains, leafy annuals. Fertilize (chemical). Graft or bud plants. Irrigate. Trim to increase growth.

I f you have an undesirable view from your yard, or if you just want to add color and texture to your garden, plant corn and strawflowers together in full sunlight instead of building a fence. To encourage larger flowers on some plants, pinch off side shoots during the growing season. In the fall, cut the flower stems, hang them upside down until dry, and then use in arrangements.

May 20
7:47 pm EDT

MAY

S	M	T	W	T	F	S
		1	2	3	4	5
6	7	8	9	10	11	12
13	14	15	16	17	18	19
20	21	22	23	24	25	26
27	28	29	30	31		

June
May 27–June 2

Education is what survives when what has been learnt has
been forgotten.   ~B. F. SKINNER

Date	Qtr.	Sign	Activity
May 30, 6:46 am– Jun 1, 8:31 am	2nd	Libra	Plant annuals for fragrance and beauty. Trim to increase growth.
Jun 1, 8:31 am– Jun 3, 8:32 am	2nd	Scorpio	Plant grains, leafy annuals. Fertilize (chemical). Graft or bud plants. Irrigate. Trim to increase growth.

The best time to pick flowers for arrangements is early in the morning. To prevent bacteria from ruining flowers, arrange them in a clean container, change the water daily, and cut the tips off the stems that have been in water every few days. Never place your arrangement in full sunlight or near a heat source.

May 28
4:16 pm EDT

JUNE

S	M	T	W	T	F	S
					1	2
3	4	5	6	7	8	9
10	11	12	13	14	15	16
17	18	19	20	21	22	23
24	25	26	27	28	29	30

♊ June 3–9

Their fluttery fledgling lips / Move slowly, / Drawing in the warm air. ~THEODORE ROETHKE, "ORCHIDS"

Date	Qtr.	Sign	Activity
Jun 1, 8:31 am– Jun 3, 8:32 am	2nd	Scorpio	Plant grains, leafy annuals. Fertilize (chemical). Graft or bud plants. Irrigate. Trim to increase growth.
Jun 4, 7:12 am– Jun 5, 8:31 am	3rd	Sagittarius	Cultivate. Destroy weeds and pests. Harvest fruits and root crops for food. Trim to retard growth.
Jun 5, 8:31 am– Jun 7, 10:17 am	3rd	Capricorn	Plant potatoes and tubers. Trim to retard growth.
Jun 7, 10:17 am– Jun 9, 3:22 pm	3rd	Aquarius	Cultivate. Destroy weeds and pests. Harvest fruits and root crops for food. Trim to retard growth.
Jun 9, 3:22 pm– Jun 11, 6:41 am	3rd	Pisces	Plant biennials, perennials, bulbs and roots. Prune. Irrigate. Fertilize (organic).

Give your flowers a little attention every day and reap the rewards all summer long.

• Deadhead and lightly prune roses to encourage more blooms; always cut above a stem with five leaves.

• Pick faded flowers off fuchsia and petunias to encourage more blooms.

• Control aphids by not overfertilizing and by spraying plants with a strong spray of water.

○
June 4
7:12 am EDT

JUNE

S	M	T	W	T	F	S
					1	2
3	4	5	6	7	8	9
10	11	12	13	14	15	16
17	18	19	20	21	22	23
24	25	26	27	28	29	30

2011 © Shannon Drawe. Image from BigStockPhoto.com

June 10–16   ♊

I swear to you there are divine things more beautiful than words can tell.   ~Walt Whitman, *Leaves of Grass*

Date	Qtr.	Sign	Activity
Jun 9, 3:22 pm– Jun 11, 6:41 am	3rd	Pisces	Plant biennials, perennials, bulbs and roots. Prune. Irrigate. Fertilize (organic).
Jun 11, 6:41 am– Jun 12, 12:21 am	4th	Pisces	Plant biennials, perennials, bulbs and roots. Prune. Irrigate. Fertilize (organic).
Jun 12, 12:21 am– Jun 14, 12:22 pm	4th	Aries	Cultivate. Destroy weeds and pests. Harvest fruits and root crops for food. Trim to retard growth.
Jun 14, 12:22 pm– Jun 17, 1:24 am	4th	Taurus	Plant potatoes and tubers. Trim to retard growth.

You can kill aphids by spraying the underside of leaves with a solution of dish soap and water. The soap causes dehydration and washes away the waxy coating that protects aphids. Use a mixture of 2 teaspoons soap to a bottle of water. This treatment must be repeated weekly. If you want to treat aphids more aggressively, insecticidal soaps are available at garden centers and hardware stores. These soaps, which interfere with the process of reproduction, do contain oils that can be hard on some plants.

2011 © WebSubstance. Image from BigStockPhoto.com

◗

June 11
6:41 am EDT

June

S	M	T	W	T	F	S
					1	2
3	4	5	6	7	8	9
10	11	12	13	14	15	16
17	18	19	20	21	22	23
24	25	26	27	28	29	30

♊ June 17–23

Summer afternoon—summer afternoon; to me those have always been the two most beautiful words in the English language.   ~HENRY JAMES (ATTRIBUTED)

Date	Qtr.	Sign	Activity
Jun 14, 12:22 pm– Jun 17, 1:24 am	4th	Taurus	Plant potatoes and tubers. Trim to retard growth.
Jun 17, 1:24 am– Jun 19, 11:02 am	4th	Gemini	Cultivate. Destroy weeds and pests. Harvest fruits and root crops for food. Trim to retard growth.
Jun 19, 1:34 pm– Jun 21, 11:47 pm	1st	Cancer	Plant grains, leafy annuals. Fertilize (chemical). Graft or bud plants. Irrigate. Trim to increase growth.

The Summer Solstice, the longest day of the year, is June 21 this year in the Northern Hemisphere. How long is the longest day? That depends on where you live, of course. Latitudes close to the equator see little variation in their day length, while the North and South Poles alternate between twenty-four hours of daylight and twenty-four hours of darkness.

●
June 19
11:02 am EDT

JUNE

S	M	T	W	T	F	S
					1	2
3	4	5	6	7	8	9
10	11	12	13	14	15	16
17	18	19	20	21	22	23
24	25	26	27	28	29	30

June 24–30 ♋

We make a living by what we get; we make a life by what we give.
                                                ~WINSTON CHURCHILL

Date	Qtr.	Sign	Activity
Jun 26, 1:15 pm– Jun 26, 11:30 pm	1st	Libra	Plant annuals for fragrance and beauty. Trim to increase growth.
Jun 26, 11:30 pm– Jun 28, 4:32 pm	2nd	Libra	Plant annuals for fragrance and beauty. Trim to increase growth.
Jun 28, 4:32 pm– Jun 30, 6:04 pm	2nd	Scorpio	Plant grains, leafy annuals. Fertilize (chemical). Graft or bud plants. Irrigate. Trim to increase growth.

Edible flowers were used by the Romans, Greeks, and Chinese centuries ago. Before you eat them, though, be sure they have not been sprayed with pesticides or fertilized with untreated manure. If you want to use flowers in recipes or to garnish foods:

• pick blossoms early in the day;

• avoid unopened or faded flowers; and

• use large-petal flowers (e.g., pansies, begonia, gladiolus, and daylilies).

See http://www.ext.colostate.edu/pubs/garden/07237.html for a more complete list of edible flowers.

2011 © June Marie. Image from BigStockPhoto.com

◑

June 26
11:30 pm EDT

			JUNE			
S	M	T	W	T	F	S
					1	2
3	4	5	6	7	8	9
10	11	12	13	14	15	16
17	18	19	20	21	22	23
24	25	26	27	28	29	30

♋ July

July 1–7

Our deeds determine us, as much as we determine our deeds.

~George Eliot

Date	Qtr.	Sign	Activity
Jul 2, 6:51 pm– Jul 3, 2:52 pm	2nd	Capricorn	Graft or bud plants. Trim to increase growth.
Jul 3, 2:52 pm– Jul 4, 8:26 pm	3rd	Capricorn	Plant potatoes and tubers. Trim to retard growth.
Jul 4, 8:26 pm– Jul 7, 12:29 am	3rd	Aquarius	Cultivate. Destroy weeds and pests. Harvest fruits and root crops for food. Trim to retard growth.
Jul 7, 12:29 am– Jul 9, 8:14 am	3rd	Pisces	Plant biennials, perennials, bulbs and roots. Prune. Irrigate. Fertilize (organic).

Keep flowerbeds watered and free of weeds to encourage plants to continue blooming. Stake and tie top-heavy plants, such as foxglove and delphiniums. Cut back baby's breath to encourage more blooms. Harvest and dry lavender blooms for use in sachets.

_____

_____

_____

○
July 3
2:52 pm EDT

July

S	M	T	W	T	F	S
1	2	3	4	5	6	7
8	9	10	11	12	13	14
15	16	17	18	19	20	21
22	23	24	25	26	27	28
29	30	31				

2011 © Goh Siok Hian. Image from BigStockPhoto.com

July 8–14 ♋

*Once the game is over, the king and the pawn go back in the
same box.*
                                        ~ITALIAN PROVERB

Date	Qtr.	Sign	Activity
Jul 7, 12:29 am– Jul 9, 8:14 am	3rd	Pisces	Plant biennials, perennials, bulbs and roots. Prune. Irrigate. Fertilize (organic).
Jul 9, 8:14 am– Jul 10, 9:48 pm	3rd	Aries	Cultivate. Destroy weeds and pests. Harvest fruits and root crops for food. Trim to retard growth.
Jul 10, 9:48 pm– Jul 11, 7:30 pm	4th	Aries	Cultivate. Destroy weeds and pests. Harvest fruits and root crops for food. Trim to retard growth.
Jul 11, 7:30 pm– Jul 14, 8:26 am	4th	Taurus	Plant potatoes and tubers. Trim to retard growth.
Jul 14, 8:26 am– Jul 16, 8:31 pm	4th	Gemini	Cultivate. Destroy weeds and pests. Harvest fruits and root crops for food. Trim to retard growth.

Many plants and vegetables are ready or near ready for harvesting this time of year. If you planted garlic, clip the flower stalks off and harvest once the leaves have turned brown. Cut sprigs of rosemary and freeze for future use. Harvest basil weekly. Harvest broccoli when the buds begin to loosen and before the yellow flowers appear.

2011 © Stephen Kirklys. Image from BigStockPhoto.com

◑
July 10
9:48 pm EDT

JULY

S	M	T	W	T	F	S
	1	2	3	4	5	6	7
8	9	10	11	12	13	14
15	16	17	18	19	20	21
22	23	24	25	26	27	28
29	30	31				

♋ July 15–21

Life ain't all beer and Skittles, and more's the pity; but what's the odds, so long as you're happy?

~GEORGE DU MAURIER

Date	Qtr.	Sign	Activity
Jul 14, 8:26 am– Jul 16, 8:31 pm	4th	Gemini	Cultivate. Destroy weeds and pests. Harvest fruits and root crops for food. Trim to retard growth.
Jul 16, 8:31 pm– Jul 19, 12:24 am	4th	Cancer	Plant biennials, perennials, bulbs and roots. Prune. Irrigate. Fertilize (organic).
Jul 19, 12:24 am– Jul 19, 6:13 am	1st	Cancer	Plant grains, leafy annuals. Fertilize (chemical). Graft or bud plants. Irrigate. Trim to increase growth.

Feed your lawn and outdoor potted plants with a slow-release nitrogen fertilizer. Use grass clippings as mulch around vegetable plants to keep moisture in and weeds out. Grass mulch can also be used on path areas to slow weed growth.

●
July 19
12:24 am EDT

JULY

S	M	T	W	T	F	S
1	2	3	4	5	6	7
8	9	10	11	12	13	14
15	16	17	18	19	20	21
22	23	24	25	26	27	28
29	30	31				

July 22–28 ♌

History is not usually what has happened. History is what some people have thought to be significant.

~IDRIES SHAH

Date	Qtr.	Sign	Activity
Jul 23, 6:38 pm–Jul 25, 10:29 pm	1st	Libra	Plant annuals for fragrance and beauty. Trim to increase growth.
Jul 25, 10:29 pm–Jul 26, 4:56 am	1st	Scorpio	Plant grains, leafy annuals. Fertilize (chemical). Graft or bud plants. Irrigate. Trim to increase growth.
Jul 26, 4:56 am–Jul 28, 1:18 am	2nd	Scorpio	Plant grains, leafy annuals. Fertilize (chemical). Graft or bud plants. Irrigate. Trim to increase growth.

Inorganic mulches, such as plastic, will not improve soil conditions, but they can help soil stay warmer and retain moisture. Clear plastic used in hot weather can kill off insects and weeds. Opaque black plastic will block sunlight and keep weeds from sprouting. Plastic mulch works well around annuals, like squash and tomatoes, but it is not a good choice for perennials like asparagus. Don't place mulch too close to plants. Leave about 6 inches of space to prevent crown or root rot and to discourage rodents from chewing on plants.

2011 © Paul Herbert. Image from BigStockPhoto.com

◑

July 26
4:56 am EDT

JULY

S	M	T	W	T	F	S
1	2	3	4	5	6	7
8	9	10	11	12	13	14
15	16	17	18	19	20	21
22	23	24	25	26	27	28
29	30	31				

ᘿ August

July 29–August 4

Mountains are the beginning and the end of all natural scenery.

~John Ruskin

Date	Qtr.	Sign	Activity
Jul 30, 3:29 am– Aug 1, 5:56 am	2nd	Capricorn	Graft or bud plants. Trim to increase growth.
Aug 1, 11:27 pm– Aug 3, 9:58 am	3rd	Aquarius	Cultivate. Destroy weeds and pests. Harvest fruits and root crops for food. Trim to retard growth.
Aug 3, 9:58 am– Aug 5, 4:59 pm	3rd	Pisces	Plant biennials, perennials, bulbs and roots. Prune. Irrigate. Fertilize (organic).

The need for supplemental fertilizer depends on what is planted in the soil. Some plants, such as thyme and cosmos, like "lean" soil. Heavy feeders, such as tomatoes and corn, or perennials like rhubarb and asparagus, can deplete soil. Watch your plants for signs that they need extra food. If plants are growing slowly or have discolored leaves, they may need fertilizing. If they are too tall or are not producing fruit and flowers, they might have too much fertilizer. You can use a soil testing kit (available online and at some garden centers) to determine nutrient needs.

○
August 1
11:27 pm EDT

August

S	M	T	W	T	F	S
			1	2	3	4
5	6	7	8	9	10	11
12	13	14	15	16	17	18
19	20	21	22	23	24	25
26	27	28	29	30	31	

2011 © Ian Nixon. Image from BigStockPhoto.com

August 5–11 ♌

The road to a friend's house is never long.

~Danish Proverb

Date	Qtr.	Sign	Activity
Aug 3, 9:58 am– Aug 5, 4:59 pm	3rd	Pisces	Plant biennials, perennials, bulbs and roots. Prune. Irrigate. Fertilize (organic).
Aug 5, 4:59 pm– Aug 8, 3:28 am	3rd	Aries	Cultivate. Destroy weeds and pests. Harvest fruits and root crops for food. Trim to retard growth.
Aug 8, 3:28 am– Aug 9, 2:55 pm	3rd	Taurus	Plant potatoes and tubers. Trim to retard growth.
Aug 9, 2:55 pm– Aug 10, 4:11 pm	4th	Taurus	Plant potatoes and tubers. Trim to retard growth.
Aug 10, 4:11 pm– Aug 13, 4:27 am	4th	Gemini	Cultivate. Destroy weeds and pests. Harvest fruits and root crops for food. Trim to retard growth.

You can extend your living area if you have space in your garden or yard to add a seating area or garden swing. Create a room by adding boundaries—shrubs, trellises, and fences—to create private outdoor rooms.

2011 © Sue Scarfe. Image from BigStockPhoto.com

◑

August 9
2:55 pm EDT

August

S	M	T	W	T	F	S
			1	2	3	4
5	6	7	8	9	10	11
12	13	14	15	16	17	18
19	20	21	22	23	24	25
26	27	28	29	30	31	

♌ August 12–18

*Most folks are about as happy as they make up their minds
to be.*　　　　　　　　　　　　　　　　　　~ABRAHAM LINCOLN

Date	Qtr.	Sign	Activity
Aug 10, 4:11 pm– Aug 13, 4:27 am	4th	Gemini	Cultivate. Destroy weeds and pests. Harvest fruits and root crops for food. Trim to retard growth.
Aug 13, 4:27 am– Aug 15, 2:05 pm	4th	Cancer	Plant biennials, perennials, bulbs and roots. Prune. Irrigate. Fertilize (organic).
Aug 15, 2:05 pm– Aug 17, 11:54 am	4th	Leo	Cultivate. Destroy weeds and pests. Harvest fruits and root crops for food. Trim to retard growth.

For fun, and before the kids go back to school, enlist their help to make a folk-art creature for your garden. Add movement to your scarecrows and creatures by attaching cloth streamers or mylar ties to them. You can make hair with reflective mylar tape or strips, put a mirror in the scarecrow's pocket, or tie reflective aluminum pie tins to their hands. Birds may not be afraid of your garden crew, but the extra movement and reflection will startle them so they fly away.

August 17
11:54 am EDT

AUGUST

S	M	T	W	T	F	S
			1	2	3	4
5	6	7	8	9	10	11
12	13	14	15	16	17	18
19	20	21	22	23	24	25
26	27	28	29	30	31	

2011 © Wendy Simmons. Image from BigStockPhoto.com

August 19–25 ♌

If life knocks you flat on your back, open your eyes: above you are the stars.

~Guy Finley, *The Secret of Letting Go*

Date	Qtr.	Sign	Activity
Aug 20, 12:45 am–Aug 22, 3:54 am	1st	Libra	Plant annuals for fragrance and beauty. Trim to increase growth.
Aug 22, 3:54 am–Aug 24, 6:50 am	1st	Scorpio	Plant grains, leafy annuals. Fertilize (chemical). Graft or bud plants. Irrigate. Trim to increase growth.

Extend your growing season by using frost protectors. Surround peppers, pumpkins, and other long-yielding crops with hay bales or trellising and hang burlap over them at night and during cold spells. Cold frames offer permanent protection to plants during cold seasons. The sides can be made from cement blocks, wood, or fiberglass. The back wall should be taller than the front, so the lid will be at about a 15-degree angle. Top the frame with a sheet of Plexiglas or clear plastic. If you want to do some extra work and make the top easier to manage, enclose the Plexiglas top in a wood frame and attach it to the back wall with hinges for easy opening on warmer days.

2011 © Jeff Gynane. Image from BigStockPhoto.com

◐

August 24
9:54 am EDT

August

S	M	T	W	T	F	S
			1	2	3	4
5	6	7	8	9	10	11
12	13	14	15	16	17	18
19	20	21	22	23	24	25
26	27	28	29	30	31	

♍ September
August 26–September 1

I am never in a hurry, and when the world slows down to my pace, I find it very agreeable.

~Hercule Poirot (Agatha Christie)

Date	Qtr.	Sign	Activity
Aug 26, 9:58 am–Aug 28, 1:38 pm	2nd	Capricorn	Graft or bud plants. Trim to increase growth.
Aug 30, 6:31 pm–Aug 31, 9:58 am	2nd	Pisces	Plant grains, leafy annuals. Fertilize (chemical). Graft or bud plants. Irrigate. Trim to increase growth.
Aug 31, 9:58 am–Sep 2, 1:37 am	3rd	Pisces	Plant biennials, perennials, bulbs and roots. Prune. Irrigate. Fertilize (organic).

To make herbal honey, add 2 teaspoons of your favorite fresh herb to a quart of honey. Warm over low heat and then place in a clean canning jar. Store the honey for two to three weeks before using to allow the flavors to develop.

_____

_____

_____

○
August 31
9:58 am EDT

Sᴇᴘᴛᴇᴍʙᴇʀ

S	M	T	W	T	F	S
						1
2	3	4	5	6	7	8
9	10	11	12	13	14	15
16	17	18	19	20	21	22
23	24	25	26	27	28	29
30						

2011 © Marilyn Barbone. Image from BigStockPhoto.com

September 2–8 ♍

We have more possibilities available in each moment than
we realize.   ~THICH NHAT HANH

Date	Qtr.	Sign	Activity
Aug 31, 9:58 am– Sep 2, 1:37 am	3rd	Pisces	Plant biennials, perennials, bulbs and roots. Prune. Irrigate. Fertilize (organic).
Sep 2, 1:37 am– Sep 4, 11:41 am	3rd	Aries	Cultivate. Destroy weeds and pests. Harvest fruits and root crops for food. Trim to retard growth.
Sep 4, 11:41 am– Sep 7, 12:10 am	3rd	Taurus	Plant potatoes and tubers. Trim to retard growth.
Sep 7, 12:10 am– Sep 8, 9:15 am	3rd	Gemini	Cultivate. Destroy weeds and pests. Harvest fruits and root crops for food. Trim to retard growth.
Sep 8, 9:15 am– Sep 9, 12:49 pm	4th	Gemini	Cultivate. Destroy weeds and pests. Harvest fruits and root crops for food. Trim to retard growth.

Most herbs can be frozen. If you want them to retain their color, and you are willing to forego some flavor, blanch the herbs before you freeze them. Most of the time, you will want to remove the leaves and discard the stems. To blanche, place the leaves in a strainer and pour hot water over them. Dry the leaves on paper towels before freezing.

2011 © Robert Beyers II. Image from BigStockPhoto.com

◑

September 8
9:15 am EDT

SEPTEMBER

S	M	T	W	T	F	S
						1
2	3	4	5	6	7	8
9	10	11	12	13	14	15
16	17	18	19	20	21	22
23	24	25	26	27	28	29
30						

♍ September 9–15

To be seventy years young is sometimes more cheerful and hopeful than to be forty years old.

~OLIVER WENDELL HOLMES

Date	Qtr.	Sign	Activity
Sep 8, 9:15 am– Sep 9, 12:49 pm	4th	Gemini	Cultivate. Destroy weeds and pests. Harvest fruits and root crops for food. Trim to retard growth.
Sep 9, 12:49 pm– Sep 11, 11:00 pm	4th	Cancer	Plant biennials, perennials, bulbs and roots. Prune. Irrigate. Fertilize (organic).
Sep 11, 11:00 pm– Sep 14, 5:30 am	4th	Leo	Cultivate. Destroy weeds and pests. Harvest fruits and root crops for food. Trim to retard growth.
Sep 14, 5:30 am– Sep 15, 10:11 pm	4th	Virgo	Cultivate, especially medicinal plants. Destroy weeds and pests. Trim to retard growth.

R ed admiral butterflies migrate south in September. After spending the spring and summer months in fields and marshy areas, these butterflies can often be seen in urban yards and gardens, where they feed on sap, rotten fruit, and, occasionally, nectar from clover and asters.

●

September 15
10:11 pm EDT

SEPTEMBER

S	M	T	W	T	F	S
						1
2	3	4	5	6	7	8
9	10	11	12	13	14	15
16	17	18	19	20	21	22
23	24	25	26	27	28	29
30						

September 16–22 ♍

Irrationally held truths may be more harmful than reasoned errors.

~T. H. HUXLEY

Date	Qtr.	Sign	Activity
Sep 16, 8:55 am– Sep 18, 10:46 am	1st	Libra	Plant annuals for fragrance and beauty. Trim to increase growth.
Sep 18, 10:46 am– Sep 20, 12:34 pm	1st	Scorpio	Plant grains, leafy annuals. Fertilize (chemical). Graft or bud plants. Irrigate. Trim to increase growth.
Sep 22, 3:20 pm– Sep 22, 3:41 pm	1st	Capricorn	Graft or bud plants. Trim to increase growth.
Sep 22, 3:41 pm– Sep 24, 7:32 pm	2nd	Capricorn	Graft or bud plants. Trim to increase growth.

The slug is another creature you may notice in September, even though most gardeners wish to never see them. They come out at night or early in the morning and leave a shiny trail of slime on sidewalks and streets. Slugs feed on plant material until it is too hard to get, and then they move to wintering spots behind boards and under stones.

September 22
3:41 pm EDT

SEPTEMBER

S	M	T	W	T	F	S
						1
2	3	4	5	6	7	8
9	10	11	12	13	14	15
16	17	18	19	20	21	22
23	24	25	26	27	28	29
30						

2011 © Christopher Howells. Image from BigStockPhoto.com

♎ September 23–29

He that plants trees loves others besides himself.

~Thomas Fuller

Date	Qtr.	Sign	Activity
Sep 22, 3:41 pm– Sep 24, 7:32 pm	2nd	Capricorn	Graft or bud plants. Trim to increase growth.
Sep 27, 1:23 am– Sep 29, 9:14 am	2nd	Pisces	Plant grains, leafy annuals. Fertilize (chemical). Graft or bud plants. Irrigate. Trim to increase growth.
Sep 29, 11:19 pm– Oct 1, 7:26 pm	3rd	Aries	Cultivate. Destroy weeds and pests. Harvest fruits and root crops for food. Trim to retard growth.

Watch the trees in your yard and neighborhood and notice how different kinds show different colors this time of year. The green chlorophyll trees use for making food during the summer breaks down when the days and nights get colder. When the chlorophyll loses its coloring, we are then able to see the yellow xanthophyll, orange carotene, and/or red anthocyanin that is also present in the leaves.

_____

_____

_____

_____

○
September 29
11:19 pm EDT

SEPTEMBER
S	M	T	W	T	F	S
						1
2	3	4	5	6	7	8
9	10	11	12	13	14	15
16	17	18	19	20	21	22
23	24	25	26	27	28	29
30						

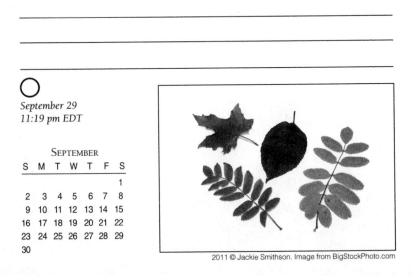

October ♎

September 30–October 6

Fox-red, leaf blond, October throws common sense away
for fluent color.   ~CHARLES SEMONES "OCTOBER"

Date	Qtr.	Sign	Activity
Sep 29, 11:19 pm– Oct 1, 7:26 pm	3rd	Aries	Cultivate. Destroy weeds and pests. Harvest fruits and root crops for food. Trim to retard growth.
Oct 1, 7:26 pm– Oct 4, 7:47 am	3rd	Taurus	Plant potatoes and tubers. Trim to retard growth.
Oct 4, 7:47 am– Oct 6, 8:45 pm	3rd	Gemini	Cultivate. Destroy weeds and pests. Harvest fruits and root crops for food. Trim to retard growth.
Oct 6, 8:45 pm– Oct 8, 3:33 am	3rd	Cancer	Plant biennials, perennials, bulbs and roots. Prune. Irrigate. Fertilize (organic).

Have lots of extra tomatoes? Make spaghetti sauce and seal it in pretty jars to give as gifts during the holiday season. Put a jar of sauce in a basket along with some dry pasta noodles and a wedge of fresh Parmesan cheese. If you really want to go all out, include a bottle of Chianti wine.

2011 © Tatjaha Gupalo. Image from BigStockPhoto.com

OCTOBER						
S	M	T	W	T	F	S
	1	2	3	4	5	6
7	8	9	10	11	12	13
14	15	16	17	18	19	20
21	22	23	24	25	26	27
28	29	30	31			

♎ October 7–13

Mistakes are part of the game. It's how well you recover from them, that's the mark of a great player.

~ALICE COOPER

Date	Qtr.	Sign	Activity
Oct 6, 8:45 pm– Oct 8, 3:33 am	3rd	Cancer	Plant biennials, perennials, bulbs and roots. Prune. Irrigate. Fertilize (organic).
Oct 8, 3:33 am– Oct 9, 7:55 am	4th	Cancer	Plant biennials, perennials, bulbs and roots. Prune. Irrigate. Fertilize (organic).
Oct 9, 7:55 am– Oct 11, 3:23 pm	4th	Leo	Cultivate. Destroy weeds and pests. Harvest fruits and root crops for food. Trim to retard growth.
Oct 11, 3:23 pm– Oct 13, 7:02 pm	4th	Virgo	Cultivate, especially medicinal plants. Destroy weeds and pests. Trim to retard growth.

When you pick pumpkins, don't store them on a bare cement floor, as they'll spoil faster. If you want to use them for Jack o' lanterns, cut the bottom out of the pumpkin instead of the top. If you do remove the top, pin a piece of aluminum foil on the underside of the lid to dissipate heat and prevent burning. After carving pumpkins, coat the cut surfaces with petroleum jelly to extend the life of your Jack o' lantern.

◗
October 8
3:33 am EDT

OCTOBER

S	M	T	W	T	F	S
	1	2	3	4	5	6
7	8	9	10	11	12	13
14	15	16	17	18	19	20
21	22	23	24	25	26	27
28	29	30	31			

2011 © onepony. Image from BigStockPhoto.com

October 14–20 ♎

The orbèd maiden, with white fire laden,
Whom mortals call the Moon.

~Percy Bysshe Shelley

Date	Qtr.	Sign	Activity
Oct 15, 8:02 am– Oct 15, 8:06 pm	1st	Libra	Plant annuals for fragrance and beauty. Trim to increase growth.
Oct 15, 8:06 pm– Oct 17, 8:26 pm	1st	Scorpio	Plant grains, leafy annuals. Fertilize (chemical). Graft or bud plants. Irrigate. Trim to increase growth.
Oct 19, 9:41 pm– Oct 21, 11:32 pm	1st	Capricorn	Graft or bud plants. Trim to increase growth.

Flower seeds and trees and shrubs that produce nuts and berries are good food sources for birds and other small creatures during colder months. Different birds need different foods, so if you want to attract specific birds to your yard, check with stores in your area that sell bird food. Dense shrubs, small trees, and vines on trees can also provide valuable shelter. A brush pile or hollow log provides good shelter and resting spots, too.

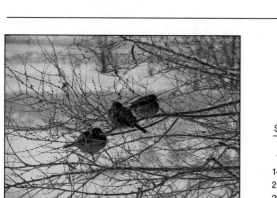

2011 © Sergey Pristyazhnyuk. Image from BigStockPhoto.com

● October 15
8:02 am EDT

October

S	M	T	W	T	F	S
	1	2	3	4	5	6
7	8	9	10	11	12	13
14	15	16	17	18	19	20
21	22	23	24	25	26	27
28	29	30	31			

♎ October 21–27

Those who wish to sing always find a song.

~SWEDISH PROVERB

Date	Qtr.	Sign	Activity
Oct 19, 9:41 pm– Oct 21, 11:32 pm	1st	Capricorn	Graft or bud plants. Trim to increase growth.
Oct 21, 11:32 pm– Oct 22, 1:02 am	2nd	Capricorn	Graft or bud plants. Trim to increase growth.
Oct 24, 7:00 am– Oct 26, 3:31 pm	2nd	Pisces	Plant grains, leafy annuals. Fertilize (chemical). Graft or bud plants. Irrigate. Trim to increase growth.

When winter settles in, in the Northern Hemisphere, a touch of color in an otherwise gray and white landscape is very welcome. Find a spot in your garden or yard that can be seen from the house (either full sunlight or partial shade). Plant winterberry (hardy to zone 3), which grows from 6 to 12 feet tall. Behind this, plant a taller evergreen shrub. When all other colors are drained from the landscape, the red berries of the winterberry against the evergreen will really pop out at you.

◑
October 21
11:32 pm EDT

OCTOBER

S	M	T	W	T	F	S
	1	2	3	4	5	6
7	8	9	10	11	12	13
14	15	16	17	18	19	20
21	22	23	24	25	26	27
28	29	30	31			

2011 © Ekaterina Dushenina. Image from BigStockPhoto.com

November ♏

October 28–November 3

Experience teaches slowly, and at the cost of mistakes.

~J. A. FROUDE

Date	Qtr.	Sign	Activity
Oct 29, 2:15 am– Oct 29, 3:49 pm	2nd	Taurus	Plant annuals for hardiness. Trim to increase growth.
Oct 29, 3:49 pm– Oct 31, 2:40 pm	3rd	Taurus	Plant potatoes and tubers. Trim to retard growth.
Oct 31, 2:40 pm– Nov 3, 3:43 am	3rd	Gemini	Cultivate. Destroy weeds and pests. Harvest fruits and root crops for food. Trim to retard growth.
Nov 3, 3:43 am– Nov 5, 2:39 pm	3rd	Cancer	Plant biennials, perennials, bulbs and roots. Prune. Irrigate. Fertilize (organic).

If you want to try leaving root crops like parsnips and carrots in the ground over winter, cover them with a deep layer of mulch. Leaves, straw, or sawdust make good mulch and will protect the vegetables for quite a while. Use a fork to loosen the soil around the plants when you are ready to harvest and use them.

2011 © Kenneth Caleno. Image from BigStockPhoto.com

○
October 29
3:49 pm EDT

NOVEMBER

S	M	T	W	T	F	S
					1	2	3
4	5	6	7	8	9	10
11	12	13	14	15	16	17
18	19	20	21	22	23	24
25	26	27	28	29	30	

♏ November 4–10

When angry, count to ten; when very angry, swear.

~MARK TWAIN

Date	Qtr.	Sign	Activity
Nov 3, 3:43 am– Nov 5, 2:39 pm	3rd	Cancer	Plant biennials, perennials, bulbs and roots. Prune. Irrigate. Fertilize (organic).
Nov 5, 2:39 pm– Nov 6, 7:36 pm	3rd	Leo	Cultivate. Destroy weeds and pests. Harvest fruits and root crops for food. Trim to retard growth.
Nov 6, 7:36 pm– Nov 7, 11:35 pm	4th	Leo	Cultivate. Destroy weeds and pests. Harvest fruits and root crops for food. Trim to retard growth.
Nov 7, 11:35 pm– Nov 10, 4:35 am	4th	Virgo	Cultivate, especially medicinal plants. Destroy weeds and pests. Trim to retard growth.

When you prune back your grapevines for winter, use the cut vines to make a decorative wreath for the upcoming holidays. Decorate your wreath with whatever you have around home—dried or artificial flowers, ribbon, lace, and pine cones work well. If you like a more natural look, make an evergreen swag from balsam fir, spruce, or cedar branches and attach it to the wreath. Decorate the swag with pine cones.

◐

November 6
7:36 pm EST
Daylight Saving Time ends
  November 4, 2:00 am

NOVEMBER						
S	M	T	W	T	F	S
					1	2	3
4	5	6	7	8	9	10
11	12	13	14	15	16	17
18	19	20	21	22	23	24
25	26	27	28	29	30	

November 11–17 ♏

I have enjoyed greatly the second blooming ... suddenly you find—at the age of 50, say—that a whole new life has opened before you.   ~AGATHA CHRISTIE

Date	Qtr.	Sign	Activity
Nov 12, 6:10 am– Nov 13, 5:08 pm	4th	Scorpio	Plant biennials, perennials, bulbs and roots. Prune. Irrigate. Fertilize (organic).
Nov 13, 5:08 pm– Nov 14, 5:52 am	1st	Scorpio	Plant grains, leafy annuals. Fertilize (chemical). Graft or bud plants. Irrigate. Trim to increase growth.
Nov 16, 5:35 am– Nov 18, 7:10 am	1st	Capricorn	Graft or bud plants. Trim to increase growth.

Now is the time to lay your clematis vines down on the ground, bring in the wind chimes, and wrap the shrubs to protect them from drying and sunburn (yes, even in winter!). If you have moved large potted plants or small trees inside for the winter, decorate them! Hang a string of small white lights on medium-sized branches to enjoy in the months ahead.

November 13
5:08 pm EST

NOVEMBER

S	M	T	W	T	F	S
				1	2	3
4	5	6	7	8	9	10
11	12	13	14	15	16	17
18	19	20	21	22	23	24
25	26	27	28	29	30	

♏ November 18–24

Chop your own wood and it will warm you twice.

~Henry Ford

Date	Qtr.	Sign	Activity
Nov 16, 5:35 am– Nov 18, 7:10 am	1st	Capricorn	Graft or bud plants. Trim to increase growth.
Nov 20, 11:55 am– Nov 22, 8:12 pm	2nd	Pisces	Plant grains, leafy annuals. Fertilize (chemical). Graft or bud plants. Irrigate. Trim to increase growth.

To make a beautiful centerpiece for the Thanksgiving table, remove the top and clean the seeds out of an 8- to 10-inch pumpkin. Select a container that fits into the opening. Fill it with water and fresh, fall-colored flowers. Fresh kale stalks are a good alternative to flowers if you want something a little different. Kale comes in curly, dinosaur, and even purple varieties.

◑

November 20
9:31 am EST

		November				
S	M	T	W	T	F	S
					1	2	3
4	5	6	7	8	9	10
11	12	13	14	15	16	17
18	19	20	21	22	23	24
25	26	27	28	29	30	

December

November 25–December 1

A happy life consists not in the absence, but in the mastery of hardships.
                                    ∼HELEN KELLER

Date	Qtr.	Sign	Activity
Nov 25, 7:18 am– Nov 27, 7:58 pm	2nd	Taurus	Plant annuals for hardiness. Trim to increase growth.
Nov 28, 9:46 am– Nov 30, 8:55 am	3rd	Gemini	Cultivate. Destroy weeds and pests. Harvest fruits and root crops for food. Trim to retard growth.
Nov 30, 8:55 am– Dec 2, 8:57 pm	3rd	Cancer	Plant biennials, perennials, bulbs and roots. Prune. Irrigate. Fertilize (organic).

If you want to give gifts to family and friends for their gardens and you have time, consider making gifts. Terra cotta pots can be made to look like antiqued brass with the application of a faux finish. You can turn 2-inch terra cotta pots into lampshades that cover bulbs on a string of lights. Carefully enlarge the drainage holes by scraping with a drill bit. Remove the bulbs and slip each light fixture through a drainage hole. Replace the bulbs. People will love these unique gifts.

2011 © Heather Nilson. Image from BigStockPhoto.com

November 28
9:46 am EST

DECEMBER

S	M	T	W	T	F	S
						1
2	3	4	5	6	7	8
9	10	11	12	13	14	15
16	17	18	19	20	21	22
23	24	25	26	27	28	29
30	31					

December 2–8

Look at the stars! Look, look up at the skies!

~Gerard Manley Hopkins

Date	Qtr.	Sign	Activity
Nov 30, 8:55 am– Dec 2, 8:57 pm	3rd	Cancer	Plant biennials, perennials, bulbs and roots. Prune. Irrigate. Fertilize (organic).
Dec 2, 8:57 pm– Dec 5, 6:51 am	3rd	Leo	Cultivate. Destroy weeds and pests. Harvest fruits and root crops for food. Trim to retard growth.
Dec 5, 6:51 am– Dec 6, 10:31 am	3rd	Virgo	Cultivate, especially medicinal plants. Destroy weeds and pests. Trim to retard growth.
Dec 6, 10:31 am– Dec 7, 1:35 pm	4th	Virgo	Cultivate, especially medicinal plants. Destroy weeds and pests. Trim to retard growth.

Most roses are too tender to withstand the cold, dry winter conditions. The graft union is especially vulnerable to freezing. In zone 5 or colder, cut the bush back to about 2 feet after the first hard frost and insulate it by mounding soil, wood chips, or sawdust around the stems. Don't use soil from the area around the plant; bring it in from somewhere else.

_____

_____

_____

December 6
10:31 am EST

December

S	M	T	W	T	F	S
						1
2	3	4	5	6	7	8
9	10	11	12	13	14	15
16	17	18	19	20	21	22
23	24	25	26	27	28	29
30	31					

2011 © Arne Trautmann. Image from BigStockPhoto.com

December 9–15

Choose food that is as beautiful as you wish to be yourself.

~Victoria Moran

Date	Qtr.	Sign	Activity
Dec 9, 4:51 pm– Dec 11, 5:22 pm	4th	Scorpio	Plant biennials, perennials, bulbs and roots. Prune. Irrigate. Fertilize (organic).
Dec 11, 5:22 pm– Dec 13, 3:42 am	4th	Sagittarius	Cultivate. Destroy weeds and pests. Harvest fruits and root crops for food. Trim to retard growth.
Dec 13, 4:43 pm– Dec 15, 4:53 pm	1st	Capricorn	Graft or bud plants. Trim to increase growth.

When you are finished with outdoor work, update your garden records. Make notes about the season's successes and failures. Write down how your planting combinations worked or didn't work. If you moved plants, make a note of where you placed them. All of this information will come in very handy when you plan next year's gardens.

2011 © Lee Miller. Image from BigStockPhoto.com

December 13
3:42 am EST

DECEMBER

S	M	T	W	T	F	S
						1
2	3	4	5	6	7	8
9	10	11	12	13	14	15
16	17	18	19	20	21	22
23	24	25	26	27	28	29
30	31					

December 16–22

We live in deeds, not years; in thoughts, not breaths; in feelings, not in figures on a dial.

~PHILIP JAMES BAILEY

Date	Qtr.	Sign	Activity
Dec 17, 7:48 pm– Dec 20, 12:19 am	1st	Pisces	Plant grains, leafy annuals. Fertilize (chemical). Graft or bud plants. Irrigate. Trim to increase growth.
Dec 20, 12:19 am– Dec 20, 2:43 am	2nd	Pisces	Plant grains, leafy annuals. Fertilize (chemical). Graft or bud plants. Irrigate. Trim to increase growth.
Dec 22, 1:25 pm– Dec 25, 2:13 am	2nd	Taurus	Plant annuals for hardiness. Trim to increase growth.

If you have flower seeds left over from earlier in the year, plant them indoors now in regular planters. If your home lacks a good south-facing window, place the plants under a grow light and enjoy a touch of summer during the coming winter months.

December 20
12:19 am EST

DECEMBER

S	M	T	W	T	F	S
						1
2	3	4	5	6	7	8
9	10	11	12	13	14	15
16	17	18	19	20	21	22
23	24	25	26	27	28	29
30	31					

December 23–29 ♑

Love all. Trust a few. Do harm to none.

~William Shakespeare

Date	Qtr.	Sign	Activity
Dec 22, 1:25 pm– Dec 25, 2:13 am	2nd	Taurus	Plant annuals for hardiness. Trim to increase growth.
Dec 27, 3:06 pm– Dec 28, 5:21 am	2nd	Cancer	Plant grains, leafy annuals. Fertilize (chemical). Graft or bud plants. Irrigate. Trim to increase growth.
Dec 28, 5:21 am– Dec 30, 2:45 am	3rd	Cancer	Plant biennials, perennials, bulbs and roots. Prune. Irrigate. Fertilize (organic).

In southern states, ferns grow and remain green all winter. In northern states, the polypody fern survives and actually lives many years on shaded, steep rocks. The polypody fern has a single midvein that has thin leaflets but displays no other branching. Their tough, leathery leaves help it cope with desiccation in the dry winter air.

○

December 28
5:21 am EST

December

S	M	T	W	T	F	S
						1
2	3	4	5	6	7	8
9	10	11	12	13	14	15
16	17	18	19	20	21	22
23	24	25	26	27	28	29
30	31					

2011 © Uschi Hering. Image from BigStockPhoto.com

♑ December 30–31

And for winter fly-fishing, it is as useful as an almanac out of date.

~Izaak Walton

Date	Qtr.	Sign	Activity
Dec 28, 5:21 am– Dec 30, 2:45 am	3rd	Cancer	Plant biennials, perennials, bulbs and roots. Prune. Irrigate. Fertilize (organic).
Dec 30, 2:45 am– Jan 1, 12:35 pm	3rd	Leo	Cultivate. Destroy weeds and pests. Harvest fruits and root crops for food. Trim to retard growth.

Gardening begins with the soil. The better the soil, the better your plants will grow. Most plants like a loose, fertile loam, which has a dark-brown color and smells earthy. Heavy soil has high-clay content, and light soil has a lot of sand in it. If you have either heavy or light soil, it can be made more loamlike by adding organic matter. Aged compost, composted leaves, or rotted manure are excellent sources of organic matter, but peat moss, while convenient, should be avoided if possible; it contains too few nutrients.

_____

_____

_____

_____

DECEMBER

S	M	T	W	T	F	S
						1
2	3	4	5	6	7	8
9	10	11	12	13	14	15
16	17	18	19	20	21	22
23	24	25	26	27	28	29
30	31					

Gardening by the Moon

Today, people often reject the notion of gardening according to the Moon's phase and sign. The usual nonbeliever is not a scientist but the city dweller who has never had any real contact with nature and little experience of natural rhythms.

Camille Flammarion, the French astronomer, testifies to the success of Moon planting, though:

"Cucumbers increase at Full Moon, as well as radishes, turnips, leeks, lilies, horseradish, and saffron; onions, on the contrary, are much larger and better nourished during the decline and old age of the Moon than at its increase, during its youth and fullness, which is the reason the Egyptians abstained from onions, on account of their antipathy to the Moon. Herbs gathered while the Moon increases are of great efficiency. If the vines are trimmed at night when the Moon is in the sign of the Lion, Sagittarius, the Scorpion, or the Bull, it will save them from field rats, moles, snails, flies, and other animals."

Dr. Clark Timmins is one of the few modern scientists to have conducted tests in Moon planting. Following is a summary of his experiments:

Beets: When sown with the Moon in Scorpio, the germination rate was 71 percent; when sown in Sagittarius, the germination rate was 58 percent.

Scotch marigold: When sown with the Moon in Cancer, the germination rate was 90 percent; when sown in Leo, the rate was 32 percent.

Carrots: When sown with the Moon in Scorpio, the germination rate was 64 percent; when sown in Sagittarius, the germination rate was 47 percent.

Tomatoes: When sown with the Moon in Cancer, the germination rate was 90 percent; but when sown with the Moon in Leo, the germination rate was 58 percent.

Two things should be emphasized. First, remember that this is only a summary of the results of the experiments; the experiments themselves were conducted in a scientific manner to eliminate any variation in soil, temperature, moisture, and so on, so that only the Moon sign is varied. Second, note that these astonishing results were obtained without regard to the phase of the Moon—the other factor we use in Moon planting, and which presumably would have increased the differential in germination rates.

Dr. Timmins also tried transplanting Cancer- and Leo-planted tomato seedlings while the Cancer Moon was waxing. The result was 100 percent survival. When transplanting was done with the waning Sagittarius Moon, there was 0 percent survival. Dr. Timmins' tests show that the Cancer-planted tomatoes had blossoms twelve days earlier than those planted under Leo; the Cancer-planted tomatoes had an average height of twenty inches at that time compared to fifteen inches for the Leo-planted; the first ripe tomatoes were gathered from the Cancer plantings eleven days ahead of the Leo plantings; and a count of the hanging fruit and its size and weight shows an advantage to the Cancer plants over the Leo plants of 45 percent.

Dr. Timmins also observed that there have been similar tests that did not indicate results favorable to the Moon planting theory. As a scientist, he asked why one set of experiments indicated a positive verification of Moon planting, and others did not. He checked these other tests and found that the experimenters had not followed the geocentric system for determining the Moon sign positions, but the heliocentric. When the times used in these other tests were converted to the geocentric system, the dates chosen often were found to be in barren, rather than fertile, signs. Without going into a technical explanation, it is sufficient to point out that geocentric and heliocentric positions often vary by as much as four days. This is a large enough differential to place the Moon in Cancer, for example, in the heliocentric system, and at the same time in Leo by the geocentric system.

Most almanacs and calendars show the Moon's signs heliocentrically—and thus incorrectly for Moon planting—while the *Moon Sign Book* is calculated correctly for planting purposes, using the geocentric system. Some readers are confused because the *Moon Sign Book* talks about first, second, third, and fourth quarters, while other almanacs refer to these same divisions as New Moon, first quarter, Full Moon, and fourth quarter. Thus the almanacs say first quarter when the *Moon Sign Book* says second quarter.

There is nothing complicated about using astrology in agriculture and horticulture in order to increase both pleasure and profit, but there is one very important rule that is often neglected—use common sense! Of course this is one rule that should be remembered in every activity we undertake, but in the case of gardening and farming by the Moon, if it is not possible to use the best dates for planting or harvesting, we must select the next best and just try to do the best we can.

This brings up the matter of the other factors to consider in your gardening work. The dates we give as best for a certain activity apply to the entire country (with slight time correction), but in your section of the country you may be buried under three feet of snow on a date we say is good to plant your flowers. So we have factors of weather, season, temperature, and moisture variations, soil conditions, your own available time and opportunity, and so forth. Some astrologers like to think it is all a matter of science, but gardening is also an art. In art, you develop an instinctive identification with your work and influence it with your feelings and wishes.

The *Moon Sign Book* gives you the place of the Moon for every day of the year so that you can select the best times once you have become familiar with the rules and practices of lunar agriculture. We give you specific, easy-to-follow directions so that you can get right down to work.

We give you the best dates for planting, and also for various related activities, including cultivation, fertilizing, harvesting, irrigation, and getting rid of weeds and pests. But we cannot tell you exactly when it's good to plant. Many of these rules were learned by observation and experience; as the body of experience grew, we could see various patterns emerging that allowed us to make judgments about new things. That's what you should do, too. After you have worked with lunar agriculture for a while and have gained a working knowledge, you will probably begin to try new things—and we hope you will share your experiments and findings with us. That's how the science grows.

Here's an example of what we mean. Years ago Llewellyn George suggested that we try to combine our bits of knowledge about what to expect in planting under each of the Moon signs in order to benefit from several lunar factors in one plant. From this came our rule for developing "thoroughbred seed." To develop thoroughbred seed, save the seed for three successive years from plants grown by the correct Moon sign and phase. You can plant in the first quarter phase and in the sign of Cancer for fruitfulness; the second year, plant seeds from the first year plants in Libra for beauty; and in the third year, plant the seeds from the second year plants in Taurus to produce hardiness. In a similar manner you can combine the fruitfulness of Cancer, the good root growth of Pisces, and the sturdiness and good vine growth of Scorpio. And don't forget the characteristics of Capricorn: hardy like Taurus, but drier and perhaps more resistant to drought and disease.

Unlike common almanacs, we consider both the Moon's phase and the Moon's sign in making our calculations for the proper timing of our work. It is perhaps a little easier to understand this if we remind you that we are all living in the center of a vast electromagnetic field that is the Earth and its environment in space. Everything that occurs within this electromagnetic field has an effect on everything else within the field. The Moon and the Sun are the most important of the factors affecting the life of the Earth, and it is their relative positions to the Earth that we project for each day of the year.

Many people claim that not only do they achieve larger crops gardening by the Moon, but that their fruits and vegetables are much tastier. A number of organic gardeners have also become lunar gardeners using the natural rhythm of life forces that we experience through the relative movements of the Sun and Moon. We provide a few basic rules and then give you day-by-day guidance for your gardening work. You will be able to choose the best dates to meet your own needs and opportunities.

Planting by the Moon's Phases

During the increasing or waxing light—from New Moon to Full Moon—plant annuals that produce their yield above the ground. An annual is a plant that completes its entire life cycle within one growing season and has to be seeded each year. During the decreasing or waning light—from Full Moon to New Moon—plant biennials, perennials, and bulb and root plants. Biennials include crops that are planted one season to winter over and produce crops the next, such as winter wheat. Perennials and bulb and root plants include all plants that grow from the same root each year.

A simpler, less-accurate rule is to plant crops that produce above the ground during the waxing Moon, and to plant crops that produce below the ground during the waning Moon. Thus the old adage, "Plant potatoes during the dark of the Moon." Llewellyn George's system divided the lunar month into quarters. The first two from New Moon to Full Moon are the first and second quarters, and the last two from Full Moon to New Moon the third and fourth quarters. Using these divisions, we can increase our accuracy in timing our efforts to coincide with natural forces.

First Quarter

Plant annuals producing their yield above the ground, which are generally of the leafy kind that produce their seed outside the fruit. Some examples are asparagus, broccoli, brussels sprouts, cabbage, cauliflower, celery, cress, endive, kohlrabi, lettuce, parsley, and spinach. Cucumbers are an exception, as they do best in the first quarter rather than the second, even though the seeds are inside the fruit. Also plant cereals and grains.

Second Quarter

Plant annuals producing their yield above the ground, which are generally of the viney kind that produce their seed inside the fruit. Some examples include beans, eggplant, melons, peas, peppers, pumpkins, squash, tomatoes, etc. These are not hard-and-fast divisions. If you can't plant during the first quarter, plant during the second, and vice versa. There are many plants that seem to do equally well planted in either quarter, such as watermelon, hay, and cereals and grains.

Third Quarter

Plant biennials, perennials, bulbs, root plants, trees, shrubs, berries, grapes, strawberries, beets, carrots, onions, parsnips, rutabagas, potatoes, radishes, peanuts, rhubarb, turnips, winter wheat, etc.

Fourth Quarter

This is the best time to cultivate, turn sod, pull weeds, and destroy pests of all kinds, especially when the Moon is in Aries, Leo, Virgo, Gemini, Aquarius, and Sagittarius.

The Moon in the Signs

Moon in Aries

Barren, dry, fiery, and masculine. Use for destroying noxious weeds.

Moon in Taurus

Productive, moist, earthy, and feminine. Use for planting many crops when hardiness is important, particularly root crops. Also used for lettuce, cabbage, and similar leafy vegetables.

Moon in Gemini

Barren and dry, airy and masculine. Use for destroying noxious growths, weeds, and pests, and for cultivation.

Moon in Cancer

Fruitful, moist, feminine. Use for planting and irrigation.

Moon in Leo

Barren, dry, fiery, masculine. Use for killing weeds or cultivation.

Moon in Virgo

Barren, moist, earthy, and feminine. Use for cultivation and destroying weeds and pests.

Moon in Libra

Semi-fruitful, moist, and airy. Use for planting crops that need good pulp growth. A very good sign for flowers and vines. Also used for seeding hay, corn fodder, and the like.

Moon in Scorpio

Very fruitful and moist, watery and feminine. Nearly as productive as Cancer; use for the same purposes. Especially good for vine growth and sturdiness.

Moon in Sagittarius

Barren and dry, fiery and masculine. Use for planting onions, seeding hay, and for cultivation.

Moon in Capricorn

Productive and dry, earthy and feminine. Use for planting potatoes and other tubers.

Moon in Aquarius

Barren, dry, airy, and masculine. Use for cultivation and destroying noxious growths and pests.

Moon in Pisces

Very fruitful, moist, watery, and feminine. Especially good for root growth.

A Guide to Planting

Plant	Quarter	Sign
Annuals	1st or 2nd	
Apple tree	2nd or 3rd	Cancer, Pisces, Virgo
Artichoke	1st	Cancer, Pisces
Asparagus	1st	Cancer, Scorpio, Pisces
Aster	1st or 2nd	Virgo, Libra
Barley	1st or 2nd	Cancer, Pisces, Libra, Capricorn, Virgo
Beans (bush & pole)	2nd	Cancer, Taurus, Pisces, Libra
Beans (kidney, white, & navy)	1st or 2nd	Cancer, Pisces
Beech tree	2nd or 3rd	Virgo, Taurus
Beets	3rd	Cancer, Capricorn, Pisces, Libra
Biennials	3rd or 4th	
Broccoli	1st	Cancer, Scorpio, Pisces, Libra
Brussels sprouts	1st	Cancer, Scorpio, Pisces, Libra
Buckwheat	1st or 2nd	Capricorn
Bulbs	3rd	Cancer, Scorpio, Pisces
Bulbs for seed	2nd or 3rd	
Cabbage	1st	Cancer, Scorpio, Pisces, Taurus, Libra
Canes (raspberry, blackberry, & gooseberry)	2nd	Cancer, Scorpio, Pisces
Cantaloupe	1st or 2nd	Cancer, Scorpio, Pisces, Taurus, Libra
Carrots	3rd	Cancer, Scorpio, Pisces, Taurus, Libra
Cauliflower	1st	Cancer, Scorpio, Pisces, Libra
Celeriac	3rd	Cancer, Scorpio, Pisces
Celery	1st	Cancer, Scorpio, Pisces
Cereals	1st or 2nd	Cancer, Scorpio, Pisces, Libra
Chard	1st or 2nd	Cancer, Scorpio, Pisces
Chicory	2nd or 3rd	Cancer, Scorpio, Pisces
Chrysanthemum	1st or 2nd	Virgo
Clover	1st or 2nd	Cancer, Scorpio, Pisces

Plant	Quarter	Sign
Coreopsis	2nd or 3rd	Libra
Corn	1st	Cancer, Scorpio, Pisces
Corn for fodder	1st or 2nd	Libra
Cosmo	2nd or 3rd	Libra
Cress	1st	Cancer, Scorpio, Pisces
Crocus	1st or 2nd	Virgo
Cucumber	1st	Cancer, Scorpio, Pisces
Daffodil	1st or 2nd	Libra, Virgo
Dahlia	1st or 2nd	Libra, Virgo
Deciduous trees	2nd or 3rd	Cancer, Scorpio, Pisces, Virgo, Libra
Eggplant	2nd	Cancer, Scorpio, Pisces, Libra
Endive	1st	Cancer, Scorpio, Pisces, Libra
Flowers	1st	Cancer, Scorpio, Pisces, Libra, Taurus, Virgo
Garlic	3rd	Libra, Taurus, Pisces
Gladiola	1st or 2nd	Libra, Virgo
Gourds	1st or 2nd	Cancer, Scorpio, Pisces, Libra
Grapes	2nd or 3rd	Cancer, Scorpio, Pisces, Virgo
Hay	1st or 2nd	Cancer, Scorpio, Pisces, Libra, Taurus
Herbs	1st or 2nd	Cancer, Scorpio, Pisces
Honeysuckle	1st or 2nd	Scorpio, Virgo
Hops	1st or 2nd	Scorpio, Libra
Horseradish	1st or 2nd	Cancer, Scorpio, Pisces
Houseplants	1st	Cancer, Scorpio, Pisces, Libra
Hyacinth	3rd	Cancer, Scorpio, Pisces
Iris	1st or 2nd	Cancer, Virgo
Kohlrabi	1st or 2nd	Cancer, Scorpio, Pisces, Libra
Leek	2nd or 3rd	Sagittarius
Lettuce	1st	Cancer, Scorpio, Pisces, Libra, Taurus
Lily	1st or 2nd	Cancer, Scorpio, Pisces
Maple tree	2nd or 3rd	Taurus, Virgo, Cancer, Pisces
Melon	2nd	Cancer, Scorpio, Pisces
Moon vine	1st or 2nd	Virgo

Plant	Quarter	Sign
Morning glory	1st or 2nd	Cancer, Scorpio, Pisces, Virgo
Oak tree	2nd or 3rd	Taurus, Virgo, Cancer, Pisces
Oats	1st or 2nd	Cancer, Scorpio, Pisces, Libra
Okra	1st or 2nd	Cancer, Scorpio, Pisces, Libra
Onion seed	2nd	Cancer, Scorpio, Sagittarius
Onion set	3rd or 4th	Cancer, Pisces, Taurus, Libra
Pansies	1st or 2nd	Cancer, Scorpio, Pisces
Parsley	1st	Cancer, Scorpio, Pisces, Libra
Parsnip	3rd	Cancer, Scorpio, Taurus, Capricorn
Peach tree	2nd or 3rd	Cancer, Taurus, Virgo, Libra
Peanuts	3rd	Cancer, Scorpio, Pisces
Pear tree	2nd or 3rd	Cancer, Scorpio, Pisces, Libra
Peas	2nd	Cancer, Scorpio, Pisces, Libra
Peony	1st or 2nd	Virgo
Peppers	2nd	Cancer, Scorpio, Pisces
Perennials	3rd	
Petunia	1st or 2nd	Libra, Virgo
Plum tree	2nd or 3rd	Cancer, Pisces, Taurus, Virgo
Poppies	1st or 2nd	Virgo
Portulaca	1st or 2nd	Virgo
Potatoes	3rd	Cancer, Scorpio, Libra, Taurus, Capricorn
Privet	1st or 2nd	Taurus, Libra
Pumpkin	2nd	Cancer, Scorpio, Pisces, Libra
Quince	1st or 2nd	Capricorn
Radishes	3rd	Cancer, Scorpio, Pisces, Libra, Capricorn
Rhubarb	3rd	Cancer, Pisces
Rice	1st or 2nd	Scorpio
Roses	1st or 2nd	Cancer, Virgo
Rutabaga	3rd	Cancer, Scorpio, Pisces, Taurus
Saffron	1st or 2nd	Cancer, Scorpio, Pisces
Sage	3rd	Cancer, Scorpio, Pisces

Plant	Quarter	Sign
Salsify	1st	Cancer, Scorpio, Pisces
Shallot	2nd	Scorpio
Spinach	1st	Cancer, Scorpio, Pisces
Squash	2nd	Cancer, Scorpio, Pisces, Libra
Strawberries	3rd	Cancer, Scorpio, Pisces
String beans	1st or 2nd	Taurus
Sunflowers	1st or 2nd	Libra, Cancer
Sweet peas	1st or 2nd	Any
Tomatoes	2nd	Cancer, Scorpio, Pisces, Capricorn
Trees, shade	3rd	Taurus, Capricorn
Trees, ornamental	2nd	Libra, Taurus
Trumpet vine	1st or 2nd	Cancer, Scorpio, Pisces
Tubers for seed	3rd	Cancer, Scorpio, Pisces, Libra
Tulips	1st or 2nd	Libra, Virgo
Turnips	3rd	Cancer, Scorpio, Pisces, Taurus, Capricorn, Libra
Valerian	1st or 2nd	Virgo, Gemini
Watermelon	1st or 2nd	Cancer, Scorpio, Pisces, Libra
Wheat	1st or 2nd	Cancer, Scorpio, Pisces, Libra

Companion Planting Guide

Plant	Companions	Hindered by
Asparagus	Tomatoes, parsley, basil	None known
Beans	Tomatoes, carrots, cucumbers, garlic, cabbage, beets, corn	Onions, gladiolas
Beets	Onions, cabbage, lettuce, mint, catnip	Pole beans
Broccoli	Beans, celery, potatoes, onions	Tomatoes
Cabbage	Peppermint, sage, thyme, tomatoes	Strawberries, grapes
Carrots	Peas, lettuce, chives, radishes, leeks, onions, sage	Dill, anise
Citrus trees	Guava, live oak, rubber trees, peppers	None known
Corn	Potatoes, beans, peas, melon, squash, pumpkin, sunflowers, soybeans	Quack grass, wheat, straw, mulch
Cucumbers	Beans, cabbage, radishes, sunflowers, lettuce, broccoli, squash	Aromatic herbs
Eggplant	Green beans, lettuce, kale	None known
Grapes	Peas, beans, blackberries	Cabbage, radishes
Melons	Corn, peas	Potatoes, gourds
Onions, leeks	Beets, chamomile, carrots, lettuce	Peas, beans, sage
Parsnip	Peas	None known
Peas	Radishes, carrots, corn, cucumbers, beans, tomatoes, spinach, turnips	Onion, garlic
Potatoes	Beans, corn, peas, cabbage, hemp, cucumbers, eggplant, catnip	Raspberries, pumpkins, tomatoes, sunflowers
Radishes	Peas, lettuce, nasturtiums, cucumbers	Hyssop
Spinach	Strawberries	None known
Squash/Pumpkin	Nasturtiums, corn, mint, catnip	Potatoes
Tomatoes	Asparagus, parsley, chives, onions, carrots, marigolds, nasturtiums, dill	Black walnut roots, fennel, potatoes
Turnips	Peas, beans, brussels sprouts	Potatoes

Plant	Companions	Uses
Anise	Coriander	Flavor candy, pastry, cheeses, cookies
Basil	Tomatoes	Dislikes rue; repels flies and mosquitoes
Borage	Tomatoes, squash	Use in teas
Buttercup	Clover	Hinders delphinium, peonies, monkshood, columbine

Plant	Companions	Uses
Catnip		Repels flea beetles
Chamomile	Peppermint, wheat, onions, cabbage	Roman chamomile may control damping-off disease; use in herbal sprays
Chervil	Radishes	Good in soups and other dishes
Chives	Carrots	Use in spray to deter black spot on roses
Coriander	Plant anywhere	Hinders seed formation in fennel
Cosmos		Repels corn earworms
Dill	Cabbage	Hinders carrots and tomatoes
Fennel	Plant in borders away from garden	Disliked by all garden plants
Horseradish		Repels potato bugs
Horsetail		Makes fungicide spray
Hyssop		Attracts cabbage fly away from cabbage; harmful to radishes
Lavender	Plant anywhere	Use in spray to control insects on cotton, repels clothes moths
Lovage		Lures horn worms away from tomatoes
Marigolds		Pest repellent; use against Mexican bean beetles and nematodes
Mint	Cabbage, tomatoes	Repels ants, flea beetles, and cabbage worm butterflies
Morning glory	Corn	Helps melon germination
Nasturtiums	Cabbage, cucumbers	Deters aphids, squash bugs, and pumpkin beetles
Okra	Eggplant	Will attract leafhopper (use to trap insects away from other plants)
Parsley	Tomatoes, asparagus	Freeze chopped up leaves to flavor foods
Purslane		Good ground cover
Rosemary		Repels cabbage moths, bean beetles, and carrot flies
Savory		Plant with onions to give them added sweetness
Tansy		Deters Japanese beetles, striped cucumber beetles, and squash bugs
Thyme		Repels cabbage worms
Yarrow		Increases essential oils of neighbors

Moon Void-of-Course

By Kim Rogers-Gallagher

The Moon circles the Earth in about twenty-eight days, moving through each zodiac sign in two-and-a-half days. As she passes through the thirty degrees of each sign, she "visits" with the planets in numerical order, forming aspects with them. Because she moves one degree in just two to two-and-a-half hours, her influence on each planet lasts only a few hours. She eventually reaches the planet that's in the highest degree of any sign and forms what will be her final aspect before leaving the sign. From this point until she enters the next sign, she is referred to as void-of-course.

Think of it this way: the Moon is the emotional "tone" of the day, carrying feelings with her particular to the sign she's "wearing" at the moment. After she has contacted each of the planets, she symbolically "rests" before changing her costume, so her instinct is temporarily on hold. It's during this time that many people feel "fuzzy" or "vague." Plans or decisions made now often do not pan out. Without the instinctual "knowing" the Moon provides as she touches each planet, we tend to be unrealistic or exercise poor judgment. The traditional definition of the void Moon is that "nothing will come of this." Actions initiated under a void Moon are often wasted, irrelevant, or incorrect—usually because information is hidden, missing, or has been overlooked.

Although it's not a good time to initiate plans, routine tasks seem to go along just fine. This period is ideal for reflection. On the lighter side, remember there are good uses for the void Moon. It is the period when the universe seems to be most open to loopholes. It's a great time to make plans you don't want to fulfill or schedule things you don't want to do. See the table on pages 76–81 for a schedule of the Moon's void-of-course times.

Last Aspect   Moon Enters New Sign

			January	
2	3:07 pm	2	Taurus	5:16 pm
5	3:46 am	5	Gemini	5:44 am
7	2:52 pm	7	Cancer	4:05 pm
9	9:25 pm	9	Leo	11:35 pm
12	3:23 am	12	Virgo	4:44 am
13	8:58 pm	14	Libra	8:28 am
16	10:29 am	16	Scorpio	11:33 am
18	1:31 pm	18	Sagittarius	2:29 pm
20	4:49 pm	20	Capricorn	5:40 pm
22	8:38 pm	22	Aquarius	9:53 pm
25	3:33 am	25	Pisces	4:11 am
26	11:53 pm	27	Aries	1:28 pm
30	1:08 am	30	Taurus	1:28 am
			February	
1	2:06 pm	1	Gemini	2:14 pm
4	12:06 am	4	Cancer	1:04 am
6	7:31 am	6	Leo	8:24 am
8	11:42 am	8	Virgo	12:32 pm
10	12:11 am	10	Libra	2:54 pm
12	4:09 pm	12	Scorpio	5:01 pm
14	12:04 pm	14	Sagittarius	7:56 pm
16	11:03 pm	17	Capricorn	12:03 am
19	4:22 am	19	Aquarius	5:28 am
21	11:17 am	21	Pisces	12:31 pm
22	9:24 pm	23	Aries	9:48 pm
26	7:52 am	26	Taurus	9:29 am
28	2:46 pm	28	Gemini	10:27 pm

Last Aspect **Moon Enters New Sign**

		March		
2	8:14 am	2	Cancer	10:08 am
4	5:17 pm	4	Leo	6:17 pm
6	8:27 pm	6	Virgo	10:27 pm
8	4:39 am	8	Libra	11:50 pm
10	10:09 pm	11	Scorpio	12:24 am
12	2:30 pm	13	Sagittarius	2:54 am
15	3:34 am	15	Capricorn	6:24 am
17	9:00 am	17	Aquarius	12:11 pm
19	4:31 pm	19	Pisces	8:05 pm
21	4:39 am	22	Aries	5:57 am
24	1:17 pm	24	Taurus	5:43 pm
27	12:35 am	27	Gemini	6:43 am
29	2:05 pm	29	Cancer	7:07 pm
		April		
1	12:20 am	1	Leo	4:35 am
3	9:47 am	3	Virgo	9:53 am
5	1:37 am	5	Libra	11:32 am
7	6:15 am	7	Scorpio	11:18 am
9	2:56 am	9	Sagittarius	11:12 am
11	7:06 am	11	Capricorn	1:02 pm
13	1:05 pm	13	Aquarius	5:48 pm
15	6:42 pm	16	Pisces	1:38 am
17	10:34 am	18	Aries	11:59 am
20	3:35 pm	21	Taurus	12:05 am
22	1:10 pm	23	Gemini	1:05 pm
25	4:31 pm	26	Cancer	1:42 am
28	3:05 am	28	Leo	12:10 pm
30	10:17 am	30	Virgo	7:02 pm

Last Aspect   **Moon Enters New Sign**

			May		
2	6:58 am	2		Libra	10:04 pm
4	2:02 pm	4		Scorpio	10:20 pm
6	8:14 am	6		Sagittarius	9:39 pm
8	9:34 pm	8		Capricorn	10:00 pm
10	3:11 pm	11		Aquarius	1:03 am
12	8:52 pm	13		Pisces	7:42 am
15	7:59 am	15		Aries	5:45 pm
17	5:44 pm	18		Taurus	6:03 am
20	8:35 am	20		Gemini	7:05 pm
22	6:51 pm	23		Cancer	7:31 am
25	10:34 am	25		Leo	6:11 pm
27	7:54 pm	28		Virgo	2:06 am
30	1:50 am	30		Libra	6:46 am
31	9:31 pm	6/1		Scorpio	8:31 am
			June		
3	5:29 am	3		Sagittarius	8:32 am
5	1:08 am	5		Capricorn	8:31 am
7	8:38 am	7		Aquarius	10:17 am
9	2:33 pm	9		Pisces	3:22 pm
11	6:41 am	12		Aries	12:21 am
13	11:09 pm	14		Taurus	12:22 pm
16	8:09 am	17		Gemini	1:24 am
19	11:02 am	19		Cancer	1:34 pm
21	12:48 pm	21		Leo	11:47 pm
23	6:26 pm	24		Virgo	7:42 am
26	6:53 am	26		Libra	1:15 pm
28	4:22 am	28		Scorpio	4:32 pm
30	3:46 pm	30		Sagittarius	6:04 pm

Last Aspect   Moon Enters New Sign

		July			
2	6:21 pm	2	Capricorn	6:51 pm
4	8:25 am	4	Aquarius	8:26 pm
6	11:49 am	7	Pisces	12:29 am
8	7:00 am	9	Aries	8:14 am
11	5:23 am	11	Taurus	7:30 pm
13	3:46 pm	14	Gemini	8:26 am
16	6:56 am	16	Cancer	8:31 pm
19	12:24 am	19	Leo	6:13 am
21	1:17 am	21	Virgo	1:24 pm
22	8:44 pm	23	Libra	6:38 pm
25	11:22 am	25	Scorpio	10:29 pm
26	11:38 am	28	Sagittarius	1:18 am
29	5:01 pm	30	Capricorn	3:29 am
31	7:30 pm	8/1	Aquarius	5:56 am
		August			
3	3:24 am	3	Pisces	9:58 am
5	1:56 pm	5	Aries	4:59 pm
7	4:04 pm	8	Taurus	3:28 am
9	2:55 pm	10	Gemini	4:11 pm
12	5:49 pm	13	Cancer	4:27 am
15	4:21 am	15	Leo	2:05 pm
17	1:55 pm	17	Virgo	8:33 pm
18	7:26 pm	20	Libra	12:45 am
22	3:13 am	22	Scorpio	3:54 am
23	5:34 am	24	Sagittarius	6:50 am
26	2:39 am	26	Capricorn	9:58 am
28	6:33 am	28	Aquarius	1:38 pm
30	1:48 pm	30	Pisces	6:31 pm

Last Aspect   **Moon Enters New Sign**

		September		
1	4:02 pm	2	Aries	1:37 am
4	7:06 am	4	Taurus	11:41 am
5	2:54 pm	7	Gemini	12:10 am
9	6:59 am	9	Cancer	12:49 pm
11	5:58 pm	11	Leo	11:00 pm
14	1:14 am	14	Virgo	5:30 am
16	7:26 am	16	Libra	8:55 am
18	7:30 am	18	Scorpio	10:46 am
20	9:11 am	20	Sagittarius	12:34 pm
22	12:45 pm	22	Capricorn	3:20 pm
24	5:19 pm	24	Aquarius	7:32 pm
26	11:33 pm	27	Pisces	1:23 am
28	10:35 pm	29	Aries	9:14 am
		October		
1	6:32 pm	1	Taurus	7:26 pm
4	3:44 am	4	Gemini	7:47 am
5	5:08 pm	6	Cancer	8:45 pm
8	3:33 am	9	Leo	7:55 am
10	5:40 pm	11	Virgo	3:23 pm
12	7:48 pm	13	Libra	7:02 pm
15	8:02 am	15	Scorpio	8:06 pm
16	10:23 pm	17	Sagittarius	8:26 pm
19	4:27 pm	19	Capricorn	9:41 pm
21	11:32 pm	22	Aquarius	1:02 am
23	9:27 pm	24	Pisces	7:00 am
26	11:04 am	26	Aries	3:31 pm
27	9:32 pm	29	Taurus	2:15 am
29	5:01 pm	31	Gemini	2:40 pm

Last Aspect   Moon Enters New Sign

		November			
2	5:21 am	3	Cancer	3:43 am
4	3:37 am	5	Leo	2:39 pm
7	10:27 am	7	Virgo	11:35 pm
9	7:27 pm	10	Libra	4:35 am
12	12:13 am	12	Scorpio	6:10 am
14	5:39 am	14	Sagittarius	5:52 am
16	4:44 am	16	Capricorn	5:35 am
18	12:54 am	18	Aquarius	7:10 am
20	9:31 am	20	Pisces	11:55 am
22	1:32 am	22	Aries	8:12 pm
23	8:34 pm	25	Taurus	7:18 am
26	7:57 pm	27	Gemini	7:58 pm
28	8:04 pm	30	Cancer	8:55 am
		December			
2	1:55 am	2	Leo	8:57 pm
4	5:08 pm	5	Virgo	6:51 am
7	5:35 am	7	Libra	1:35 pm
8	7:37 pm	9	Scorpio	4:51 pm
11	8:08 am	11	Sagittarius	5:22 pm
13	3:42 am	13	Capricorn	4:43 pm
15	4:15 pm	15	Aquarius	4:53 pm
17	1:12 pm	17	Pisces	7:48 pm
20	12:19 am	20	Aries	2:43 am
22	7:57 am	22	Taurus	1:25 pm
25	12:58 am	25	Gemini	2:13 am
27	1:50 am	27	Cancer	3:06 pm
28	9:43 am	30	Leo	2:45 am
31	4:52 pm	1/1/2013	Virgo	7:48 pm

The Moon's Rhythm

The Moon journeys around Earth in an elliptical orbit that takes about 27.33 days, which is known as a sidereal month (period of revolution of one body about another). She can move up to 15 degrees or as few as 11 degrees in a day, with the fastest motion occurring when the Moon is at perigee (closest approach to Earth). The Moon is never retrograde, but when her motion is slow, the effect is similar to a retrograde period.

Astrologers have observed that people born on a day when the Moon is fast will process information differently from those who are born when the Moon is slow in motion. People born when the Moon is fast process information quickly and tend to react quickly, while those born during a slow Moon will be more deliberate.

The time from New Moon to New Moon is called the synodic month (involving a conjunction), and the average time span between this Sun-Moon alignment is 29.53 days. Since 29.53

won't divide into 365 evenly, we can have a month with two Full Moons or two New Moons.

Moon Aspects

The aspects the Moon will make during the times you are considering are also important. A trine or sextile, and sometimes a conjunction, are considered favorable aspects. A trine or sextile between the Sun and Moon is an excellent foundation for success. Whether or not a conjunction is considered favorable depends upon the planet the Moon is making a conjunction to. If it's joining the Sun, Venus, Mercury, Jupiter, or even Saturn, the aspect is favorable. If the Moon joins Pluto or Mars, however, that would not be considered favorable. There may be exceptions, but it would depend on what you are electing to do. For example, a trine to Pluto might hasten the end of a relationship you want to be free of.

It is important to avoid times when the Moon makes an aspect to or is conjoining any retrograde planet, unless, of course, you want the thing started to end in failure.

After the Moon has completed an aspect to a planet, that planetary energy has passed. For example, if the Moon squares Saturn at 10:00 am, you can disregard Saturn's influence on your activity if it will occur after that time. You should always look ahead at aspects the Moon will make on the day in question, though, because if the Moon opposes Mars at 11:30 pm on that day, you can expect events that stretch into the evening to be affected by the Moon-Mars aspect. A testy conversation might lead to an argument, or more.

Moon Signs

Much agricultural work is ruled by earth signs—Virgo, Capricorn, and Taurus; and the air signs—Gemini, Aquarius, and Libra—rule flying and intellectual pursuits.

Each planet has one or two signs in which its characteristics are enhanced or "dignified," and the planet is said to "rule" that sign. The Sun rules Leo and the Moon rules Cancer, for example. The ruling planet for each sign is listed below. These should not be considered complete lists. We recommend that you purchase a book of planetary rulerships for more complete information.

Aries Moon

The energy of an Aries Moon is masculine, dry, barren, and fiery. Aries provides great start-up energy, but things started at this time may be the result of impulsive action that lacks research or necessary support. Aries lacks staying power.

Use this assertive, outgoing Moon sign to initiate change, but have a plan in place for someone to pick up the reins when you're impatient to move on to the next thing. Work that requires skillful, but not necessarily patient, use of tools—hammering, cutting down trees, etc.—is appropriate in Aries. Expect things to occur rapidly but to also quickly pass. If you are prone to injury or accidents, exercise caution and good judgment in Aries-related activities.

RULER: Mars

IMPULSE: Action

RULES: Head and face

Taurus Moon

A Taurus Moon's energy is feminine, semi-fruitful, and earthy. The Moon is exalted—very strong—in Taurus. Taurus is known as the farmer's sign because of its associations with farmland and precipitation that is the typical day-long "soaker" variety. Taurus energy is good to incorporate into your plans when patience, practicality, and perseverance are needed. Be aware, though, that you may also experience stubbornness in this sign.

Things started in Taurus tend to be long lasting and to increase in value. This can be very supportive energy in a marriage election. On the downside, the fixed energy of this sign resists change or the letting go of even the most difficult situations. A divorce following a marriage that occurred during a Taurus Moon may be difficult and costly to end. Things begun now tend to become habitual and hard to alter. If you want to make changes in something you started, it would be better to wait for Gemini. This is a good time to get a loan, but expect the people in charge of money to be cautious and slow to make decisions.

RULER: Venus

IMPULSE: Stability

RULES: Neck, throat, and voice

Gemini Moon

A Gemini Moon's energy is masculine, dry, barren, and airy. People are more changeable than usual and may prefer to follow intellectual pursuits and play mental games rather than apply themselves to practical concerns.

This sign is not favored for agricultural matters, but it is an excellent time to prepare for activities, to run errands, and write letters. Plan to use a Gemini Moon to exchange ideas, meet people, go on vacations that include walking or biking, or be in situations that require versatility and quick thinking on your feet.

RULER: Mercury

IMPULSE: Versatility

RULES: Shoulders, hands, arms, lungs, and nervous system

Cancer Moon

A Cancer Moon's energy is feminine, fruitful, moist, and very strong. Use this sign when you want to grow things—flowers, fruits, vegetables, commodities, stocks, or collections—for example. This sensitive sign stimulates rapport between people. Considered the most fertile of the signs, it is often associated with mothering. You can use this moontime to build personal friendships that support mutual growth.

Cancer is associated with emotions and feelings. Prominent Cancer energy promotes growth, but it can also turn people pouty and prone to withdrawing into their shells.

RULER: The Moon

IMPULSE: Tenacity

RULES: Chest area, breasts, and stomach

Leo Moon

A Leo Moon's energy is masculine, hot, dry, fiery, and barren. Use it whenever you need to put on a show, make a presentation, or entertain colleagues or guests. This is a proud yet playful energy that exudes self-confidence and is often associated with romance.

This is an excellent time for fund-raisers and ceremonies or to be straightforward, frank, and honest about something. It is advisable not to put yourself in a position of needing public approval or where you might have to cope with underhandedness, as trouble in these areas can bring out the worst Leo traits. There is a tendency in this sign to become arrogant or self-centered.

RULER: The Sun

IMPULSE: I am

RULES: Heart and upper back

Virgo Moon

A Virgo Moon is feminine, dry, barren, earthy energy. It is favorable for anything that needs painstaking attention—especially those things where exactness rather than innovation is preferred.

Use this sign for activities when you must analyze information or when you must determine the value of something. Virgo is the sign of bargain hunting. It's friendly toward agricultural matters with an emphasis on animals and harvesting vegetables. It is an excellent time to care for animals, especially training them and veterinary work.

This sign is most beneficial when decisions have already been made and now need to be carried out. The inclination here is to see details rather than the bigger picture.

There is a tendency in this sign to overdo. Precautions should be taken to avoid becoming too dull from all work and no play. Build a little relaxation and pleasure into your routine from the beginning.

RULER: Mercury

IMPULSE: Discriminating

RULES: Abdomen and intestines

Libra Moon

A Libra Moon's energy is masculine, semi-fruitful, and airy. This energy will benefit any attempt to bring beauty to a place or thing. Libra is considered good energy for starting things of an intellectual nature. Libra is the sign of partnership and unions, which make it an excellent time to form partnerships of any kind, to make agreements, and to negotiate. Even though this sign is good for initiating things, it is crucial to work with a partner who will provide incentive and encouragement, however. A Libra Moon accentuates teamwork (particularly teams of two) and artistic work (especially work that involves color). Make use of this sign when you are decorating your home or shopping for better-quality clothing.

RULER: Venus

IMPULSE: Balance

RULES: Lower back, kidneys, and buttocks

Scorpio Moon

The Scorpio Moon is feminine, fruitful, cold, and moist. It is useful when intensity (that sometimes borders on obsession) is needed. Scorpio is considered a very psychic sign. Use this Moon sign when you must back up something you strongly believe in, such as union or employer relations. There is strong group loyalty here, but a Scorpio Moon is also a good time to end connections thoroughly. This is also a good time to conduct research.

The desire nature is so strong here that there is a tendency to manipulate situations to get what one wants or to not see one's responsibility in an act.

RULER: Pluto, Mars (traditional)

IMPULSE: Transformation

RULES: Reproductive organs, genitals, groin, and pelvis

Sagittarius Moon

The Moon's energy is masculine, dry, barren, and fiery in Sagittarius, encouraging flights of imagination and confidence in the flow of life. Sagittarius is the most philosophical sign. Candor and honesty are enhanced when the Moon is here. This is an excellent time to "get things off your chest" and to deal with institutions of higher learning, publishing companies, and the law. It's also a good time for sport and adventure.

Sagittarians are the crusaders of this world. This is a good time to tackle things that need improvement, but don't try to be the diplomat while influenced by this energy. Opinions can run strong, and the tendency to proselytize is increased.

RULER: Jupiter

IMPULSE: Expansion

RULES: Thighs and hips

Capricorn Moon

In Capricorn the Moon's energy is feminine, semi-fruitful, and earthy. Because Cancer and Capricorn are polar opposites, the Moon's energy is thought to be weakened here. This energy encourages the need for structure, discipline, and organization. This is a good time to set goals and plan for the future, tend to family business, and to take care of details requiring patience or a businesslike manner. Institutional activities are favored. This sign should be avoided if you're seeking favors, as those in authority can be insensitive under this influence.

RULER: Saturn

IMPULSE: Ambitious

RULES: Bones, skin, and knees

Aquarius Moon

An Aquarius Moon's energy is masculine, barren, dry, and airy. Activities that are unique, individualistic, concerned with humanitarian issues, society as a whole, and making improvements are favored under this Moon. It is this quality of making improvements that has caused this sign to be associated with inventors and new inventions.

An Aquarius Moon promotes the gathering of social groups for friendly exchanges. People tend to react and speak from an intellectual rather than emotional viewpoint when the Moon is in this sign.

RULER: Uranus and Saturn

IMPULSE: Reformer

RULES: Calves and ankles

Pisces Moon

A Pisces Moon is feminine, fruitful, cool, and moist. This is an excellent time to retreat, meditate, sleep, pray, or make that dreamed-of escape into a fantasy vacation. However, things are not always what they seem to be with the Moon in Pisces. Personal boundaries tend to be fuzzy, and you may not be seeing things clearly. People tend to be idealistic under this sign, which can prevent them from seeing reality.

There is a live-and-let-live philosophy attached to this sign, which in the idealistic world may work well enough, but chaos is frequently the result. That's why this sign is also associated with alcohol and drug abuse, drug trafficking, and counterfeiting. On the lighter side, many musicians and artists are ruled by Pisces. It's only when they move too far away from reality that the dark side of substance abuse, suicide, or crime takes away life.

RULER: Jupiter and Neptune

IMPULSE: Empathetic

RULES: Feet

More About Zodiac Signs

Element (Triplicity)

Each of the zodiac signs is classified as belonging to an element; these are the four basic elements:

Fire Signs

Aries, Sagittarius, and Leo are action-oriented, outgoing, energetic, and spontaneous.

Earth Signs

Taurus, Capricorn, and Virgo are stable, conservative, practical, and oriented to the physical and material realm.

Air Signs

Gemini, Aquarius, and Libra are sociable and critical, and they tend to represent intellectual responses rather than feelings.

Water Signs

Cancer, Scorpio, and Pisces are emotional, receptive, intuitive, and can be very sensitive.

Quality (Quadruplicity)

Each zodiac sign is further classified as being cardinal, mutable, or fixed. There are four signs in each quadruplicity, one sign from each element.

Cardinal Signs

Aries, Cancer, Libra, and Capricorn represent beginnings and newly initiated action. They initiate each new season in the cycle of the year.

Fixed Signs

Taurus, Leo, Scorpio, and Aquarius want to maintain the status quo through stubbornness and persistence; they represent that "between" time. For example, Leo is the month when summer really feels like summer.

Mutable Signs

Pisces, Gemini, Virgo, and Sagittarius adapt to change and tolerate situations. They represent the last month of each season, when things are changing in preparation for the coming season.

Nature and Fertility

In addition to a sign's element and quality, each sign is further classified as either fruitful, semi-fruitful, or barren. This classification is the most important for readers who use the gardening information in the *Moon Sign Book* because the timing of most events depends on the fertility of the sign occupied by the Moon. The water signs of Cancer, Scorpio, and Pisces are the most fruitful. The semi-fruitful signs are the earth signs Taurus and Capricorn, and the air sign Libra. The barren signs correspond to fire-signs Aries, Leo, and Sagittarius; air-signs Gemini and Aquarius; and earth-sign Virgo.

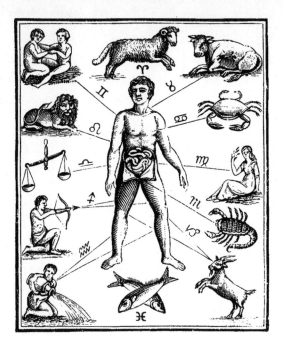

Good Timing

By Sharon Leah

E lectional astrology is the art of electing times to begin any undertaking. Say, for example, you want to start a business. That business will experience ups and downs, as well as reach its potential, according to the promise held in the universe at the time the business was started—its birth time. The horoscope (birth chart) set for the date, time, and place that a business starts would indicate the outcome—its potential to succeed.

So, you might ask yourself the question: If the horoscope for a business start can show success or failure, why not begin at a time that is more favorable to the venture? Well, you can.

While no time is perfect, there are better times and better days to undertake specific activities. There are thousands of examples that prove electional astrology is not only practical, but that it can make a difference in our lives. There are rules for electing times to begin various activities—even shopping. You'll find detailed instructions about how to make elections beginning on page 107.

Personalizing Elections

The election rules in this almanac are based upon the planetary positions at the time for which the election is made. They do not depend on any type of birth chart. However, a birth chart based upon the time, date, and birthplace of an event has advantages. No election is effective for every person. For example, you may leave home to begin a trip at the same time as a friend, but each of you will have a different experience according to whether or not your birth chart favors the trip.

Not all elections require a birth chart, but the timing of very important events—business starts, marriages, etc.—would benefit from the additional accuracy a birth chart provides. To order a birth chart for yourself or a planned event, visit our Web site at www.llewellyn.com.

Some Things to Consider

You've probably experienced good timing in your life. Maybe you were at the right place at the right time to meet a friend whom you hadn't seen in years. Frequently, when something like that happens, it is the result of following an intuitive impulse—that "gut instinct." Consider for a moment that you were actually responding to planetary energies. Electional astrology is a tool that can help you to align with energies, present and future, that are available to us through planetary placements.

Significators

Decide upon the important significators (planet, sign, and house ruling the matter) for which the election is being made. The Moon is the most important significator in any election, so the

Moon should always be fortified (strong by sign and making favorable aspects to other planets). The Moon's aspects to other planets are more important than the sign the Moon is in.

Other important considerations are the significators of the Ascendant and Midheaven—the house ruling the election matter and the ruler of the sign on that house cusp. Finally, any planet or sign that has a general rulership over the matter in question should be taken into consideration.

Nature and Fertility

Determine the general nature of the sign that is appropriate for your election. For example, much agricultural work is ruled by the earth signs of Virgo, Capricorn, and Taurus; while the air signs—Gemini, Aquarius, and Libra—rule intellectual pursuits.

One Final Comment

Use common sense. If you must do something, like plant your garden or take an airplane trip on a day that doesn't have the best aspects, proceed anyway, but try to minimize problems. For example, leave early for the airport to avoid being left behind due to delays in the security lanes. When you have no other choice, do the best that you can under the circumstances at the time.

If you want to personalize your elections, please turn to page 107 for more information. If you want a quick and easy answer, you can refer to Llewellyn's Astro Almanac.

Llewellyn's Astro Almanac

The Astro Almanac tables, beginning on the next page, can help you find the dates best suited to particular activities. The dates provided are determined from the Moon's sign, phase, and aspects to other planets. Please note that the Astro Almanac does not take personal factors, such as your Sun and Moon sign, into account. The dates are general, and they will apply for everyone. Some activities will not have suitable dates during a particular month, so no dates will be shown.

Activity	January
Animals (Neuter or spay)	18, 19, 21, 22
Animals (Sell or buy)	7, 25, 31
Automobile (Buy)	5, 7, 12, 22
Brewing	17, 18
Build (Start foundation)	25
Business (Conducting for self and others)	3, 13, 18, 28
Business (Start new)	
Can Fruits and Vegetables	9, 17
Can Preserves	9, 17
Concrete (Pour)	10, 11
Construction (Begin new)	3, 7, 12, 13, 20, 28
Consultants (Begin work with)	1, 2, 7, 12, 17, 20, 22, 25, 27, 30
Contracts (Bid on)	1, 2, 7, 8, 25, 27, 30
Cultivate	23
Decorating	5, 6, 7, 23, 24, 25
Demolition	10, 11, 18, 19
Electronics (Buy)	5, 23
Entertain Guests	3, 4, 5, 7, 8, 31
Floor Covering (Laying new)	10, 11, 12, 13, 14, 15, 16, 22, 23
Habits (Break)	21
Hair (Cut to increase growth)	2, 3, 4, 5, 6, 25, 26, 30, 31
Hair (Cut to decrease growth)	18, 19, 20, 21
Harvest (Grain for storage)	10, 11, 12
Harvest (Root crops)	10, 11, 18, 19, 20
Investments (New)	3, 13
Loan (Ask for)	2, 3, 4, 5, 9, 30, 31
Massage (Relaxing)	31
Mow Lawn (Decrease growth)	10, 11, 12, 13, 14, 15, 16, 17, 18, 19, 20, 21
Mow Lawn (Increase growth)	1, 2, 3, 4, 5, 6, 7, 24, 25, 26, 27, 28, 29, 30
Mushrooms (Pick)	8, 9, 10
Negotiate (Business for the elderly)	7, 20
Prune for Better Fruit	16, 17, 18, 19, 20
Prune to Promote Healing	21, 22
Wean Children	19, 20, 21, 22, 23, 24, 25
Wood Floors (Installing)	20, 21, 22
Write Letters or Contracts	5, 10, 18, 22, 23

Activity	February
Animals (Neuter or spay)	14, 15, 17, 18, 19, 21
Animals (Sell or buy)	4, 6
Automobile (Buy)	1, 2, 4, 17, 29
Brewing	13, 14
Build (Start foundation)	
Business (Conducting for self and others)	2, 12, 16, 27
Business (Start new)	
Can Fruits and Vegetables	13, 14
Can Preserves	13, 14
Concrete (Pour)	20
Construction (Begin new)	2, 4, 8, 12, 16, 17, 27
Consultants (Begin work with)	2, 4, 8, 12, 17, 21, 22, 26, 28
Contracts (Bid on)	2, 4, 22, 26, 28
Cultivate	19, 20, 21
Decorating	1, 2, 3, 4, 29
Demolition	7, 14, 15, 16
Electronics (Buy)	1, 2, 12, 19, 29
Entertain Guests	2, 4, 5, 27, 28, 29
Floor Covering (Laying new)	8, 9, 10, 11, 12, 19, 20
Habits (Break)	17, 18, 20
Hair (Cut to increase growth)	1, 2, 3, 4, 6, 22, 26, 27, 28, 29
Hair (Cut to decrease growth)	14, 15, 16, 17, 18
Harvest (Grain for storage)	8, 14
Harvest (Root crops)	8, 14, 15, 16, 19, 20
Investments (New)	2, 12
Loan (Ask for)	1, 6, 7, 26, 27, 28
Massage (Relaxing)	6, 20
Mow Lawn (Decrease growth)	8, 9, 10, 11, 12, 13, 14, 15, 16, 17, 18, 19, 20
Mow Lawn (Increase growth)	1, 2, 3, 4, 5, 6, 22, 23, 24, 25, 26, 27, 28, 29
Mushrooms (Pick)	6, 7, 8
Negotiate (Business for the elderly)	8, 16, 21
Prune for Better Fruit	12, 13, 14, 16
Prune to Promote Healing	17, 18, 19
Wean Children	15, 16, 17, 18, 19, 20, 21
Wood Floors (Installing)	17, 18, 19
Write Letters or Contracts	1, 6, 15, 19, 22, 29

Activity	March
Animals (Neuter or spay)	14, 15, 16, 17, 19, 21, 22
Animals (Sell or buy)	2, 3, 30
Automobile (Buy)	2, 27, 29
Brewing	11, 20, 21
Build (Start foundation)	
Business (Conducting for self and others)	3, 12, 17, 27
Business (Start new)	7
Can Fruits and Vegetables	11, 20, 21
Can Preserves	6, 19, 20
Concrete (Pour)	18, 19
Construction (Begin new)	3, 7, 16, 17, 27, 30
Consultants (Begin work with)	3, 4, 7, 13, 16, 17, 20, 22, 25, 27, 30, 31
Contracts (Bid on)	3, 4, 7, 25, 27, 30, 31
Cultivate	13, 14, 18, 19, 22
Decorating	1, 2, 27, 28, 29
Demolition	13, 14, 22
Electronics (Buy)	17, 27
Entertain Guests	2, 3, 25, 26, 28, 29, 30, 31
Floor Covering (Laying new)	9, 10, 17, 18
Habits (Break)	15, 16, 17, 19
Hair (Cut to increase growth)	1, 4, 24, 25, 26, 27, 28
Hair (Cut to decrease growth)	13, 14, 15, 16, 19, 20, 21
Harvest (Grain for storage)	13, 14
Harvest (Root crops)	13, 14, 17, 18, 19
Investments (New)	3, 12
Loan (Ask for)	4, 5, 6, 25, 26
Massage (Relaxing)	3, 26
Mow Lawn (Decrease growth)	9, 10, 11, 12, 13, 14, 15, 16, 17, 18, 19, 20, 21
Mow Lawn (Increase growth)	1, 2, 3, 4, 5, 6, 7, 23, 24, 25, 26, 27, 28, 29, 30, 31
Mushrooms (Pick)	7, 8, 9
Negotiate (Business for the elderly)	2, 6, 19, 29
Prune for Better Fruit	11, 12, 13, 14
Prune to Promote Healing	15, 16, 17
Wean Children	13, 14, 15, 16, 17, 18, 19
Wood Floors (Installing)	15, 16, 17
Write Letters or Contracts	5, 13, 17, 22, 27

Activity	April
Animals (Neuter or spay)	10, 11, 12, 13, 17, 18
Animals (Sell or buy)	1, 4, 5, 27, 30
Automobile (Buy)	13, 24, 25
Brewing	8, 16, 17
Build (Start foundation)	
Business (Conducting for self and others)	2, 10, 15, 26
Business (Start new)	4
Can Fruits and Vegetables	8, 16, 17
Can Preserves	8
Concrete (Pour)	14
Construction (Begin new)	2, 4, 10, 12, 15, 26, 27
Consultants (Begin work with)	4, 9, 12, 13, 17, 18, 22, 24, 27, 29
Contracts (Bid on)	4, 22, 24, 27, 29
Cultivate	10, 11, 14, 15, 19, 20
Decorating	5, 6, 23, 24, 25
Demolition	9, 10, 18, 19, 20
Electronics (Buy)	14, 24
Entertain Guests	5, 21, 22, 24, 25, 26, 27, 30
Floor Covering (Laying new)	7, 13, 14, 15
Habits (Break)	14, 18, 19, 20
Hair (Cut to increase growth)	1, 21, 22, 23, 24, 25, 28
Hair (Cut to decrease growth)	9, 10, 11, 12, 16, 17
Harvest (Grain for storage)	9, 10, 11, 13
Harvest (Root crops)	9, 10, 11, 13, 14, 15, 18, 19, 20
Investments (New)	2, 10
Loan (Ask for)	1, 2, 21, 22, 23, 28, 29, 30
Massage (Relaxing)	1, 5, 14, 30
Mow Lawn (Decrease growth)	7, 8, 9, 10, 11, 12, 13, 14, 15, 16, 17, 18, 19, 20
Mow Lawn (Increase growth)	1, 2, 3, 4, 5, 22, 23, 24, 25, 26, 27, 28, 29, 30
Mushrooms (Pick)	5, 6, 7
Negotiate (Business for the elderly)	15, 25, 30
Prune for Better Fruit	7, 8, 9, 10
Prune to Promote Healing	12, 13
Wean Children	10, 11, 12, 13, 14, 15
Wood Floors (Installing)	11, 12, 13
Write Letters or Contracts	1, 9, 14, 18, 24, 29

Activity	May
Animals (Neuter or spay)	6, 8, 9, 10, 14, 15
Animals (Sell or buy)	2, 4, 25, 27, 31
Automobile (Buy)	21, 22
Brewing	6, 14, 15
Build (Start foundation)	27
Business (Conducting for self and others)	1, 10, 15, 26, 30
Business (Start new)	2, 30
Can Fruits and Vegetables	6, 14, 15
Can Preserves	6, 19, 20
Concrete (Pour)	11, 12, 19
Construction (Begin new)	1, 2, 10, 25, 26, 30
Consultants (Begin work with)	2, 8, 10, 14, 15, 20, 25, 26, 30, 31
Contracts (Bid on)	2, 22, 25, 26, 30, 31
Cultivate	7, 8, 12, 16, 17
Decorating	3, 4, 20, 21, 22, 30, 31
Demolition	7, 16, 17
Electronics (Buy)	11, 21, 31
Entertain Guests	4, 18, 19, 20, 22, 23, 24, 27, 31
Floor Covering (Laying new)	11, 12, 18, 19, 20
Habits (Break)	16, 17
Hair (Cut to increase growth)	21, 22, 25
Hair (Cut to decrease growth)	7, 8, 9, 10, 13, 14, 18, 19, 20
Harvest (Grain for storage)	6, 7, 8, 11, 12
Harvest (Root crops)	7, 8, 11, 12, 16, 17
Investments (New)	1, 10, 30
Loan (Ask for)	26, 27
Massage (Relaxing)	4, 12, 27, 31
Mow Lawn (Decrease growth)	6, 7, 8, 9, 10, 11, 12, 13, 14, 15, 16, 17, 18, 19
Mow Lawn (Increase growth)	1, 2, 3, 4, 21, 22, 23, 24, 25, 26, 27, 28, 29, 30, 31
Mushrooms (Pick)	4, 5, 6
Negotiate (Business for the elderly)	8, 12, 22, 27
Prune for Better Fruit	5, 6, 7, 8
Prune to Promote Healing	9, 10
Wean Children	7, 8, 9, 10, 11, 12
Wood Floors (Installing)	9, 10
Write Letters or Contracts	7, 20, 21, 26

Activity	June
Animals (Neuter or spay)	5, 6, 7, 9, 10
Animals (Sell or buy)	22, 27
Automobile (Buy)	17, 18
Brewing	10
Build (Start foundation)	23
Business (Conducting for self and others)	8, 13, 24, 29
Business (Start new)	24
Can Fruits and Vegetables	10
Can Preserves	15
Concrete (Pour)	8, 9, 15
Construction (Begin new)	7, 8, 12, 13, 22, 24, 26
Consultants (Begin work with)	7, 10, 12, 15, 17, 21, 22, 26
Contracts (Bid on)	21, 22, 26, 29
Cultivate	4, 5, 12, 13, 17, 18
Decorating	1, 19, 26, 27, 28
Demolition	4, 12, 13
Electronics (Buy)	8, 17, 26
Entertain Guests	15, 16, 17, 19, 20, 22, 27
Floor Covering (Laying new)	7, 8, 14, 15, 16, 17, 18
Habits (Break)	12, 13, 17
Hair (Cut to increase growth)	3, 21, 30
Hair (Cut to decrease growth)	5, 6, 9, 10, 11, 14, 15, 16, 17, 18
Harvest (Grain for storage)	5, 7, 8, 9
Harvest (Root crops)	4, 7, 8, 9, 12, 13, 17, 18
Investments (New)	8, 29
Loan (Ask for)	21, 22, 23
Massage (Relaxing)	8, 22, 27
Mow Lawn (Decrease growth)	5, 6, 7, 8, 9, 10, 11, 12, 13,14, 15, 16, 17, 18
Mow Lawn (Increase growth)	1, 2, 3, 20, 21, 22, 23, 24, 25, 26, 27, 28, 29, 30
Mushrooms (Pick)	3, 4, 5
Negotiate (Business for the elderly)	4, 18, 23
Prune for Better Fruit	4
Prune to Promote Healing	5, 6, 7
Wean Children	3, 4, 5, 6, 7, 8, 9
Wood Floors (Installing)	5, 6, 7
Write Letters or Contracts	3, 8, 17, 21, 22

Activity	July
Animals (Neuter or spay)	3, 7, 8
Animals (Sell or buy)	20, 25
Automobile (Buy)	15, 16
Brewing	7, 8, 17
Build (Start foundation)	21
Business (Conducting for self and others)	13, 23, 28
Business (Start new)	22
Can Fruits and Vegetables	7, 8, 17, 18
Can Preserves	12, 13, 17, 18
Concrete (Pour)	5, 12, 13
Construction (Begin new)	5, 9, 13, 19, 23, 24, 28
Consultants (Begin work with)	1, 5, 9, 10, 14, 15, 19, 20, 24, 28
Contracts (Bid on)	1, 20, 24, 28
Cultivate	10, 11, 15, 16
Decorating	23, 24, 25
Demolition	9, 10
Electronics (Buy)	5, 15, 24
Entertain Guests	12, 13, 14, 15, 16, 20, 25
Floor Covering (Laying new)	4, 5, 6, 7, 8, 12, 13, 14, 15, 16
Habits (Break)	11, 14, 15, 16
Hair (Cut to increase growth)	1, 2, 19, 28, 29, 30, 31
Hair (Cut to decrease growth)	3, 7, 8, 11, 12, 13, 14, 15
Harvest (Grain for storage)	4, 5, 9, 10
Harvest (Root crops)	4, 5, 6, 9, 10, 11, 14, 15, 16
Investments (New)	8, 28
Loan (Ask for)	19, 20, 21
Massage (Relaxing)	2, 20, 25
Mow Lawn (Decrease growth)	4, 5, 6, 7, 8, 9, 10, 11, 12, 13, 14, 15, 16, 17
Mow Lawn (Increase growth)	1, 2, 20, 21, 22, 23, 24, 25, 26, 27, 28, 29, 30, 31
Mushrooms (Pick)	2, 3, 4, 31
Negotiate (Business for the elderly)	6, 29
Prune for Better Fruit	
Prune to Promote Healing	3, 4
Wean Children	1, 2, 3, 4, 5, 6, 28, 29, 30
Wood Floors (Installing)	3, 4
Write Letters or Contracts	1, 5, 15, 19, 20, 28

Activity	August
Animals (Neuter or spay)	3, 4, 5, 31
Animals (Sell or buy)	18, 20, 23, 29
Automobile (Buy)	10, 11, 12
Brewing	4, 5, 14, 15
Build (Start foundation)	
Business (Conducting for self and others)	12, 22, 26
Business (Start new)	18
Can Fruits and Vegetables	4, 5, 14
Can Preserves	8, 9, 10, 14
Concrete (Pour)	2, 8, 9, 10, 16
Construction (Begin new)	1, 6, 12, 16, 20, 22, 26, 29
Consultants (Begin work with)	1, 5, 6, 10, 11, 15, 16, 20, 25, 29
Contracts (Bid on)	1, 20, 22, 25, 29
Cultivate	11, 12, 16, 17
Decorating	1, 20, 21, 22, 28, 29, 30
Demolition	5, 6, 7, 15, 16
Electronics (Buy)	1, 10, 11, 20, 29
Entertain Guests	8, 9, 10, 11, 12, 13, 14
Floor Covering (Laying new)	2, 8, 9, 10, 11, 12, 15, 16, 17
Habits (Break)	10, 11, 12, 16
Hair (Cut to increase growth)	24, 25, 26, 27, 30
Hair (Cut to decrease growth)	3, 4, 8, 9, 10, 11, 12, 15
Harvest (Grain for storage)	2, 5, 6, 7
Harvest (Root crops)	2, 5, 6, 7, 10, 11, 12, 15, 16
Investments (New)	6, 26
Loan (Ask for)	17
Massage (Relaxing)	8, 13
Mow Lawn (Decrease growth)	2, 3, 4, 5, 6, 7, 8, 9, 10, 11, 12, 13, 14, 15, 16
Mow Lawn (Increase growth)	18, 19, 20, 21, 22, 23, 24, 25, 26, 27, 28, 29, 30
Mushrooms (Pick)	1, 2, 30, 31
Negotiate (Business for the elderly)	2, 12, 17, 30
Prune for Better Fruit	
Prune to Promote Healing	
Wean Children	1, 2, 3, 24, 25, 26, 27, 28, 29, 30
Wood Floors (Installing)	
Write Letters or Contracts	1, 11, 15, 16, 24, 29

Activity	September
Animals (Neuter or spay)	1
Animals (Sell or buy)	17, 21
Automobile (Buy)	7, 9, 16
Brewing	10, 11
Build (Start foundation)	
Business (Conducting for self and others)	5, 11, 20, 24
Business (Start new)	
Can Fruits and Vegetables	10, 11
Can Preserves	5, 10, 11
Concrete (Pour)	5, 12, 13
Construction (Begin new)	3, 5, 11, 13, 17, 24, 26, 30
Consultants (Begin work with)	3, 5, 8, 11, 13, 16, 17, 21, 25, 26, 30
Contracts (Bid on)	16, 17, 21, 25, 26
Cultivate	8, 9, 12, 13, 14, 15
Decorating	16, 17, 18, 24, 25, 26
Demolition	2, 3, 12, 13, 29, 30
Electronics (Buy)	7, 25
Entertain Guests	6, 7, 8, 9, 10, 17
Floor Covering (Laying new)	4, 5, 6, 7, 8, 12, 13, 14, 15
Habits (Break)	9, 13, 14
Hair (Cut to increase growth)	20, 21, 22, 23, 27, 28
Hair (Cut to decrease growth)	1, 4, 5, 6, 7, 8, 11
Harvest (Grain for storage)	2, 3, 7, 8, 30
Harvest (Root crops)	2, 3, 7, 8, 9, 12, 13, 30
Investments (New)	5, 24
Loan (Ask for)	
Massage (Relaxing)	12, 17
Mow Lawn (Decrease growth)	1, 2, 3, 4, 5, 6, 7, 8, 9, 10, 11, 12, 13, 14, 30
Mow Lawn (Increase growth)	16, 17, 18, 19, 20, 21, 22, 23, 24, 25, 26, 27, 28
Mushrooms (Pick)	1, 28, 29, 30
Negotiate (Business for the elderly)	22, 26
Prune for Better Fruit	
Prune to Promote Healing	
Wean Children	21, 22, 23, 24, 25
Wood Floors (Installing)	
Write Letters or Contracts	7, 12, 16, 21, 25

Activity	October
Animals (Neuter or spay)	
Animals (Sell or buy)	16, 23, 27
Automobile (Buy)	4, 11, 12, 20, 21
Brewing	7, 8
Build (Start foundation)	
Business (Conducting for self and others)	5, 10, 19, 24
Business (Start new)	20
Can Fruits and Vegetables	7, 8
Can Preserves	2, 3, 7, 8, 30
Concrete (Pour)	2, 3, 10, 11, 30
Construction (Begin new)	5, 10, 14, 19, 23, 27
Consultants (Begin work with)	5, 7, 10, 12, 14, 16, 21, 23, 26, 27
Contracts (Bid on)	16, 21, 23, 26, 27
Cultivate	10, 11, 12
Decorating	15, 22, 23
Demolition	9, 10
Electronics (Buy)	4, 22
Entertain Guests	2, 3, 5, 6, 7, 8, 30, 31
Floor Covering (Laying new)	1, 2, 3, 4, 5, 9, 10, 11, 12, 13, 14, 15, 30, 31
Habits (Break)	9, 10
Hair (Cut to increase growth)	17, 18, 19, 20, 21, 24, 25, 29
Hair (Cut to decrease growth)	1, 2, 3, 4, 5, 9, 30, 31
Harvest (Grain for storage)	1, 4, 5, 6, 31
Harvest (Root crops)	1, 4, 5, 6, 9, 10, 11, 31
Investments (New)	5, 24
Loan (Ask for)	29
Massage (Relaxing)	7, 31
Mow Lawn (Decrease growth)	1, 2, 3, 4, 5, 6, 7, 8, 9, 10, 11, 12, 13, 14, 30, 31
Mow Lawn (Increase growth)	16, 17, 18, 19, 20, 21, 22, 23, 24, 25, 26, 27, 28
Mushrooms (Pick)	28, 29, 30
Negotiate (Business for the elderly)	6, 11, 24
Prune for Better Fruit	
Prune to Promote Healing	
Wean Children	18, 19, 20, 21, 22, 23
Wood Floors (Installing)	
Write Letters or Contracts	4, 9, 16, 18, 22

Activity	November
Animals (Neuter or spay)	
Animals (Sell or buy)	15, 19
Automobile (Buy)	1, 8, 16, 17, 28
Brewing	3
Build (Start foundation)	
Business (Conducting for self and others)	4, 9, 18, 22
Business (Start new)	16
Can Fruits and Vegetables	3, 13
Can Preserves	3, 13
Concrete (Pour)	6, 7
Construction (Begin new)	4, 6, 9, 11, 18, 19, 22, 23
Consultants (Begin work with)	1, 5, 6, 10, 11, 14, 17, 19, 22, 23, 28
Contracts (Bid on)	14, 17, 19, 22, 23
Cultivate	6, 7, 8, 9
Decorating	18, 19, 20, 27, 28
Demolition	5, 6
Electronics (Buy)	1, 10, 18, 28
Entertain Guests	1, 3, 4, 6, 11, 26, 27, 28, 29, 30
Floor Covering (Laying new)	1, 2, 5, 6, 7, 8, 9, 10, 11, 12, 29
Habits (Break)	7
Hair (Cut to increase growth)	14, 15, 16, 17, 20, 21, 25, 26, 27
Hair (Cut to decrease growth)	1, 2, 5, 29
Harvest (Grain for storage)	1, 2, 5, 6, 29
Harvest (Root crops)	1, 2, 5, 6, 7, 28, 29
Investments (New)	4, 22
Loan (Ask for)	25, 26, 27
Massage (Relaxing)	6, 11, 20
Mow Lawn (Decrease growth)	1, 2, 3, 5, 6, 7, 8, 9, 10, 11, 12, 29, 30
Mow Lawn (Increase growth)	14, 15, 16, 17, 18, 19, 20, 21, 22, 23, 24, 25, 26, 27
Mushrooms (Pick)	27, 28, 29
Negotiate (Business for the elderly)	3, 16, 20, 30
Prune for Better Fruit	12, 13
Prune to Promote Healing	
Wean Children	14, 15, 16, 17, 18, 19, 20
Wood Floors (Installing)	
Write Letters or Contracts	1, 6, 14, 18, 28

Activity	December
Animals (Neuter or spay)	11, 12, 13
Animals (Sell or buy)	16
Automobile (Buy)	5, 7, 14, 25
Brewing	1, 2, 10, 11
Build (Start foundation)	
Business (Conducting for self and others)	3, 8, 17, 22
Business (Start new)	14
Can Fruits and Vegetables	1, 2, 10, 11
Can Preserves	1, 2, 10, 11
Concrete (Pour)	3, 4, 30, 31
Construction (Begin new)	3, 8, 16, 17, 20, 22, 30
Consultants (Begin work with)	2, 3, 7, 8, 11, 16, 20, 21, 25, 30
Contracts (Bid on)	16, 20, 21, 25, 30
Cultivate	6, 7
Decorating	16, 17, 25, 26, 27
Demolition	2, 3, 4, 11, 12, 30, 31
Electronics (Buy)	16, 25
Entertain Guests	2, 24, 25, 26, 27, 28, 29, 31
Floor Covering (Laying new)	2, 3, 4, 5, 6, 7, 8, 9, 30, 31
Habits (Break)	
Hair (Cut to increase growth)	13, 14, 17, 18, 19, 20, 22, 23, 24, 25, 26
Hair (Cut to decrease growth)	2, 11, 12
Harvest (Grain for storage)	2, 3, 4, 5, 30, 31
Harvest (Root crops)	2, 3, 4, 11, 12, 30, 31
Investments (New)	3, 22
Loan (Ask for)	23, 24
Massage (Relaxing)	1, 31
Mow Lawn (Decrease growth)	1, 2, 3, 4, 5, 6, 7, 8, 9, 10, 11, 12, 29, 30, 31
Mow Lawn (Increase growth)	14, 15, 16, 17, 18, 19, 20, 21, 22, 23, 24, 25, 26, 27
Mushrooms (Pick)	27, 28, 29
Negotiate (Business for the elderly)	5, 18, 28
Prune for Better Fruit	9, 10, 11
Prune to Promote Healing	
Wean Children	12, 13, 14, 15, 16, 17
Wood Floors (Installing)	
Write Letters or Contracts	3, 11, 12, 16, 25, 30

Choose the Best Time for Your Activities

When rules for elections refer to "favorable" and "unfavorable" aspects to your Sun or other planets, please refer to the Favorable and Unfavorable Days Tables and Lunar Aspectarian for more information. You'll find instructions beginning on page 129 and the tables beginning on page 136.

The material in this section came from several sources including: *The New A to Z Horoscope Maker and Delineator* by Llewellyn George (Llewellyn, 1999), *Moon Sign Book* (Llewellyn, 1945), and *Electional Astrology* by Vivian Robson (Slingshot Publishing, 2000). Robson's book was originally published in 1937.

Advertise (Internet)

The Moon should be conjunct, sextile, or trine Mercury or Uranus and in the sign of Gemini, Capricorn, or Aquarius.

Advertise (Print)

Write ads on a day favorable to your Sun. The Moon should be conjunct, sextile, or trine Mercury or Venus. Avoid hard aspects to Mars and Saturn. Ad campaigns produce the best results when the Moon is well aspected in Gemini (to enhance communication) or Capricorn (to build business).

Animals

Take home new pets when the day is favorable to your Sun, or when the Moon is trine, sextile, or conjunct Mercury, Venus, or Jupiter, or in the sign of Virgo or Pisces. However, avoid days when the Moon is either square or opposing the Sun, Mars, Saturn, Uranus, Neptune, or Pluto. When selecting a pet, have the Moon well aspected by the planet that rules the animal. Cats are ruled by the Sun, dogs by Mercury, birds by Venus, horses by Jupiter, and fish by Neptune. Buy large animals when the Moon is in Sagittarius or Pisces and making favorable aspects to Jupiter or Mercury. Buy animals smaller than sheep when the Moon is in Virgo with favorable aspects to Mercury or Venus.

Animals (Breed)

Animals are easiest to handle when the Moon is in Taurus, Cancer, Libra, or Pisces, but try to avoid the Full Moon. To encourage healthy births, animals should be mated so births occur when the Moon is increasing in Taurus, Cancer, Pisces, or Libra. Those born during a semi-fruitful sign (Taurus and Capricorn) will produce leaner meat. Libra yields beautiful animals for showing and racing.

Animals (Declaw)

Declaw cats for medical purposes in the dark of the Moon. Avoid the week before and after the Full Moon and the sign of Pisces.

Animals (Neuter or spay)

Have livestock and pets neutered or spayed when the Moon is in Sagittarius, Capricorn, or Pisces, after it has passed through Scorpio, the sign that rules reproductive organs. Avoid the week before and after the Full Moon.

Animals (Sell or buy)

In either buying or selling, it is important to keep the Moon and Mercury free from any aspect to Mars. Aspects to Mars will create discord and increase the likelihood of wrangling over price and quality. The Moon should be passing from the first quarter to full and sextile or trine Venus or Jupiter. When buying racehorses, let the Moon be in an air sign. The Moon should be in air signs when you buy birds. If the birds are to be pets, let the Moon be in good aspect to Venus.

Animals (Train)

Train pets when the Moon is in Virgo or trine to Mercury.

Animals (Train dogs to hunt)

Let the Moon be in Aries in conjunction with Mars, which makes them courageous and quick to learn. But let Jupiter also be in aspect to preserve them from danger in hunting.

Automobiles

When buying an automobile, select a time when the Moon is conjunct, sextile, or trine to Mercury, Saturn, or Uranus and in the sign of Gemini or Capricorn. Avoid times when Mercury is in retrograde motion.

Baking Cakes

Your cakes will have a lighter texture if you see that the Moon is in Gemini, Libra, or Aquarius and in good aspect to Venus or

Mercury. If you are decorating a cake or confections are being made, have the Moon placed in Libra.

Beauty Treatments (Massage, etc.)

See that the Moon is in Taurus, Cancer, Leo, Libra, or Aquarius and in favorable aspect to Venus. In the case of plastic surgery, aspects to Mars should be avoided, and the Moon should not be in the sign ruling the part to be operated on.

Borrow (Money or goods)

See that the Moon is not placed between 15 degrees Libra and 15 degrees Scorpio. Let the Moon be waning and in Leo, Scorpio (16 to 30 degrees), Sagittarius, or Pisces. Venus should be in good aspect to the Moon, and the Moon should not be square, opposing, or conjunct either Saturn or Mars.

Brewing

Start brewing during the third or fourth quarter, when the Moon is in Cancer, Scorpio, or Pisces.

Build (Start foundation)

Turning the first sod for the foundation marks the beginning of the building. For best results, excavate the site when the Moon is in the first quarter of a fixed sign and making favorable aspects to Saturn.

Business (Start new)

When starting a business, have the Moon be in Taurus, Virgo, or Capricorn and increasing. The Moon should be sextile or trine Jupiter or Saturn, but avoid oppositions or squares. The planet ruling the business should be well aspected, too.

Buy Goods

Buy during the third quarter, when the Moon is in Taurus for quality or in a mutable sign (Gemini, Sagittarius, Virgo, or Pisces) for savings. Good aspects to Venus or the Sun are desirable. If you are buying for yourself, it is good if the day is favorable for your Sun sign. You may also apply rules for buying specific items.

Canning

Can fruits and vegetables when the Moon is in either the third or fourth quarter and in the water sign Cancer or Pisces. Preserves and jellies use the same quarters and the signs Cancer, Pisces, or Taurus.

Clothing

Buy clothing on a day that is favorable for your Sun sign and when Venus or Mercury is well aspected. Avoid aspects to Mars and Saturn. Buy your clothing when the Moon is in Taurus if you want to remain satisfied. Do not buy clothing or jewelry when the Moon is in Scorpio or Aries. See that the Moon is sextile or trine the Sun during the first or second quarters.

Collections

Try to make collections on days when your Sun is well aspected. Avoid days when the Moon is opposing or square Mars or

Saturn. If possible, the Moon should be in a cardinal sign (Aries, Cancer, Libra, or Capricorn). It is more difficult to collect when the Moon is in Taurus or Scorpio.

Concrete

Pour concrete when the Moon is in the third quarter of the fixed sign Taurus, Leo, or Aquarius.

Construction (Begin new)

The Moon should be sextile or trine Jupiter. According to Hermes, no building should be begun when the Moon is in Scorpio or Pisces. The best time to begin building is when the Moon is in Aquarius.

Consultants (Work with)

The Moon should be conjunct, sextile, or trine Mercury or Jupiter.

Contracts (Bid on)

The Moon should be in Gemini or Capricorn and either the Moon or Mercury should be conjunct, sextile, or trine Jupiter.

Copyrights/Patents

The Moon should be conjunct, trine, or sextile either Mercury or Jupiter.

Coronations and Installations

Let the Moon be in Leo and in favorable aspect to Venus, Jupiter, or Mercury. The Moon should be applying to these planets.

Cultivate

Cultivate when the Moon is in a barren sign and waning, ideally the fourth quarter in Aries, Gemini, Leo, Virgo, or Aquarius. The third quarter in the sign of Sagittarius will also work.

Cut Timber

Timber cut during the waning Moon does not become worm-eaten; it will season well and not warp, decay, or snap during burning. Cut when the Moon is in Taurus, Gemini, Virgo, or Capricorn—especially in August. Avoid the water signs. Look for favorable aspects to Mars.

Decorating or Home Repairs

Have the Moon waxing and in the sign of Libra, Gemini, or Aquarius. Avoid squares or oppositions to either Mars or Saturn. Venus in good aspect to Mars or Saturn is beneficial.

Demolition

Let the waning Moon be in Leo, Sagittarius, or Aries.

Dental and Dentists

Visit the dentist when the Moon is in Virgo, or pick a day marked favorable for your Sun sign. Mars should be marked sextile, conjunct, or trine; avoid squares or oppositions to Saturn, Uranus, or Jupiter.

Teeth are best removed when the Moon is in Gemini, Virgo, Sagittarius, or Pisces and during the first or second quarter. Avoid the Full Moon! The day should be favorable for your lunar cycle, and Mars and Saturn should be marked conjunct, trine, or sextile. Fillings should be done in the third or fourth quarters in the sign of Taurus, Leo, Scorpio, or Pisces. The same applies for dentures.

Dressmaking

William Lilly wrote in 1676: "Make no new clothes, or first put them on when the Moon is in Scorpio or afflicted by Mars, for they will be apt to be torn and quickly worn out." Design, repair, and sew clothes in the first and second quarters of Taurus, Leo, or Libra on a day marked favorable for your Sun sign. Venus,

Jupiter, and Mercury should be favorably aspected, but avoid hard aspects to Mars or Saturn.

Egg-setting (see p. 161)

Eggs should be set so chicks will hatch during fruitful signs. To set eggs, subtract the number of days given for incubation or gestation from the fruitful dates. Chickens incubate in twenty-one days, turkeys and geese in twenty-eight days.

A freshly laid egg loses quality rapidly if it is not handled properly. Use plenty of clean litter in the nests to reduce the number of dirty or cracked eggs. Gather eggs daily in mild weather and at least two times daily in hot or cold weather. The eggs should be placed in a cooler immediately after gathering and stored at 50 to 55 degrees Fahrenheit. Do not store eggs with foods or products that give off pungent odors since eggs may absorb the odors.

Eggs saved for hatching purposes should not be washed. Only clean and slightly soiled eggs should be saved for hatching. Dirty eggs should not be incubated. Eggs should be stored in a cool place with the large ends up. It is not advisable to store the eggs longer than one week before setting them in an incubator.

Electricity and Gas (Install)

The Moon should be in a fire sign, and there should be no squares, oppositions, or conjunctions with Uranus (ruler of electricity), Neptune (ruler of gas), Saturn, or Mars. Hard aspects to Mars can cause fires.

Electronics (Buying)

Choose a day when the Moon is in an air sign (Gemini, Libra, Aquarius) and well aspected by Mercury and/or Uranus when buying electronics.

Electronics (Repair)

The Moon should be sextile or trine Mars or Uranus and in a fixed sign (Taurus, Leo, Scorpio, Aquarius).

Entertain Friends

Let the Moon be in Leo or Libra and making good aspects to Venus. Avoid squares or oppositions to either Mars or Saturn by the Moon or Venus.

Eyes and Eyeglasses

Have your eyes tested and glasses fitted on a day marked favorable for your Sun sign, and on a day that falls during your favorable lunar cycle. Mars should not be in aspect with the Moon. The same applies for any treatment of the eyes, which should also be started during the Moon's first or second quarter.

Fence Posts

Set posts when the Moon is in the third or fourth quarter of the fixed sign Taurus or Leo.

Fertilize and Compost

Fertilize when the Moon is in a fruitful sign (Cancer, Scorpio, Pisces). Organic fertilizers are best when the Moon is waning. Use chemical fertilizers when the Moon is waxing. Start compost when the Moon is in the fourth quarter in a water sign.

Find Hidden Treasure

Let the Moon be in good aspect to Jupiter or Venus. If you erect a horoscope for this election, place the Moon in the Fourth House.

2011 © ponybrowne. Image from BigStockPhoto.com

Find Lost Articles

Search for lost articles during the first quarter and when your Sun sign is marked favorable. Also check to see that the planet ruling the lost item is trine, sextile, or conjunct the Moon. The Moon rules household utensils; Mercury rules letters and books; and Venus rules clothing, jewelry, and money.

Fishing

During the summer months, the best time of the day to fish is from sunrise to three hours after and from two hours before sunset until one hour after. Fish do not bite in cooler months until the air is warm, from noon to 3 pm. Warm, cloudy days are good. The most favorable winds are from the south and southwest. Easterly winds are unfavorable. The best days of the month for fishing are when the Moon changes quarters, especially if the change occurs on a day when the Moon is in a water sign (Cancer, Scorpio, Pisces). The best period in any month is the day after the Full Moon.

Friendship

The need for friendship is greater when the Moon is in Aquarius or when Uranus aspects the Moon. Friendship prospers when Venus or Uranus is trine, sextile, or conjunct the Moon. The Moon in Gemini facilitates the chance meeting of acquaintances and friends.

Grafting or Budding

Grafting is the process of introducing new varieties of fruit on less desirable trees. For this process you should use the increasing phase of the Moon in fruitful signs such as Cancer, Scorpio, or Pisces. Capricorn may be used, too. Cut your grafts while trees are dormant, from December to March. Keep them in a cool, dark place, not too dry or too damp. Do the grafting before the sap starts to flow and while the Moon is waxing, preferably while it is in Cancer, Scorpio, or Pisces. The type of plant should determine both cutting and planting times.

Habit (Breaking)

To end an undesirable habit, and this applies to ending everything from a bad relationship to smoking, start on a day when the Moon is in the fourth quarter and in the barren sign of Gemini, Leo, or Aquarius. Aries, Virgo, and Capricorn may be suitable as well, depending on the habit you want to be rid of. Make sure that your lunar cycle is favorable. Avoid lunar aspects to Mars or Jupiter. However, favorable aspects to Pluto are helpful.

Haircuts

Cut hair when the Moon is in Gemini, Sagittarius, Pisces, Taurus, or Capricorn, but not in Virgo. Look for favorable aspects to Venus. For faster growth, cut hair when the Moon is increasing in Cancer or Pisces. To make hair grow thicker, cut when the Moon is full in the signs of Taurus, Cancer, or Leo. If you want your hair to grow more slowly, have the Moon be decreasing in Aries, Gemini, or Virgo, and have the Moon square or opposing Saturn.

Permanents, straightening, and hair coloring will take well if the Moon is in Taurus or Leo and trine or sextile Venus. Avoid hair treatments if Mars is marked as square or in opposition, especially if heat is to be used. For permanents, a trine to Jupiter is helpful. The Moon also should be in the first quarter. Check the lunar cycle for a favorable day in relation to your Sun sign.

Harvest Crops

Harvest root crops when the Moon is in a dry sign (Aries, Leo, Sagittarius, Gemini, Aquarius) and waning. Harvest grain for storage just after the Full Moon, avoiding Cancer, Scorpio, or Pisces. Harvest in the third and fourth quarters in dry signs. Dry crops in the third quarter in fire signs.

Health

A diagnosis is more likely to be successful when the Moon is in Aries, Cancer, Libra, or Capricorn and less so when in Gemini, Sagittarius, Pisces, or Virgo. Begin a recuperation program when the Moon is in a cardinal or fixed sign and the day is favorable to your Sun sign. Enter hospitals at these times, too. For surgery, see "Surgical Procedures." Buy medicines when the Moon is in Virgo or Scorpio.

Home (Buy new)

If you desire a permanent home, buy when the New Moon is in a fixed sign—Taurus or Leo—for example. Each sign will affect your decision in a different way. A house bought when the Moon is in Taurus is likely to be more practical and have a country look—right down to the split-rail fence. A house purchased when the Moon is in Leo will more likely be a real showplace.

If you're buying for speculation and a quick turnover, be certain that the Moon is in a cardinal sign (Aries, Cancer, Libra, Capricorn). Avoid buying when the Moon is in a fixed sign (Leo, Scorpio, Aquarius, Taurus).

Home (Make repairs)

In all repairs, avoid squares, oppositions, or conjunctions to the planet ruling the place or thing to be repaired. For example, bathrooms are ruled by Scorpio and Cancer. You would not want to start a project in those rooms when the Moon or Pluto is receiving hard aspects. The front entrance, hall, dining room, and porch are ruled by the Sun. So you would want to avoid times when Saturn or Mars are square, opposing, or conjunct the Sun. Also, let the Moon be waxing.

Home (Sell)

Make a strong effort to list your property for sale when the Sun is marked favorable in your sign and in good aspect to Jupiter. Avoid adverse aspects to as many planets as possible.

Home Furnishings (Buy new)

Saturn days (Saturday) are good for buying, and Jupiter days (Thursday) are good for selling. Items bought on days when Saturn is well aspected tend to wear longer and purchases tend to be more conservative.

Job (Start new)

Jupiter and Venus should be sextile, trine, or conjunct the Moon. A day when your Sun is receiving favorable aspects is preferred.

Legal Matters

Good Moon-Jupiter aspects improve the outcome in legal decisions. To gain damages through a lawsuit, begin the process during the increasing Moon. To avoid paying damages, a court date during the decreasing Moon is desirable. Good Moon-Sun aspects strengthen your chance of success. A well-aspected Moon in Cancer or Leo, making good aspects to the Sun, brings the best results in custody cases. In divorce cases, a favorable Moon-Venus aspect is best.

Loan (Ask for)

A first and second quarter phase favors the lender, the third and fourth quarters favor the borrower. Good aspects of Jupiter and Venus to the Moon are favorable to both, as is having the Moon in Leo or Taurus.

Machinery, Appliances, or Tools (Buy)

Tools, machinery, and other implements should be bought on days when your lunar cycle is favorable and when Mars and Uranus are trine, sextile, or conjunct the Moon. Any quarter of the Moon is suitable. When buying gas or electrical appliances, the Moon should be in Aquarius.

Make a Will

Let the Moon be in a fixed sign (Taurus, Leo, Scorpio, or Aquarius) to ensure permanence. If the Moon is in a cardinal sign (Aries, Cancer, Libra, or Capricorn), the will could be altered. Let the Moon be waxing—increasing in light—and in good aspect to Saturn, Venus, or Mercury. In case the will is made in an emergency during illness and the Moon is slow in motion, void-of-course, combust, or under the Sun's beams, the testator will die and the will remain unaltered. There is some danger that it will be lost or stolen, however.

Marriage

The best time for marriage to take place is when the Moon is increasing, but not yet full. Good signs for the Moon to be in are Taurus, Cancer, Leo, or Libra.

The Moon in Taurus produces the most steadfast marriages, but if the partners later want to separate, they may have a difficult time. Make sure that the Moon is well aspected, especially to Venus or Jupiter. Avoid aspects to Mars, Uranus, or Pluto and the signs Aries, Gemini, Virgo, Scorpio, or Aquarius.

The values of the signs are as follows:

- Aries is not favored for marriage
- Taurus from 0 to 19 degrees is good, the remaining degrees are less favorable
- Cancer is unfavorable unless you are marrying a widow
- Leo is favored, but it may cause one party to deceive the other as to his or her money or possessions

- Virgo is not favored except when marrying a widow
- Libra is good for engagements but not for marriage
- Scorpio from 0 to 15 degrees is good, but the last 15 degrees are entirely unfortunate. The woman may be fickle, envious, and quarrelsome
- Sagittarius is neutral
- Capricorn, from 0 to 10 degrees, is difficult for marriage; however, the remaining degrees are favorable, especially when marrying a widow
- Aquarius is not favored
- Pisces is favored, although marriage under this sign can incline a woman to chatter a lot

These effects are strongest when the Moon is in the sign. If the Moon and Venus are in a cardinal sign, happiness between the couple may not continue long.

On no account should the Moon apply to Saturn or Mars, even by good aspect.

Medical Treatment for the Eyes

Let the Moon be increasing in light and motion and making favorable aspects to Venus or Jupiter and be unaspected by Mars. Keep the Moon out of Taurus, Capricorn, or Virgo. If an aspect between the Moon and Mars is unavoidable, let it be separating.

Medical Treatment for the Head

If possible, have Mars and Saturn free of hard aspects. Let the Moon be in Aries or Taurus, decreasing in light, in conjunction or aspect with Venus or Jupiter and free of hard aspects. The Sun should not be in any aspect to the Moon.

Medical Treatment for the Nose

Let the Moon be in Cancer, Leo, or Virgo and not aspecting Mars or Saturn and also not in conjunction with a retrograde or weak planet.

Mining

Saturn rules mining. Begin work when Saturn is marked conjunct, trine, or sextile. Mine for gold when the Sun is marked conjunct, trine, or sextile. Mercury rules quicksilver, Venus rules copper, Jupiter rules tin, Saturn rules lead and coal, Uranus rules radioactive elements, Neptune rules oil, the Moon rules water. Mine for these items when the ruling planet is marked conjunct, trine, or sextile.

Move to New Home

If you have a choice, and sometimes you don't, make sure that Mars is not aspecting the Moon. Move on a day favorable to your Sun sign or when the Moon is conjunct, sextile, or trine the Sun.

Mow Lawn

Mow in the first and second quarters (waxing phase) to increase growth and lushness, and in the third and fourth quarters (waning phase) to decrease growth.

Negotiate

When you are choosing a time to negotiate, consider what the meeting is about and what you want to have happen. If it is agreement or compromise between two parties that you desire, have the Moon be in the sign of Libra. When you are making contracts, it is best to have the Moon in the same element. For example, if your concern is communication, then elect a time when the Moon is in an air sign. If, on the other hand, your concern is about possessions, an earth sign would be more appropriate. Fixed signs are unfavorable, with the exception of Leo; so are cardinal signs, except for Capricorn. If you are negotiating the end of something, use the rules that apply to ending habits.

2011 © CandyBox Photography. Image from BigStockPhoto.com

Occupational Training

When you begin training, see that your lunar cycle is favorable that day and that the planet ruling your occupation is marked conjunct or trine.

Paint

Paint buildings during the waning Libra or Aquarius Moon. If the weather is hot, paint when the Moon is in Taurus. If the weather is cold, paint when the Moon is in Leo. Schedule the painting to start in the fourth quarter as the wood is drier and paint will penetrate wood better. Avoid painting around the New Moon, though, as the wood is likely to be damp, making the paint subject to scalding when hot weather hits it. If the temperature is below 70 degrees Fahrenheit, it is not advisable to paint while the Moon is in Cancer, Scorpio, or Pisces as the paint is apt to creep, check, or run.

Party (Host or attend)

A party timed so the Moon is in Gemini, Leo, Libra, or Sagittarius, with good aspects to Venus and Jupiter, will be fun and well attended. There should be no aspects between the Moon and Mars or Saturn.

Pawn

Do not pawn any article when Jupiter is receiving a square or opposition from Saturn or Mars or when Jupiter is within 17 degrees of the Sun, for you will have little chance to redeem the items.

Pick Mushrooms

Mushrooms, one of the most promising traditional medicines in the world, should be gathered at the Full Moon.

Plant

Root crops, like carrots and potatoes, are best if planted in the sign Taurus or Capricorn. Beans, peas, tomatoes, peppers, and other fruit-bearing plants are best if planted in a sign that supports seed growth. Leaf plants, like lettuce, broccoli, or cauliflower, are best planted when the Moon is in a water sign.

It is recommended that you transplant during a decreasing Moon, when forces are streaming into the lower part of the plant. This helps root growth.

Promotion (Ask for)

Choose a day favorable to your Sun sign. Mercury should be marked conjunct, trine, or sextile. Avoid days when Mars or Saturn is aspected.

Prune

Prune during the third and fourth quarter of a Scorpio Moon to retard growth and to promote better fruit. Prune when the Moon is in cardinal Capricorn to promote healing.

Reconcile with People

If the reconciliation is with a woman, let Venus be strong and well aspected. If elders or superiors are involved, see that Saturn is receiving good aspects; if the reconciliation is between young people or between an older and younger person, see that Mercury is well aspected.

Romance

There is less control of when a romance starts, but romances begun under an increasing Moon are more likely to be permanent or satisfying, while those begun during the decreasing Moon tend to transform the participants. The tone of the relationship can be guessed from the sign the Moon is in. Romances begun with the Moon in Aries may be impulsive. Those begun in Capricorn will take greater effort to bring to a desirable conclusion, but they may be very rewarding. Good aspects between the Moon and Venus will have a positive influence on the relationship. Avoid unfavorable aspects to Mars, Uranus, and Pluto. A decreasing Moon, particularly the fourth quarter, facilitates ending a relationship and causes the least pain.

Roof a Building

Begin roofing a building during the third or fourth quarter, when the Moon is in Aries or Aquarius. Shingles laid during the New Moon have a tendency to curl at the edges.

Sauerkraut

The best-tasting sauerkraut is made just after the Full Moon in the fruitful signs of Cancer, Scorpio, or Pisces.

Select a Child's Sex

Count from the last day of menstruation to the first day of the next cycle and divide the interval between the two dates in half. Pregnancy in the first half produces females, but copulation should take place with the Moon in a feminine sign. Pregnancy in the latter half, up to three days before the beginning of menstruation, produces males, but copulation should take place with the Moon in a masculine sign. The three-day period before the next period again produces females.

Sell or Canvass

Begin these activities during a day favorable to your Sun sign. Otherwise, sell on days when Jupiter, Mercury, or Mars is trine, sextile, or conjunct the Moon. Avoid days when Saturn is square or opposing the Moon, for that always hinders business and causes discord. If the Moon is passing from the first quarter to full, it is best to have the Moon swift in motion and in good aspect with Venus and/or Jupiter.

Sign Papers

Sign contracts or agreements when the Moon is increasing in a fruitful sign and on a day when the Moon is making favorable aspects to Mercury. Avoid days when Mars, Saturn, or Neptune are square or opposite the Moon.

Spray and Weed

Spray pests and weeds during the fourth quarter when the Moon is in the barren sign Leo or Aquarius and making favorable aspects to Pluto. Weed during a waning Moon in a barren sign.

Staff (Fire)

Have the Moon in the third or fourth quarter, but not full. The Moon should not be square any planets.

Staff (Hire)

The Moon should be in the first or second quarter, and preferably in the sign of Gemini or Virgo. The Moon should be conjunct, trine, or sextile Mercury or Jupiter.

Stocks (Buy)

The Moon should be in Taurus or Capricorn, and there should be a sextile or trine to Jupiter or Saturn.

Surgical Procedures

Blood flow, like ocean tides, appears to be related to Moon phases. To reduce hemorrhage after a surgery, schedule it within one week before or after a New Moon. Schedule surgery to occur during the increase of the Moon if possible, as wounds heal better and vitality is greater than during the decrease of the Moon. Avoid surgery within one week before or after the Full Moon. Select a date when the Moon is past the sign governing the part of the body involved in the operation. For example, abdominal operations should be done when the Moon is in Sagittarius, Capricorn, or Aquarius. The further removed the Moon sign is from the sign ruling the afflicted part of the body, the better.

For successful operations, avoid times when the Moon is applying to any aspect of Mars. (This tends to promote inflammation and complications.) See the Lunar Aspectarian on odd pages 137–159 to find days with negative Mars aspects and positive Venus and Jupiter aspects. Never operate with the Moon in the same sign as a person's Sun sign or Ascendant. Let the Moon be in a fixed sign and avoid square or opposing aspects. The Moon should not be void-of-course. Cosmetic surgery should be done in the increase of the Moon, when the Moon is not square or in opposition to Mars. Avoid days when the Moon is square or opposing Saturn or the Sun.

Travel (Air)

Start long trips when the Moon is making favorable aspects to the Sun. For enjoyment, aspects to Jupiter are preferable; for visiting, look for favorable aspects to Mercury. To prevent accidents, avoid squares or oppositions to Mars, Saturn, Uranus, or

Pluto. Choose a day when the Moon is in Sagittarius or Gemini and well aspected to Mercury, Jupiter, or Uranus. Avoid adverse aspects of Mars, Saturn, or Uranus.

Visit

On setting out to visit a person, let the Moon be in aspect with any retrograde planet, for this ensures that the person you're visiting will be at home. If you desire to stay a long time in a place, let the Moon be in good aspect to Saturn. If you desire to leave the place quickly, let the Moon be in a cardinal sign.

Wean Children

To wean a child successfully, do so when the Moon is in Sagittarius, Capricorn, Aquarius, or Pisces—signs that do not rule vital human organs. By observing this astrological rule, much trouble for parents and child may be avoided.

Weight (Reduce)

If you want to lose weight, the best time to get started is when the Moon is in the third or fourth quarter and in the barren sign of Virgo. Review the section on How to Use the Moon Tables and Lunar Aspectarian beginning on page 136 to help you select a date that is favorable to begin your weight-loss program.

Wine and Drink Other Than Beer

Start brewing when the Moon is in Pisces or Taurus. Sextiles or trines to Venus are favorable, but avoid aspects to Mars or Saturn.

Write

Write for pleasure or publication when the Moon is in Gemini. Mercury should be making favorable aspects to Uranus and Neptune.

How to Use the Moon Tables and Lunar Aspectarian

Timing activities is one of the most important things you can do to ensure success. In many Eastern countries, timing by the planets is so important that practically no event takes place without first setting up a chart for it. Weddings have occurred in the middle of the night because the influences were best then. You may not want to take it that far, but you can still make use of the influences of the Moon whenever possible. It's easy and it works!

Llewellyn's Moon Sign Book has information to help you plan just about any activity: weddings, fishing, making purchases, cutting your hair, traveling, and more. We provide the guidelines you need to pick the best day out of the several from which you have to choose. The Moon Tables are the *Moon Sign Book's* primary method for choosing dates. Following are instructions, examples, and directions on how to read the Moon Tables. More advanced information on using the tables containing the Lunar Aspectarian and favorable and unfavorable days (found on odd-numbered pages opposite the Moon Tables), Moon void-of-course and retrograde information to choose the dates best for you is also included.

The Five Basic Steps

Step 1: Directions for Choosing Dates

Look up the directions for choosing dates for the activity that you wish to begin, then go to step 2.

Step 2: Check the Moon Tables

You'll find two tables for each month of the year beginning on page 136. The Moon Tables (on the left-hand pages) include the day, date, and sign the Moon is in; the element and nature of the sign; the Moon's phase; and when it changes sign or phase. If there is a time listed after a date, that time is the time when the Moon moves into that zodiac sign. Until then, the Moon is considered to be in the sign for the previous day.

The abbreviation Full signifies Full Moon and New signifies New Moon. The times listed with dates indicate when the Moon changes sign. The times listed after the phase indicate when the Moon changes phase.

Turn to the month you would like to begin your activity. You will be using the Moon's sign and phase information most often when you begin choosing your own dates. Use the Time Zone Map on page 164 and the Time Zone Conversions table on page 165 to convert time to your own time zone.

When you find dates that meet the criteria for the correct Moon phase and sign for your activity, you may have completed the process. For certain simple activities, such as getting a haircut, the phase and sign information is all that is needed. If the directions for your activity include information on certain lunar aspects, however, you should consult the Lunar Aspectarian. An example of this would be if the directions told you not to perform a certain activity when the Moon is square (Q) Jupiter.

Step 3: Check the Lunar Aspectarian

On the pages opposite the Moon Tables you will find tables containing the Lunar Aspectarian and Favorable and Unfavorable Days. The Lunar Aspectarian gives the aspects (or angles) of the Moon to other planets. Some aspects are favorable, while others are not. To use the Lunar Aspectarian, find the planet that the directions list as favorable for your activity, and run down the column to the date desired. For example, you should avoid aspects to Mars if you are planning surgery. So you would look for Mars across the top and then run down that column looking for days where there are no aspects to Mars (as signified by empty boxes). If you want to find a favorable aspect (sextile (X) or trine (T)) to Mercury, run your finger down the column under Mercury until you find an X or T. Adverse aspects to planets are squares (Q) or oppositions (O). A conjunction (C) is sometimes beneficial, sometimes not, depending on the activity or planets involved.

Step 4: Favorable and Unfavorable Days

The tables listing favorable and unfavorable days are helpful when you want to choose your personal best dates because your Sun sign is taken into consideration. The twelve Sun signs are listed on the right side of the tables. Once you have determined which days meet your criteria for phase, sign, and aspects, you can determine whether or not those days are positive for you by checking the favorable and unfavorable days for your Sun sign.

To find out if a day is positive for you, find your Sun sign and then look down the column. If it is marked F, it is very favorable. The Moon is in the same sign as your Sun on a favorable day. If it is marked f, it is slightly favorable; U is very unfavorable; and u means slightly unfavorable. A day marked very unfavorable (U) indicates that the Moon is in the sign opposing your Sun.

Once you have selected good dates for the activity you are about to begin, you can go straight to "Using What You've Learned," beginning on the next page. To learn how to fine-tune your selections even further, read on.

Step 5: Void-of-Course Moon and Retrogrades

This last step is perhaps the most advanced portion of the procedure. It is generally considered poor timing to make decisions, sign important papers, or start special activities during a Moon void-of-course period or during a Mercury retrograde. Once you have chosen the best date for your activity based on steps one through four, you can check the Void-of-Course tables, beginning on page 76, to find out if any of the dates you have chosen have void periods.

The Moon is said to be void-of-course after it has made its last aspect to a planet within a particular sign, but before it has moved into the next sign. Put simply, the Moon is "resting" during the void-of-course period, so activities initiated at this time generally don't come to fruition. You will notice that there are many void periods during the year, and it is nearly impossible to avoid all of them. Some people choose to ignore these altogether and do not take them into consideration when planning activities.

Next, you can check the Retrograde Planets tables on page 160 to see what planets are retrograde during your chosen date(s).

A planet is said to be retrograde when it appears to move backward in the sky as viewed from the Earth. Generally, the farther a planet is away from the Sun, the longer it can stay retrograde. Some planets will retrograde for several months at a time. Avoiding retrogrades is not as important in lunar planning as avoiding the Moon void-of-course, with the exception of the planet Mercury.

Mercury rules thought and communication, so it is advisable not to sign important papers, initiate important business or legal work, or make crucial decisions during these times. As with the Moon void-of-course, it is difficult to avoid all planetary retrogrades when beginning events, and you may choose to ignore this step of the process. Following are some examples using some or all of the steps outlined above.

Using What You've Learned

Let's say it's a new year and you want to have your hair cut. It's thin and you would like it to look fuller, so you find the directions for hair care and you see that for thicker hair you should cut hair while the Moon is Full and in the sign of Taurus, Cancer, or Leo. You should avoid the Moon in Aries, Gemini, or Virgo. Look at the January Moon Table on page 136. You see that the Full Moon is on January 9 at 2:30 am. The Moon moves into the sign of Leo at 11:35 pm that day and remains in Leo until January 12 at 4:44 am, so January 10–11 meets both the phase and sign criteria.

Let's move on to a more difficult example using the sign and phase of the Moon. You want to buy a permanent home. After checking the instructions for purchasing a house: "Home (Buy new)" on page 118, you see that you should buy a home when the Moon is in Taurus, Cancer, or Leo. You need to get a loan, so you should also look under "Loan (Ask for)" on page 119. Here it says that the third and fourth quarters favor the borrower (you). You are going to buy the house in October so go to page 154. The Moon is in the third quarter October 1–8. The Moon is in Cancer from 8:45 pm on October 6 until October 9 at 7:55 am. The best day for obtaining a loan would be October 7, while the Moon is in Cancer.

Just match up the best sign and phase (quarter) to come up with the best date. With all activities, be sure to check the favorable and unfavorable days for your Sun sign in the table adjoining the Lunar Aspectarian. If there is a choice between several dates, pick the one most favorable for you. Because buying a home is an important business decision, you may also wish to see if the Moon is void or if Mercury is retrograde during these dates.

Now let's look at an example that uses signs, phases, and aspects. Our example is starting new home construction. We will use the month of April. Look under "Build (Start foundation)" on page 110 and you'll see that the Moon should be in the first quarter of Taurus or Leo. You should select a time when the Moon is not making unfavorable aspects to Saturn. (Conjunctions are usually considered good if they are not to Mars, Saturn, or Neptune.) Look in the April Moon Table. You will see that the Moon is in the first quarter April 21–29. The Moon is in Taurus from 12:05 am on April 21 until April 23 at 1:05 pm. Now, look to the April Lunar Aspectarian. We see that there are no squares or oppositions to Saturn April 21–23. These are good dates to start a foundation.

A Note About Time and Time Zones

All tables in the *Moon Sign Book* use Eastern Time. You must calculate the difference between your time zone and the Eastern Time Zone. Please refer to the Time Zone Conversions chart on 165 for help with time conversions. The sign the Moon is in at midnight is the sign shown in the Aspectarian and Favorable and Unfavorable Days tables.

How Does the Time Matter?

Due to the three-hour time difference between the East and West Coasts of the United States, those of you living on the East Coast may be, for example, under the influence of a Virgo Moon, while those of you living on the West Coast will still have a Leo Moon influence.

We follow a commonly held belief among astrologers: whatever sign the Moon is in at the start of a day—12:00 am Eastern

Time—is considered the dominant influence of the day. That sign is indicated in the Moon Tables. If the date you select for an activity shows the Moon changing signs, you can decide how important the sign change may be for your specific election and adjust your election date and time accordingly.

Use Common Sense

Some activities depend on outside factors. Obviously, you can't go out and plant when there is a foot of snow on the ground. You should adjust to the conditions at hand. If the weather was bad during the first quarter, when it was best to plant crops, do it during the second quarter while the Moon is in a fruitful sign. If the Moon is not in a fruitful sign during the first or second quarter, choose a day when it is in a semi-fruitful sign. The best advice is to choose either the sign or phase that is most favorable, when the two don't coincide.

To Summarize

First, look up the activity under the proper heading, then look for the information given in the tables. Choose the best date considering the number of positive factors in effect. If most of the dates are favorable, there is no problem choosing the one that will fit your schedule. However, if there aren't any really good dates, pick the ones with the least number of negative influences. Please keep in mind that the information found here applies in the broadest sense to the events you want to plan or are considering. To be the most effective, when you use electional astrology, you should also consider your own birth chart in relation to a chart drawn for the time or times you have under consideration. The best advice we can offer you is: read the entire introduction to each section.

January Moon Table

Date	Sign	Element	Nature	Phase
1 Sun	Aries	Fire	Barren	2nd 1:15 am
2 Mon 5:16 pm	Taurus	Earth	Semi-fruitful	2nd
3 Tue	Taurus	Earth	Semi-fruitful	2nd
4 Wed	Taurus	Earth	Semi-fruitful	2nd
5 Thu 5:44 am	Gemini	Air	Barren	2nd
6 Fri	Gemini	Air	Barren	2nd
7 Sat 4:05 pm	Cancer	Water	Fruitful	2nd
8 Sun	Cancer	Water	Fruitful	2nd
9 Mon 11:35 pm	Leo	Fire	Barren	Full 2:30 am
10 Tue	Leo	Fire	Barren	3rd
11 Wed	Leo	Fire	Barren	3rd
12 Thu 4:44 am	Virgo	Earth	Barren	3rd
13 Fri	Virgo	Earth	Barren	3rd
14 Sat 8:28 am	Libra	Air	Semi-fruitful	3rd
15 Sun	Libra	Air	Semi-fruitful	3rd
16 Mon 11:33 am	Scorpio	Water	Fruitful	4th 4:08 am
17 Tue	Scorpio	Water	Fruitful	4th
18 Wed 2:29 pm	Sagittarius	Fire	Barren	4th
19 Thu	Sagittarius	Fire	Barren	4th
20 Fri 5:40 pm	Capricorn	Earth	Semi-fruitful	4th
21 Sat	Capricorn	Earth	Semi-fruitful	4th
22 Sun 9:53 pm	Aquarius	Air	Barren	4th
23 Mon	Aquarius	Air	Barren	New 2:39 am
24 Tue	Aquarius	Air	Barren	1st
25 Wed 4:11 am	Pisces	Water	Fruitful	1st
26 Thu	Pisces	Water	Fruitful	1st
27 Fri 1:28 pm	Aries	Fire	Barren	1st
28 Sat	Aries	Fire	Barren	1st
29 Sun	Aries	Fire	Barren	1st
30 Mon 1:28 am	Taurus	Earth	Semi-fruitful	2nd 11:10 pm
31 Tue	Taurus	Earth	Semi-fruitful	2nd

January Aspectarian/Favorable & Unfavorable Days

Date	Sun	Mercury	Venus	Mars	Jupiter	Saturn	Uranus	Neptune	Pluto
1	Q	T	X						
2				C	O			X	
3	T								T
4			Q	T					
5							X	Q	
6		T	Q						
7		O		X	T	Q	T		
8									O
9	O			X		Q			
10					Q		T		
11									
12		T	O		T	X		O	T
13	T			C					
14							O		Q
15		Q							
16	Q		T		O	C		T	
17		X							X
18	X			X			T	Q	
19			Q						
20				Q	T	X	Q	X	
21		X							C
22		C		T	Q				
23	C				Q		X		
24									
25					X	T		C	X
26			C	O					
27		X					C		
28	X								Q
29									
30	Q	Q				C	O	X	T
31				X	T				

Date	Aries	Taurus	Gemini	Cancer	Leo	Virgo	Libra	Scorpio	Sagittarus	Capricorn	Aquarius	Pisces
1	F		f	u	f		U		f	u	f	
2	F		f	u	f		U		f	u	f	
3		F		f	u	f		U		f	u	f
4		F		f	u	f		U		f	u	f
5	f		F		f	u	f		U		f	u
6	f		F		f	u	f		U		f	u
7	f		F		f	u	f		U		f	u
8	u	f		F		f	u	f		U		f
9	u	f		F		f	u	f		U		f
10	f	u	f		F		f	u	f		U	
11	f	u	f		F		f	u	f		U	
12		f	u	f		F		f	u	f		U
13		f	u	f		F		f	u	f		U
14	U		f	u	f		F		f	u	f	
15	U		f	u	f		F		f	u	f	
16		U		f	u	f		F		f	u	f
17		U		f	u	f		F		f	u	f
18		U		f	u	f		F		f	u	f
19	f		U		f	u	f		F		f	u
20	f		U		f	u	f		F		f	u
21	u	f		U		f	u	f		F		f
22	u	f		U		f	u	f		F		f
23	f	u	f		U		f	u	f		F	
24	f	u	f		U		f	u	f		F	
25		f	u	f		U		f	u	f		F
26		f	u	f		U		f	u	f		F
27		f	u	f		U		f	u	f		F
28	F		f	u	f		U		f	u	f	
29	F		f	u	f		U		f	u	f	
30		F		f	u	f		U		f	u	f
31		F		f	u	f		U		f	u	f

February Moon Table

Date	Sign	Element	Nature	Phase
1 Wed 2:14 pm	Gemini	Air	Barren	2nd
2 Thu	Gemini	Air	Barren	2nd
3 Fri	Gemini	Air	Barren	2nd
4 Sat 1:04 am	Cancer	Water	Fruitful	2nd
5 Sun	Cancer	Water	Fruitful	2nd
6 Mon 8:24 am	Leo	Fire	Barren	2nd
7 Tue	Leo	Fire	Barren	Full 4:54 pm
8 Wed 12:32 pm	Virgo	Earth	Barren	3rd
9 Thu	Virgo	Earth	Barren	3rd
10 Fri 2:54 pm	Libra	Air	Semi-fruitful	3rd
11 Sat	Libra	Air	Semi-fruitful	3rd
12 Sun 5:01 pm	Scorpio	Water	Fruitful	3rd
13 Mon	Scorpio	Water	Fruitful	3rd
14 Tue 7:56 pm	Sagittarius	Fire	Barren	4th 12:04 pm
15 Wed	Sagittarius	Fire	Barren	4th
16 Thu	Sagittarius	Fire	Barren	4th
17 Fri 12:03 am	Capricorn	Earth	Semi-fruitful	4th
18 Sat	Capricorn	Earth	Semi-fruitful	4th
19 Sun 5:28 am	Aquarius	Air	Barren	4th
20 Mon	Aquarius	Air	Barren	4th
21 Tue 12:31 pm	Pisces	Water	Fruitful	New 5:35 pm
22 Wed	Pisces	Water	Fruitful	1st
23 Thu 9:48 pm	Aries	Fire	Barren	1st
24 Fri	Aries	Fire	Barren	1st
25 Sat	Aries	Fire	Barren	1st
26 Sun 9:29 am	Taurus	Earth	Semi-fruitful	1st
27 Mon	Taurus	Earth	Semi-fruitful	1st
28 Tue 10:27 pm	Gemini	Air	Barren	1st
29 Wed	Gemini	Air	Barren	2nd 8:21 pm

February Aspectarian/Favorable & Unfavorable Days

Date	Sun	Mercury	Venus	Mars	Jupiter	Saturn	Uranus	Neptune	Pluto
1							X	Q	
2	T	T							
3			Q	Q					
4					X	T	Q	T	O
5				X					
6		T			Q	Q	T		
7	O	O							
8					T	X		O	
9									T
10		O	C				O		
11									Q
12	T	T				C		T	
13				O					X
14	Q	Q		X				Q	
15			T					T	
16	X			Q		X			
17		X	Q		T		Q	X	C
18						T			
19					Q	Q	X		
20			X						
21	C				X	T		C	
22		C	O						X
23									
24							C		Q
25			C						
26					C	O		X	
27	X			T					T
28		X							
29	Q						X	Q	

Date	Aries	Taurus	Gemini	Cancer	Leo	Virgo	Libra	Scorpio	Sagittarus	Capricorn	Aquarius	Pisces
1		F		f	u	f		U		f	u	f
2	f		F		f	u	f		U		f	u
3	f		F		f	u	f		U		f	u
4	u	f		F		f	u	f		U		f
5	u	f		F		f	u	f		U		f
6	f	u	f		F		f	u	f		U	
7	f	u	f		F		f	u	f		U	
8	f	u	f		F		f	u	f		U	
9		f	u	f		F		f	u	f		U
10		f	u	f		F		f	u	f		U
11	U		f	u	f		F		f	u	f	
12	U		f	u	f		F		f	u	f	
13		U		f	u	f		F		f	u	f
14		U		f	u	f		F		f	u	f
15	f		U		f	u	f		F		f	u
16	f		U		f	u	f		F		f	u
17	u	f		U		f	u	f		F		f
18	u	f		U		f	u	f		F		f
19	f	u	f		U		f	u	f		F	
20	f	u	f		U		f	u	f		F	
21	f	u	f		U		f	u	f		F	
22		f	u	f		U		f	u	f		F
23		f	u	f		U		f	u	f		F
24	F		f	u	f		U		f	u	f	
25	F		f	u	f		U		f	u	f	
26		F		f	u	f		U		f	u	f
27		F		f	u	f		U		f	u	f
28		F		f	u	f		U		f	u	f
29	f		F		f	u	f		U		f	u

March Moon Table

Date	Sign	Element	Nature	Phase
1 Thu	Gemini	Air	Barren	2nd
2 Fri 10:08 am	Cancer	Water	Fruitful	2nd
3 Sat	Cancer	Water	Fruitful	2nd
4 Sun 6:17 pm	Leo	Fire	Barren	2nd
5 Mon	Leo	Fire	Barren	2nd
6 Tue 10:27 pm	Virgo	Earth	Barren	2nd
7 Wed	Virgo	Earth	Barren	2nd
8 Thu 11:50 pm	Libra	Air	Semi-fruitful	Full 4:39 am
9 Fri	Libra	Air	Semi-fruitful	3rd
10 Sat	Libra	Air	Semi-fruitful	3rd
11 Sun 12:24 am	Scorpio	Water	Fruitful	3rd
12 Mon	Scorpio	Water	Fruitful	3rd
13 Tue 2:54 am	Sagittarius	Fire	Barren	3rd
14 Wed	Sagittarius	Fire	Barren	4th 9:25 pm
15 Thu 6:24 am	Capricorn	Earth	Semi-fruitful	4th
16 Fri	Capricorn	Earth	Semi-fruitful	4th
17 Sat 12:11 pm	Aquarius	Air	Barren	4th
18 Sun	Aquarius	Air	Barren	4th
19 Mon 8:05 pm	Pisces	Water	Fruitful	4th
20 Tue	Pisces	Water	Fruitful	4th
21 Wed	Pisces	Water	Fruitful	4th
22 Thu 5:57 am	Aries	Fire	Barren	New 10:37 am
23 Fri	Aries	Fire	Barren	1st
24 Sat 5:43 pm	Taurus	Earth	Semi-fruitful	1st
25 Sun	Taurus	Earth	Semi-fruitful	1st
26 Mon	Taurus	Earth	Semi-fruitful	1st
27 Tue 6:43 am	Gemini	Air	Barren	1st
28 Wed	Gemini	Air	Barren	1st
29 Thu 7:07 pm	Cancer	Water	Fruitful	1st
30 Fri	Cancer	Water	Fruitful	2nd 3:41 pm
31 Sat	Cancer	Water	Fruitful	2nd

March Aspectarian/Favorable & Unfavorable Days

Date	Sun	Mercury	Venus	Mars	Jupiter	Saturn	Uranus	Neptune	Pluto
1			Q						
2		Q	X			T	Q	T	
3	T			X	X				O
4		T	Q			Q			
5					Q		T		
6						X			
7			T	C	T			O	T
8	O								
9		O					O		Q
10					C				
11			O	X	O			T	X
12	T								
13		T		Q			T	Q	
14	Q								
15		Q		T		X	Q	X	C
16			T		T				
17	X	X					Q	X	
18			Q		Q				
19						T		C	
20			O	X					X
21			X						
22	C	C					C		
23									Q
24						O	X		
25				T	C				T
26		C							
27	X	X		Q			X	Q	
28									
29		Q				T		T	
30	Q			X	X		Q		O
31		T				Q			

Date	Aries	Taurus	Gemini	Cancer	Leo	Virgo	Libra	Scorpio	Sagittarus	Capricorn	Aquarius	Pisces
1	f		F		f	u	f		U		f	u
2	u	f		F		f	u	f		U		f
3	u	f		F		f	u	f		U		f
4	u	f		F		f	u	f		U		f
5	f	u	f		F		f	u	f		U	
6	f	u	f		F		f	u	f		U	
7		f	u	f		F		f	u	f		U
8		f	u	f		F		f	u	f		U
9	U		f	u	f		F		f	u	f	
10	U		f	u	f		F		f	u	f	
11		U		f	u	f		F		f	u	f
12		U		f	u	f		F		f	u	f
13	f		U		f	u	f		F		f	u
14	f		U		f	u	f		F		f	u
15	u	f		U		f	u	f		F		f
16	u	f		U		f	u	f		F		f
17	u	f		U		f	u	f		F		f
18	f	u	f		U		f	u	f		F	
19	f	u	f		U		f	u	f		F	
20		f	u	f		U		f	u	f		F
21		f	u	f		U		f	u	f		F
22	F		f	u	f		U		f	u	f	
23	F		f	u	f		U		f	u	f	
24	F		f	u	f		U		f	u	f	
25		F		f	u	f		U		f	u	f
26		F		f	u	f		U		f	u	f
27	f		F		f	u	f		U		f	u
28	f		F		f	u	f		U		f	u
29	f		F		f	u	f		U		f	u
30	u	f		F		f	u	f		U		f
31	u	f		F		f	u	f		U		f

April Moon Table

Date	Sign	Element	Nature	Phase
1 Sun 4:35 am	Leo	Fire	Barren	2nd
2 Mon	Leo	Fire	Barren	2nd
3 Tue 9:53 am	Virgo	Earth	Barren	2nd
4 Wed	Virgo	Earth	Barren	2nd
5 Thu 11:32 am	Libra	Air	Semi-fruitful	2nd
6 Fri	Libra	Air	Semi-fruitful	Full 3:19 pm
7 Sat 11:18 am	Scorpio	Water	Fruitful	3rd
8 Sun	Scorpio	Water	Fruitful	3rd
9 Mon 11:12 am	Sagittarius	Fire	Barren	3rd
10 Tue	Sagittarius	Fire	Barren	3rd
11 Wed 1:02 pm	Capricorn	Earth	Semi-fruitful	3rd
12 Thu	Capricorn	Earth	Semi-fruitful	3rd
13 Fri 5:48 pm	Aquarius	Air	Barren	4th 6:50 am
14 Sat	Aquarius	Air	Barren	4th
15 Sun	Aquarius	Air	Barren	4th
16 Mon 1:38 am	Pisces	Water	Fruitful	4th
17 Tue	Pisces	Water	Fruitful	4th
18 Wed 11:59 am	Aries	Fire	Barren	4th
19 Thu	Aries	Fire	Barren	4th
20 Fri	Aries	Fire	Barren	4th
21 Sat 12:05 am	Taurus	Earth	Semi-fruitful	New 3:18 am
22 Sun	Taurus	Earth	Semi-fruitful	1st
23 Mon 1:05 pm	Gemini	Air	Barren	1st
24 Tue	Gemini	Air	Barren	1st
25 Wed	Gemini	Air	Barren	1st
26 Thu 1:42 am	Cancer	Water	Fruitful	1st
27 Fri	Cancer	Water	Fruitful	1st
28 Sat 12:10 pm	Leo	Fire	Barren	1st
29 Sun	Leo	Fire	Barren	2nd 5:57 am
30 Mon 7:02 pm	Virgo	Earth	Barren	2nd

April Aspectarian/Favorable & Unfavorable Days

Date	Sun	Mercury	Venus	Mars	Jupiter	Saturn	Uranus	Neptune	Pluto
1			X					T	
2	T				Q				
3			Q	C		X		O	
4					T				T
5		O	T					O	
6	O								Q
7				X		C		T	
8				O					X
9		T	O	Q				T	Q
10	T								
11		Q		T		X	Q	X	
12					T				C
13	Q	X				Q			
14			T				X		
15	X				Q	T			
16			Q	O				C	X
17					X				
18		C				C			
19			X						Q
20							O		
21	C			T				X	T
22					C				
23			Q					Q	
24		X	C				X		
25						T			
26	X			X			Q	T	O
27		Q			X				
28						Q			
29	Q	T						T	
30			X		Q	X			

Date	Aries	Taurus	Gemini	Cancer	Leo	Virgo	Libra	Scorpio	Sagittarius	Capricorn	Aquarius	Pisces
1	f	u	f		F		f	u	f		U	
2	f	u	f		F		f	u	f		U	
3		f	u	f		F		f	u	f		U
4		f	u	f		F		f	u	f		U
5	U		f	u	f		F		f	u	f	
6	U		f	u	f		F		f	u	f	
7		U		f	u	f		F		f	u	f
8		U		f	u	f		F		f	u	f
9	f		U		f	u	f		F		f	u
10	f		U		f	u	f		F		f	u
11	f		U		f	u	f		F		f	u
12	u	f		U		f	u	f		F		f
13	u	f		U		f	u	f		F		f
14	f	u	f		U		f	u	f		F	
15	f	u	f		U		f	u	f		F	
16		f	u	f		U		f	u	f		F
17		f	u	f		U		f	u	f		F
18	F		f	u	f		U		f	u	f	
19	F		f	u	f		U		f	u	f	
20	F		f	u	f		U		f	u	f	
21		F		f	u	f		U		f	u	f
22		F		f	u	f		U		f	u	f
23		F		f	u	f		U		f	u	f
24	f		F		f	u	f		U		f	u
25	f		F		f	u	f		U		f	u
26	u	f		F		f	u	f		U		f
27	u	f		F		f	u	f		U		f
28	u	f		F		f	u	f		U		f
29	f	u	f		F		f	u	f		U	
30	f	u	f		F		f	u	f		U	

May Moon Table

Date	Sign	Element	Nature	Phase
1 Tue	Virgo	Earth	Barren	2nd
2 Wed 10:04 pm	Libra	Air	Semi-fruitful	2nd
3 Thu	Libra	Air	Semi-fruitful	2nd
4 Fri 10:20 pm	Scorpio	Water	Fruitful	2nd
5 Sat	Scorpio	Water	Fruitful	Full 11:35 pm
6 Sun 9:39 pm	Sagittarius	Fire	Barren	3rd
7 Mon	Sagittarius	Fire	Barren	3rd
8 Tue 10:00 pm	Capricorn	Earth	Semi-fruitful	3rd
9 Wed	Capricorn	Earth	Semi-fruitful	3rd
10 Thu	Capricorn	Earth	Semi-fruitful	3rd
11 Fri 1:03 am	Aquarius	Air	Barren	3rd
12 Sat	Aquarius	Air	Barren	4th 5:47 pm
13 Sun 7:42 am	Pisces	Water	Fruitful	4th
14 Mon	Pisces	Water	Fruitful	4th
15 Tue 5:45 pm	Aries	Fire	Barren	4th
16 Wed	Aries	Fire	Barren	4th
17 Thu	Aries	Fire	Barren	4th
18 Fri 6:03 am	Taurus	Earth	Semi-fruitful	4th
19 Sat	Taurus	Earth	Semi-fruitful	4th
20 Sun 7:05 pm	Gemini	Air	Barren	New 7:47 pm
21 Mon	Gemini	Air	Barren	1st
22 Tue	Gemini	Air	Barren	1st
23 Wed 7:31 am	Cancer	Water	Fruitful	1st
24 Thu	Cancer	Water	Fruitful	1st
25 Fri 6:11 pm	Leo	Fire	Barren	1st
26 Sat	Leo	Fire	Barren	1st
27 Sun	Leo	Fire	Barren	1st
28 Mon 2:06 am	Virgo	Earth	Barren	2nd 4:16 pm
29 Tue	Virgo	Earth	Barren	2nd
30 Wed 6:46 am	Libra	Air	Semi-fruitful	2nd
31 Thu	Libra	Air	Semi-fruitful	2nd

May Aspectarian/Favorable & Unfavorable Days

Date	Sun	Mercury	Venus	Mars	Jupiter	Saturn	Uranus	Neptune	Pluto
1	T			C				O	T
2			Q	T					
3							O		Q
4		O	T			C			
5	O			X				T	X
6					O				
7				Q				T	Q
8		T	O			X			
9				T			Q	X	C
10	T					T	Q		
11		Q					X		
12	Q		T		Q	T			
13			O					C	
14		X							X
15	X		Q	X					
16							C		Q
17			X			O			
18							X		
19			T						T
20	C	C			C				
21				Q			X	Q	
22		C				T			
23							Q	T	
24				X					O
25						X	Q		
26	X	X					T		
27			X		Q	X			
28	Q	Q						O	T
29			Q	C					
30	T					T		O	Q
31		T	T			C			

Date	Aries	Taurus	Gemini	Cancer	Leo	Virgo	Libra	Scorpio	Sagittarus	Capricorn	Aquarius	Pisces
1		f	u	f		F		f	u	f		U
2		f	u	f		F		f	u	f		U
3	U		f	u	f		F		f	u	f	
4	U		f	u	f		F		f	u	f	
5		U		f	u	f		F		f	u	f
6		U		f	u	f		F		f	u	f
7	f		U		f	u	f		F		f	u
8	f		U		f	u	f		F		f	u
9	u	f		U		f	u	f		F		f
10	u	f		U		f	u	f		F		f
11	f	u	f		U		f	u	f		F	
12	f	u	f		U		f	u	f		F	
13		f	u	f		U		f	u	f		F
14		f	u	f		U		f	u	f		F
15		f	u	f		U		f	u	f		F
16	F		f	u	f		U		f	u	f	
17	F		f	u	f		U		f	u	f	
18		F		f	u	f		U		f	u	f
19		F		f	u	f		U		f	u	f
20		F		f	u	f		U		f	u	f
21	f		F		f	u	f		U		f	u
22	f		F		f	u	f		U		f	u
23	u	f		F		f	u	f		U		f
24	u	f		F		f	u	f		U		f
25	u	f		F		f	u	f		U		f
26	f	u	f		F		f	u	f		U	
27	f	u	f		F		f	u	f		U	
28		f	u	f		F		f	u	f		U
29		f	u	f		F		f	u	f		U
30	U		f	u	f		F		f	u	f	
31	U		f	u	f		F		f	u	f	

June Moon Table

Date	Sign	Element	Nature	Phase
1 Fri 8:31 am	Scorpio	Water	Fruitful	2nd
2 Sat	Scorpio	Water	Fruitful	2nd
3 Sun 8:32 am	Sagittarius	Fire	Barren	2nd
4 Mon	Sagittarius	Fire	Barren	Full 7:12 am
5 Tue 8:31 am	Capricorn	Earth	Semi-fruitful	3rd
6 Wed	Capricorn	Earth	Semi-fruitful	3rd
7 Thu 10:17 am	Aquarius	Air	Barren	3rd
8 Fri	Aquarius	Air	Barren	3rd
9 Sat 3:22 pm	Pisces	Water	Fruitful	3rd
10 Sun	Pisces	Water	Fruitful	3rd
11 Mon	Pisces	Water	Fruitful	4th 6:41 am
12 Tue 12:21 am	Aries	Fire	Barren	4th
13 Wed	Aries	Fire	Barren	4th
14 Thu 12:22 pm	Taurus	Earth	Semi-fruitful	4th
15 Fri	Taurus	Earth	Semi-fruitful	4th
16 Sat	Taurus	Earth	Semi-fruitful	4th
17 Sun 1:24 am	Gemini	Air	Barren	4th
18 Mon	Gemini	Air	Barren	4th
19 Tue 1:34 pm	Cancer	Water	Fruitful	New 11:02 am
20 Wed	Cancer	Water	Fruitful	1st
21 Thu 11:47 pm	Leo	Fire	Barren	1st
22 Fri	Leo	Fire	Barren	1st
23 Sat	Leo	Fire	Barren	1st
24 Sun 7:42 am	Virgo	Earth	Barren	1st
25 Mon	Virgo	Earth	Barren	1st
26 Tue 1:15 pm	Libra	Air	Semi-fruitful	2nd 11:30 pm
27 Wed	Libra	Air	Semi-fruitful	2nd
28 Thu 4:32 pm	Scorpio	Water	Fruitful	2nd
29 Fri	Scorpio	Water	Fruitful	2nd
30 Sat 6:04 pm	Sagittarius	Fire	Barren	2nd

June Aspectarian/Favorable & Unfavorable Days

Date	Sun	Mercury	Venus	Mars	Jupiter	Saturn	Uranus	Neptune	Pluto
1								T	X
2			X						
3					O		T	Q	
4	O		O	Q		X			
5	O						Q	X	C
6						T	Q		
7						T			
8	T		T				X		
9					Q	T		C	
10		T	Q						X
11	Q			O					
12		Q	X		X		C		Q
13	X					O			
14								X	
15		X							T
16				T					
17			C		C		X	Q	
18				Q		T			
19	C							T	
20							Q		O
21		C		X	Q				
22			X	X		T			
23						X			
24	X		Q	Q				O	T
25									
26	Q	X			C	T			
27			T				O		Q
28		Q				C		T	
29	T								X
30				X				Q	

Date	Aries	Taurus	Gemini	Cancer	Leo	Virgo	Libra	Scorpio	Sagittarus	Capricorn	Aquarius	Pisces
1		U		f	u	f		F		f	u	f
2		U		f	u	f		F		f	u	f
3	f		U		f	u	f		F		f	u
4	f		U		f	u	f		F		f	u
5	u	f		U		f	u	f		F		f
6	u	f		U		f	u	f		F		f
7	f	u	f		U		f	u	f		F	
8	f	u	f		U		f	u	f		F	
9	f	u	f		U		f	u	f		F	
10		f	u	f		U		f	u	f		F
11		f	u	f		U		f	u	f		F
12	F		f	u	f		U		f	u	f	
13	F		f	u	f		U		f	u	f	
14	F		f	u	f		U		f	u	f	
15		F		f	u	f		U		f	u	f
16		F		f	u	f		U		f	u	f
17	f		F		f	u	f		U		f	u
18	f		F		f	u	f		U		f	u
19	f		F		f	u	f		U		f	u
20	u	f		F		f	u	f		U		f
21	u	f		F		f	u	f		U		f
22	f	u	f		F		f	u	f		U	
23	f	u	f		F		f	u	f		U	
24		f	u	f		F		f	u	f		U
25		f	u	f		F		f	u	f		U
26		f	u	f		F		f	u	f		U
27	U		f	u	f		F		f	u	f	
28	U		f	u	f		F		f	u	f	
29		U		f	u	f		F		f	u	f
30		U		f	u	f		F		f	u	f

July Moon Table

Date	Sign	Element	Nature	Phase
1 Sun	Sagittarius	Fire	Barren	2nd
2 Mon 6:51 pm	Capricorn	Earth	Semi-fruitful	2nd
3 Tue	Capricorn	Earth	Semi-fruitful	Full 2:52 pm
4 Wed 8:26 pm	Aquarius	Air	Barren	3rd
5 Thu	Aquarius	Air	Barren	3rd
6 Fri	Aquarius	Air	Barren	3rd
7 Sat 12:29 am	Pisces	Water	Fruitful	3rd
8 Sun	Pisces	Water	Fruitful	3rd
9 Mon 8:14 am	Aries	Fire	Barren	3rd
10 Tue	Aries	Fire	Barren	4th 9:48 pm
11 Wed 7:30 pm	Taurus	Earth	Semi-fruitful	4th
12 Thu	Taurus	Earth	Semi-fruitful	4th
13 Fri	Taurus	Earth	Semi-fruitful	4th
14 Sat 8:26 am	Gemini	Air	Barren	4th
15 Sun	Gemini	Air	Barren	4th
16 Mon 8:31 pm	Cancer	Water	Fruitful	4th
17 Tue	Cancer	Water	Fruitful	4th
18 Wed	Cancer	Water	Fruitful	4th
19 Thu 6:13 am	Leo	Fire	Barren	New 12:24 am
20 Fri	Leo	Fire	Barren	1st
21 Sat 1:24 pm	Virgo	Earth	Barren	1st
22 Sun	Virgo	Earth	Barren	1st
23 Mon 6:38 pm	Libra	Air	Semi-fruitful	1st
24 Tue	Libra	Air	Semi-fruitful	1st
25 Wed 10:29 pm	Scorpio	Water	Fruitful	1st
26 Thu	Scorpio	Water	Fruitful	2nd 4:56 am
27 Fri	Scorpio	Water	Fruitful	2nd
28 Sat 1:18 am	Sagittarius	Fire	Barren	2nd
29 Sun	Sagittarius	Fire	Barren	2nd
30 Mon 3:29 am	Capricorn	Earth	Semi-fruitful	2nd
31 Tue	Capricorn	Earth	Semi-fruitful	2nd

July Aspectarian/Favorable & Unfavorable Days

Date	Sun	Mercury	Venus	Mars	Jupiter	Saturn	Uranus	Neptune	Pluto
1		T	O		O		T		
2			Q		X			X	
3	O						Q		C
4				T	Q				
5		O	T		T		X		
6						T			
7			Q		Q			C	X
8	T								
9				O	X				Q
10	Q	T	X			C			
11						O			
12		Q						X	T
13	X								
14				T	C			Q	
15		X	C				X		
16						T			
17				Q			Q	T	O
18					Q				
19	C			X	X		T		
20		C	X						
21						X		O	
22			Q		Q				T
23	X								
24		X		C	T		O		Q
25			T			C			
26	Q	Q						T	X
27									
28	T	T			O		T	Q	
29			O	X		X			
30							Q	X	C
31				Q	Q				

Date	Aries	Taurus	Gemini	Cancer	Leo	Virgo	Libra	Scorpio	Sagittarus	Capricorn	Aquarius	Pisces
1	f		U		f	u	f		F		f	u
2	f		U		f	u	f		F		f	u
3	u	f		U		f	u	f		F		f
4	u	f		U		f	u	f		F		f
5	f	u	f		U		f	u	f		F	
6	f	u	f		U		f	u	f		F	
7		f	u	f		U		f	u	f		F
8		f	u	f		U		f	u	f		F
9	F		f	u	f		U		f	u	f	
10	F		f	u	f		U		f	u	f	
11	F		f	u	f		U		f	u	f	
12		F		f	u	f		U		f	u	f
13		F		f	u	f		U		f	u	f
14	f		F		f	u	f		U		f	u
15	f		F		f	u	f		U		f	u
16	f		F		f	u	f		U		f	u
17	u	f		F		f	u	f		U		f
18	u	f		F		f	u	f		U		f
19	f	u	f		F		f	u	f		U	
20	f	u	f		F		f	u	f		U	
21	f	u	f		F		f	u	f		U	
22		f	u	f		F		f	u	f		U
23		f	u	f		F		f	u	f		U
24	U		f	u	f		F		f	u	f	
25	U		f	u	f		F		f	u	f	
26		U		f	u	f		F		f	u	f
27		U		f	u	f		F		f	u	f
28	f		U		f	u	f		F		f	u
29	f		U		f	u	f		F		f	u
30	u	f		U		f	u	f		F		f
31	u	f		U		f	u	f		F		f

August Moon Table

Date	Sign	Element	Nature	Phase
1 Wed 5:56 am	Aquarius	Air	Barren	Full 11:27 pm
2 Thu	Aquarius	Air	Barren	3rd
3 Fri 9:58 am	Pisces	Water	Fruitful	3rd
4 Sat	Pisces	Water	Fruitful	3rd
5 Sun 4:59 pm	Aries	Fire	Barren	3rd
6 Mon	Aries	Fire	Barren	3rd
7 Tue	Aries	Fire	Barren	3rd
8 Wed 3:28 am	Taurus	Earth	Semi-fruitful	3rd
9 Thu	Taurus	Earth	Semi-fruitful	4th 2:55 pm
10 Fri 4:11 pm	Gemini	Air	Barren	4th
11 Sat	Gemini	Air	Barren	4th
12 Sun	Gemini	Air	Barren	4th
13 Mon 4:27 am	Cancer	Water	Fruitful	4th
14 Tue	Cancer	Water	Fruitful	4th
15 Wed 2:05 pm	Leo	Fire	Barren	4th
16 Thu	Leo	Fire	Barren	4th
17 Fri 8:33 pm	Virgo	Earth	Barren	New 11:54 am
18 Sat	Virgo	Earth	Barren	1st
19 Sun	Virgo	Earth	Barren	1st
20 Mon 12:45 am	Libra	Air	Semi-fruitful	1st
21 Tue	Libra	Air	Semi-fruitful	1st
22 Wed 3:54 am	Scorpio	Water	Fruitful	1st
23 Thu	Scorpio	Water	Fruitful	1st
24 Fri 6:50 am	Sagittarius	Fire	Barren	2nd 9:54 am
25 Sat	Sagittarius	Fire	Barren	2nd
26 Sun 9:58 am	Capricorn	Earth	Semi-fruitful	2nd
27 Mon	Capricorn	Earth	Semi-fruitful	2nd
28 Tue 1:38 pm	Aquarius	Air	Barren	2nd
29 Wed	Aquarius	Air	Barren	2nd
30 Thu 6:31 pm	Pisces	Water	Fruitful	2nd
31 Fri	Pisces	Water	Fruitful	Full 9:58 am

August Aspectarian/Favorable & Unfavorable Days

Date	Sun	Mercury	Venus	Mars	Jupiter	Saturn	Uranus	Neptune	Pluto
1	O	O			T		X		
2			T			T			
3		T						C	X
4				Q					
5		T	Q						
6	T				X	C			Q
7				O		O			
8		Q	X					X	T
9	Q								
10		X						Q	
11					C		X		
12	X			T		T			
13			C				Q	T	O
14									
15			C	Q	Q				
16					X	T			
17	C			X		X		O	
18			X	Q					T
19									
20		X	Q		T			O	Q
21						C			
22	X			C				T	X
23		Q	T						
24	Q							T	Q
25		T				O			
26	T				X	X	Q	X	C
27		O							
28				Q		Q			
29						T	X		
30		O					T		C
31	O				T	Q			X

Date	Aries	Taurus	Gemini	Cancer	Leo	Virgo	Libra	Scorpio	Sagittarius	Capricorn	Aquarius	Pisces
1	f	u	f		U		f	u	f		F	
2	f	u	f		U		f	u	f		F	
3		f	u	f		U		f	u	f		F
4		f	u	f		U		f	u	f		F
5		f	u	f		U		f	u	f		F
6	F		f	u	f		U		f	u	f	
7	F		f	u	f		U		f	u	f	
8		F		f	u	f		U		f	u	f
9		F		f	u	f		U		f	u	f
10		F		f	u	f		U		f	u	f
11	f		F		f	u	f		U		f	u
12	f		F		f	u	f		U		f	u
13	u	f		F		f	u	f		U		f
14	u	f		F		f	u	f		U		f
15	u	f		F		f	u	f		U		f
16	f	u	f		F		f	u	f		U	
17	f	u	f		F		f	u	f		U	
18		f	u	f		F		f	u	f		U
19		f	u	f		F		f	u	f		U
20	U		f	u	f		F		f	u	f	
21	U		f	u	f		F		f	u	f	
22		U		f	u	f		F		f	u	f
23		U		f	u	f		F		f	u	f
24	f		U		f	u	f		F		f	u
25	f		U		f	u	f		F		f	u
26	u	f		U		f	u	f		F		f
27	u	f		U		f	u	f		F		f
28	u	f		U		f	u	f		F		f
29	f	u	f		U		f	u	f		F	
30	f	u	f		U		f	u	f		F	
31		f	u	f		U		f	u	f		F

September Moon Table

Date	Sign	Element	Nature	Phase
1 Sat	Pisces	Water	Fruitful	3rd
2 Sun 1:37 am	Aries	Fire	Barren	3rd
3 Mon	Aries	Fire	Barren	3rd
4 Tue 11:41 am	Taurus	Earth	Semi-fruitful	3rd
5 Wed	Taurus	Earth	Semi-fruitful	3rd
6 Thu	Taurus	Earth	Semi-fruitful	3rd
7 Fri 12:10 am	Gemini	Air	Barren	3rd
8 Sat	Gemini	Air	Barren	4th 9:15 am
9 Sun 12:49 pm	Cancer	Water	Fruitful	4th
10 Mon	Cancer	Water	Fruitful	4th
11 Tue 11:00 pm	Leo	Fire	Barren	4th
12 Wed	Leo	Fire	Barren	4th
13 Thu	Leo	Fire	Barren	4th
14 Fri 5:30 am	Virgo	Earth	Barren	4th
15 Sat	Virgo	Earth	Barren	New 10:11 pm
16 Sun 8:55 am	Libra	Air	Semi-fruitful	1st
17 Mon	Libra	Air	Semi-fruitful	1st
18 Tue 10:46 am	Scorpio	Water	Fruitful	1st
19 Wed	Scorpio	Water	Fruitful	1st
20 Thu 12:34 pm	Sagittarius	Fire	Barren	1st
21 Fri	Sagittarius	Fire	Barren	1st
22 Sat 3:20 pm	Capricorn	Earth	Semi-fruitful	2nd 3:41 pm
23 Sun	Capricorn	Earth	Semi-fruitful	2nd
24 Mon 7:32 pm	Aquarius	Air	Barren	2nd
25 Tue	Aquarius	Air	Barren	2nd
26 Wed	Aquarius	Air	Barren	2nd
27 Thu 1:23 am	Pisces	Water	Fruitful	2nd
28 Fri	Pisces	Water	Fruitful	2nd
29 Sat 9:14 am	Aries	Fire	Barren	Full 11:19 pm
30 Sun	Aries	Fire	Barren	3rd

September Aspectarian/Favorable & Unfavorable Days

Date	Sun	Mercury	Venus	Mars	Jupiter	Saturn	Uranus	Neptune	Pluto
1			T						
2							C		Q
3				X					
4			Q			O	X		
5	T	T		O					T
6									
7			X				X	Q	
8	Q	Q			C				
9						T		T	
10				T			Q		O
11	X	X				Q			
12			C	Q				T	
13					X				
14						X		O	T
15	C				X	Q			
16		C						O	Q
17			X		T				
18						C		T	X
19		Q	C						
20	X							Q	
21		X	T		O		T		
22	Q					X		X	
23		Q					Q		C
24	T			X	Q				
25		T					X		
26			O	Q	T	T			
27								C	X
28					T	Q			
29	O							C	Q
30				X					

Date	Aries	Taurus	Gemini	Cancer	Leo	Virgo	Libra	Scorpio	Sagittarus	Capricorn	Aquarius	Pisces
1		f	u	f		U		f	u	f		F
2	F		f	u	f		U		f	u	f	
3	F		f	u	f		U		f	u	f	
4		F		f	u	f		U		f	u	f
5		F		f	u	f		U		f	u	f
6		F		f	u	f		U		f	u	f
7	f		F		f	u	f		U		f	u
8	f		F		f	u	f		U		f	u
9	f		F		f	u	f		U		f	u
10	u	f		F		f	u	f		U		f
11	u	f		F		f	u	f		U		f
12	f	u	f		F		f	u	f		U	
13	f	u	f		F		f	u	f		U	
14		f	u	f		F		f	u	f		U
15		f	u	f		F		f	u	f		U
16	U		f	u	f		F		f	u	f	
17	U		f	u	f		F		f	u	f	
18		U		f	u	f		F		f	u	f
19		U		f	u	f		F		f	u	f
20		U		f	u	f		F		f	u	f
21	f		U		f	u	f		F		f	u
22	f		U		f	u	f		F		f	u
23	u	f		U		f	u	f		F		f
24	u	f		U		f	u	f		F		f
25	f	u	f		U		f	u	f		F	
26	f	u	f		U		f	u	f		F	
27		f	u	f		U		f	u	f		F
28		f	u	f		U		f	u	f		F
29	F		f	u	f		U		f	u	f	
30	F		f	u	f		U		f	u	f	

October Moon Table

Date	Sign	Element	Nature	Phase
1 Mon 7:26 pm	Taurus	Earth	Semi-fruitful	3rd
2 Tue	Taurus	Earth	Semi-fruitful	3rd
3 Wed	Taurus	Earth	Semi-fruitful	3rd
4 Thu 7:47 am	Gemini	Air	Barren	3rd
5 Fri	Gemini	Air	Barren	3rd
6 Sat 8:45 pm	Cancer	Water	Fruitful	3rd
7 Sun	Cancer	Water	Fruitful	3rd
8 Mon	Cancer	Water	Fruitful	4th 3:33 am
9 Tue 7:55 am	Leo	Fire	Barren	4th
10 Wed	Leo	Fire	Barren	4th
11 Thu 3:23 pm	Virgo	Earth	Barren	4th
12 Fri	Virgo	Earth	Barren	4th
13 Sat 7:02 pm	Libra	Air	Semi-fruitful	4th
14 Sun	Libra	Air	Semi-fruitful	4th
15 Mon 8:06 pm	Scorpio	Water	Fruitful	New 8:02 am
16 Tue	Scorpio	Water	Fruitful	1st
17 Wed 8:26 pm	Sagittarius	Fire	Barren	1st
18 Thu	Sagittarius	Fire	Barren	1st
19 Fri 9:41 pm	Capricorn	Earth	Semi-fruitful	1st
20 Sat	Capricorn	Earth	Semi-fruitful	1st
21 Sun	Capricorn	Earth	Semi-fruitful	2nd 11:32 pm
22 Mon 1:02 am	Aquarius	Air	Barren	2nd
23 Tue	Aquarius	Air	Barren	2nd
24 Wed 7:00 am	Pisces	Water	Fruitful	2nd
25 Thu	Pisces	Water	Fruitful	2nd
26 Fri 3:31 pm	Aries	Fire	Barren	2nd
27 Sat	Aries	Fire	Barren	2nd
28 Sun	Aries	Fire	Barren	2nd
29 Mon 2:15 am	Taurus	Earth	Semi-fruitful	Full 3:49 pm
30 Tue	Taurus	Earth	Semi-fruitful	3rd
31 Wed 2:40 pm	Gemini	Air	Barren	3rd

October Aspectarian/Favorable & Unfavorable Days

Date	Sun	Mercury	Venus	Mars	Jupiter	Saturn	Uranus	Neptune	Pluto
1		O	T			O		X	
2									T
3									
4			Q	O			X	Q	
5	T				C				
6						T		T	
7		T	X				Q		O
8	Q								
9		Q		T		Q	T		
10	X			X					
11				Q			X	O	
12		X	C		Q				T
13									
14				X	T		O		Q
15	C					C	T		
16		C	X						X
17								Q	
18					C	O	T		
19	X		Q					X	
20						X	Q		C
21	Q	X	T						
22				X		Q	X		
23		Q				T			
24	T					T		C	X
25				Q	Q				
26		T	O						
27					T	X		C	Q
28									
29	O					O		X	T
30									
31		O	T					Q	

Date	Aries	Taurus	Gemini	Cancer	Leo	Virgo	Libra	Scorpio	Sagittarius	Capricorn	Aquarius	Pisces
1	F		f	u	f		U			f	u	f
2	F		f	u	f		U			f	u	f
3	F		f	u	f		U			f	u	f
4	f	F		f	u	f		U			f	u
5	f	F		f	u	f		U			f	u
6	f	F		f	u	f		U			f	u
7	u	f	F		f	u	f		U			f
8	u	f	F		f	u	f		U			f
9	f	u	f	F		f	u	f		U		
10	f	u	f	F		f	u	f		U		
11		f	u	f	F		f	u	f		U	
12		f	u	f	F		f	u	f		U	
13			f	u	f	F		f	u	f		U
14	U			f	u	f	F		f	u	f	
15	U			f	u	f	F		f	u	f	
16		U			f	u	f	F		f	u	f
17		U			f	u	f	F		f	u	f
18	f		U			f	u	f	F		f	u
19	f		U			f	u	f	F		f	u
20	u	f		U			f	u	f	F		f
21	u	f		U			f	u	f	F		f
22	f	u	f		U			f	u	f	F	
23	f	u	f		U			f	u	f	F	
24		f	u	f		U			f	u	f	F
25		f	u	f		U			f	u	f	F
26		f	u	f		U			f	u	f	F
27	F		f	u	f		U			f	u	f
28	F		f	u	f		U			f	u	f
29	f	F		f	u	f		U			f	u
30	f	F		f	u	f		U			f	u
31	f	F		f	u	f		U			f	u

November Moon Table

Date	Sign	Element	Nature	Phase
1 Thu	Gemini	Air	Barren	3rd
2 Fri	Gemini	Air	Barren	3rd
3 Sat 3:43 am	Cancer	Water	Fruitful	3rd
4 Sun	Cancer	Water	Fruitful	3rd
5 Mon 2:39 pm	Leo	Fire	Barren	3rd
6 Tue	Leo	Fire	Barren	4th 7:36 pm
7 Wed 11:35 pm	Virgo	Earth	Barren	4th
8 Thu	Virgo	Earth	Barren	4th
9 Fri	Virgo	Earth	Barren	4th
10 Sat 4:35 am	Libra	Air	Semi-fruitful	4th
11 Sun	Libra	Air	Semi-fruitful	4th
12 Mon 6:10 am	Scorpio	Water	Fruitful	4th
13 Tue	Scorpio	Water	Fruitful	New 5:08 pm
14 Wed 5:52 am	Sagittarius	Fire	Barren	1st
15 Thu	Sagittarius	Fire	Barren	1st
16 Fri 5:35 am	Capricorn	Earth	Semi-fruitful	1st
17 Sat	Capricorn	Earth	Semi-fruitful	1st
18 Sun 7:10 am	Aquarius	Air	Barren	1st
19 Mon	Aquarius	Air	Barren	1st
20 Tue 11:55 am	Pisces	Water	Fruitful	2nd 9:31 am
21 Wed	Pisces	Water	Fruitful	2nd
22 Thu 8:12 pm	Aries	Fire	Barren	2nd
23 Fri	Aries	Fire	Barren	2nd
24 Sat	Aries	Fire	Barren	2nd
25 Sun 7:18 am	Taurus	Earth	Semi-fruitful	2nd
26 Mon	Taurus	Earth	Semi-fruitful	2nd
27 Tue 7:58 pm	Gemini	Air	Barren	2nd
28 Wed	Gemini	Air	Barren	Full 9:46 am
29 Thu	Gemini	Air	Barren	3rd
30 Fri 8:55 am	Cancer	Water	Fruitful	3rd

November Aspectarian/Favorable & Unfavorable Days

Date	Sun	Mercury	Venus	Mars	Jupiter	Saturn	Uranus	Neptune	Pluto
1				C		X			
2			O						
3		Q			T	Q	T	O	
4	T								
5	T					Q			
6	Q		X		X	T			
7				T					
8		Q				X		O	T
9	X			Q	Q				
10		X					O		Q
11			C	T					
12				X	C		T		X
13	C								
14		C					T	Q	
15			X	O					
16			C		X	Q	X		C
17		X	Q						
18	X					Q	X		
19		Q			T				
20	Q		T	X	T		C		
21				Q					X
22	T	T							
23				Q	X		C		Q
24									
25			O	T		O		X	T
26		O							
27								Q	
28	O				C	X			
29									
30							T	Q	T

Date	Aries	Taurus	Gemini	Cancer	Leo	Virgo	Libra	Scorpio	Sagittarus	Capricorn	Aquarius	Pisces
1	f		F		f	u	f		U		f	u
2	f		F		f	u	f		U		f	u
3	u	f		F		f	u	f		U		f
4	u	f		F		f	u	f		U		f
5	u	f		F		f	u	f		U		f
6	f	u	f		F		f	u	f		U	
7	f	u	f		F		f	u	f		U	
8		f	u	f		F		f	u	f		U
9		f	u	f		F		f	u	f		U
10	U		f	u	f		F		f	u	f	
11	U		f	u	f		F		f	u	f	
12		U		f	u	f		F		f	u	f
13		U		f	u	f		F		f	u	f
14	f		U		f	u	f		F		f	u
15	f		U		f	u	f		F		f	u
16	u	f		U		f	u	f		F		f
17	u	f		U		f	u	f		F		f
18	f	u	f		U		f	u	f		F	
19	f	u	f		U		f	u	f		F	
20		f	u	f		U		f	u	f		F
21		f	u	f		U		f	u	f		F
22		f	u	f		U		f	u	f		F
23	F		f	u	f		U		f	u	f	
24	F		f	u	f		U		f	u	f	
25		F		f	u	f		U		f	u	f
26		F		f	u	f		U		f	u	f
27		F		f	u	f		U		f	u	f
28	f		F		f	u	f		U		f	u
29	f		F		f	u	f		U		f	u
30	u	f		F		f	u	f		U		f

December Moon Table

Date	Sign	Element	Nature	Phase
1 Sat	Cancer	Water	Fruitful	3rd
2 Sun 8:57 pm	Leo	Fire	Barren	3rd
3 Mon	Leo	Fire	Barren	3rd
4 Tue	Leo	Fire	Barren	3rd
5 Wed 6:51 am	Virgo	Earth	Barren	3rd
6 Thu	Virgo	Earth	Barren	4th 10:31 am
7 Fri 1:35 pm	Libra	Air	Semi-fruitful	4th
8 Sat	Libra	Air	Semi-fruitful	4th
9 Sun 4:51 pm	Scorpio	Water	Fruitful	4th
10 Mon	Scorpio	Water	Fruitful	4th
11 Tue 5:22 pm	Sagittarius	Fire	Barren	4th
12 Wed	Sagittarius	Fire	Barren	4th
13 Thu 4:43 pm	Capricorn	Earth	Semi-fruitful	New 3:42 am
14 Fri	Capricorn	Earth	Semi-fruitful	1st
15 Sat 4:53 pm	Aquarius	Air	Barren	1st
16 Sun	Aquarius	Air	Barren	1st
17 Mon 7:48 pm	Pisces	Water	Fruitful	1st
18 Tue	Pisces	Water	Fruitful	1st
19 Wed	Pisces	Water	Fruitful	1st
20 Thu 2:43 am	Aries	Fire	Barren	2nd 12:19 am
21 Fri	Aries	Fire	Barren	2nd
22 Sat 1:25 pm	Taurus	Earth	Semi-fruitful	2nd
23 Sun	Taurus	Earth	Semi-fruitful	2nd
24 Mon	Taurus	Earth	Semi-fruitful	2nd
25 Tue 2:13 am	Gemini	Air	Barren	2nd
26 Wed	Gemini	Air	Barren	2nd
27 Thu 3:06 pm	Cancer	Water	Fruitful	2nd
28 Fri	Cancer	Water	Fruitful	Full 5:21 am
29 Sat	Cancer	Water	Fruitful	3rd
30 Sun 2:45 am	Leo	Fire	Barren	3rd
31 Mon	Leo	Fire	Barren	3rd

December Aspectarian/Favorable & Unfavorable Days

Date	Sun	Mercury	Venus	Mars	Jupiter	Saturn	Uranus	Neptune	Pluto
1			T	O					O
2		T							
3	T				X	Q	T		
4		Q	Q						
5						X		O	T
6	Q		X	T	Q				
7		X						O	
8	X				Q	T			Q
9								T	
10				X		C			X
11		C	C					Q	
12					O		T		
13	C							X	
14						X	Q		C
15			X	C					
16		X			T	Q	X		
17	X							C	
18		Q	Q		Q	T			X
19				X					
20	Q		T		X		C		Q
21		T							
22	T			Q				X	
23						O			T
24									
25					T	C	X	Q	
26			O						
27		O						T	
28	O					T	Q		O
29									
30					O	X	Q	T	
31			T						

Date	Aries	Taurus	Gemini	Cancer	Leo	Virgo	Libra	Scorpio	Sagittarus	Capricorn	Aquarius	Pisces
1	u	f		F		f	u	f		U		f
2	u	f		F		f	u	f		U		f
3	f	u	f		F		f	u	f		U	
4	f	u	f		F		f	u	f		U	
5		f	u	f		F		f	u	f		U
6		f	u	f		F		f	u	f		U
7		f	u	f		F		f	u	f		U
8	U		f	u	f		F		f	u	f	
9	U		f	u	f		F		f	u	f	
10		U		f	u	f		F		f	u	f
11		U		f	u	f		F		f	u	f
12	f		U		f	u	f		F		f	u
13	f		U		f	u	f		F		f	u
14	u	f		U		f	u	f		F		f
15	u	f		U		f	u	f		F		f
16	f	u	f		U		f	u	f		F	
17	f	u	f		U		f	u	f		F	
18		f	u	f		U		f	u	f		F
19		f	u	f		U		f	u	f		F
20	F		f	u	f		U		f	u	f	
21	F		f	u	f		U		f	u	f	
22	F		f	u	f		U		f	u	f	
23		F		f	u	f		U		f	u	f
24		F		f	u	f		U		f	u	f
25	f		F		f	u	f		U		f	u
26	f		F		f	u	f		U		f	u
27	f		F		f	u	f		U		f	u
28	u	f		F		f	u	f		U		f
29	u	f		F		f	u	f		U		f
30	f	u	f		F		f	u	f		U	
31	f	u	f		F		f	u	f		U	

2012 Retrograde Planets

Planet	Begin	Eastern	Pacific	End	Eastern	Pacific
Mars	01/23/12	7:54 pm	4:54 pm	04/13/12	11:53 pm	8:53 pm
Saturn	02/07/12	9:03 am	6:03 am	06/25/12	4:00 am	1:00 am
Mercury	03/12/12	3:49 am	12:49 am	04/04/12	6:11 am	3:11 am
Pluto	04/10/12	12:21 pm	9:21 am	09/17/12		10:07 pm
				09/18/12	1:07 am	
Venus	05/15/12	10:33 am	7:33 am	06/27/12	11:07 am	8:07 am
Neptune	06/04/12	5:03 pm	2:03 pm	11/10/12		11:52 pm
				11/11/12	2:52 am	
Uranus	07/13/12	5:49 am	2:49 am	12/13/12	7:02 am	4:02 am
Mercury	07/14/12	10:16 pm	7:16 pm	08/07/12		10:40 pm
				08/08/12	1:40 am	
Jupiter	10/04/12	9:18 am	6:18 am	01/30/13	6:37 am	3:37 am
Mercury	11/06/12	6:04 pm	3:04 pm	11/26/12	5:48 pm	2:48 pm

Eastern Time in plain type, **Pacific Time in bold type**

	Dec 11	Jan 12	Feb	Mar	Apr	May	Jun	Jul	Aug	Sep	Oct	Nov	Dec	Jan 13
☿														
♀														
♂														
♃														
♄														
♅														
♆														
♇														

Egg-Setting Dates

To Have Eggs by this Date	Sign	Qtr.	Date to Set Eggs
Jan 2, 5:16 pm–Jan 5, 5:44 am	Taurus	2nd	Dec 12, 2011
Jan 7, 4:05 pm–Jan 9, 2:30 am	Cancer	2nd	Dec 17, 2011
Jan 25, 4:11 am–Jan 27, 1:28 pm	Pisces	1st	Jan 04, 2012
Jan 30, 1:28 am–Feb 1, 2:14 pm	Taurus	1st	Jan 09
Feb 4, 1:04 am–Feb 6, 8:24 am	Cancer	2nd	Jan 14
Feb 21, 5:35 pm–Feb 23, 9:48 pm	Pisces	1st	Jan 31
Feb 26, 9:29 am–Feb 28, 10:27 pm	Taurus	1st	Feb 05
Mar 2, 10:08 am–Mar 4, 6:17 pm	Cancer	2nd	Feb 10
Mar 24, 5:43 pm–Mar 27, 6:43 am	Taurus	1st	Mar 03
Mar 29, 7:07 pm–Apr 1, 4:35 am	Cancer	1st	Mar 08
Apr 5, 11:32 am–Apr 6, 3:19 pm	Libra	2nd	Mar 15
Apr 21, 3:18 am–Apr 23, 1:05 pm	Taurus	1st	Mar 31
Apr 26, 1:42 am–Apr 28, 12:10 pm	Cancer	1st	Apr 05
May 2, 10:04 pm–May 4, 10:20 pm	Libra	2nd	Apr 11
May 23, 7:31 am–May 25, 6:11 pm	Cancer	1st	May 02
May 30, 6:46 am–Jun 1, 8:31 am	Libra	2nd	May 09
Jun 19, 1:34 pm–Jun 21, 11:47 pm	Cancer	1st	May 29
Jun 26, 1:15 pm–Jun 28, 4:32 pm	Libra	1st	Jun 05
Jul 19, 12:24 am–Jul 19, 6:13 am	Cancer	1st	Jun 28
Jul 23, 6:38 pm–Jul 25, 10:29 pm	Libra	1st	Jul 02
Aug 20, 12:45 am–Aug 22, 3:54 am	Libra	1st	Jul 30
Aug 30, 6:31 pm–Aug 31, 9:58 am	Pisces	2nd	Aug 09
Sep 16, 8:55 am–Sep 18, 10:46 am	Libra	1st	Aug 26
Sep 27, 1:23 am–Sep 29, 9:14 am	Pisces	2nd	Sep 06
Oct 15, 8:02 am–Oct 15, 8:06 pm	Libra	1st	Sep 24
Oct 24, 7:00 am–Oct 26, 3:31 pm	Pisces	2nd	Oct 03
Oct 29, 2:15 am–Oct 29, 3:49 pm	Taurus	2nd	Oct 08
Nov 20, 11:55 am–Nov 22, 8:12 pm	Pisces	2nd	Oct 30
Nov 25, 7:18 am–Nov 27, 7:58 pm	Taurus	2nd	Nov 04
Dec 17, 7:48 pm–Dec 20, 2:43 am	Pisces	1st	Nov 26
Dec 22, 1:25 pm–Dec 25, 2:13 am	Taurus	2nd	Dec 01
Dec 27, 3:06 pm–Dec 28, 5:21 am	Cancer	2nd	Dec 06

Dates to Hunt and Fish

Date	Quarter	Sign
Jan 1, 1:15 am–Jan 2, 5:16 pm	2nd	Aries
Jan 7, 4:05 pm–Jan 9, 11:35 pm	2nd	Cancer
Jan 16, 11:33 am–Jan 18, 2:29 pm	4th	Scorpio
Jan 25, 4:11 am–Jan 27, 1:28 pm	1st	Pisces
Feb 4, 1:04 am–Feb 6, 8:24 am	2nd	Cancer
Feb 12, 5:01 pm–Feb 14, 7:56 pm	3rd	Scorpio
Feb 21, 12:31 pm–Feb 23, 9:48 pm	4th	Pisces
Mar 2, 10:08 am–Mar 4, 6:17 pm	2nd	Cancer
Mar 11, 12:24 am–Mar 13, 2:54 am	3rd	Scorpio
Mar 13, 2:54 am–Mar 15, 6:24 am	3rd	Sagittarius
Mar 19, 8:05 pm–Mar 22, 5:57 am	4th	Pisces
Mar 29, 7:07 pm–Apr 1, 4:35 am	1st	Cancer
Apr 7, 11:18 am–Apr 9, 11:12 am	3rd	Scorpio
Apr 9, 11:12 am–Apr 11, 1:02 pm	3rd	Sagittarius
Apr 16, 1:38 am–Apr 18, 11:59 am	4th	Pisces
Apr 26, 1:42 am–Apr 28, 12:10 pm	1st	Cancer
May 4, 10:20 pm–May 6, 9:39 pm	2nd	Scorpio
May 6, 9:39 pm–May 8, 10:00 pm	3rd	Sagittarius
May 13, 7:42 am–May 15, 5:45 pm	4th	Pisces
May 23, 7:31 am–May 25, 6:11 pm	1st	Cancer
Jun 1, 8:31 am–Jun 3, 8:32 am	2nd	Scorpio
Jun 3, 8:32 am–Jun 5, 8:31 am	2nd	Sagittarius
Jun 9, 3:22 pm–Jun 12, 12:21 am	3rd	Pisces
Jun 19, 1:34 pm–Jun 21, 11:47 pm	1st	Cancer
Jun 28, 4:32 pm–Jun 30, 6:04 pm	2nd	Scorpio
Jun 30, 6:04 pm–Jul 2, 6:51 pm	2nd	Sagittarius
Jul 7, 12:29 am–Jul 9, 8:14 am	3rd	Pisces
Jul 9, 8:14 am–Jul 11, 7:30 pm	3rd	Aries
Jul 16, 8:31 pm–Jul 19, 6:13 am	4th	Cancer
Jul 25, 10:29 pm–Jul 28, 1:18 am	1st	Scorpio
Jul 28, 1:18 am–Jul 30, 3:29 am	2nd	Sagittarius
Aug 3, 9:58 am–Aug 5, 4:59 pm	3rd	Pisces
Aug 5, 4:59 pm–Aug 8, 3:28 am	3rd	Aries
Aug 13, 4:27 am–Aug 15, 2:05 pm	4th	Cancer
Aug 22, 3:54 am–Aug 24, 6:50 am	1st	Scorpio
Aug 30, 6:31 pm–Sep 2, 1:37 am	2nd	Pisces
Sep 2, 1:37 am–Sep 4, 11:41 am	3rd	Aries
Sep 9, 12:49 pm–Sep 11, 11:00 pm	4th	Cancer
Sep 18, 10:46 am–Sep 20, 12:34 pm	1st	Scorpio
Sep 27, 1:23 am–Sep 29, 9:14 am	2nd	Pisces
Sep 29, 9:14 am–Oct 1, 7:26 pm	2nd	Aries
Oct 6, 8:45 pm–Oct 9, 7:55 am	3rd	Cancer
Oct 15, 8:06 pm–Oct 17, 8:26 pm	1st	Scorpio
Oct 24, 7:00 am–Oct 26, 3:31 pm	2nd	Pisces
Oct 26, 3:31 pm–Oct 29, 2:15 am	2nd	Aries
Nov 3, 3:43 am–Nov 5, 2:39 pm	3rd	Cancer
Nov 12, 6:10 am–Nov 14, 5:52 am	4th	Scorpio
Nov 20, 11:55 am–Nov 22, 8:12 pm	2nd	Pisces
Nov 22, 8:12 pm–Nov 25, 7:18 am	2nd	Aries
Nov 30, 8:55 am–Dec 2, 8:57 pm	3rd	Cancer
Dec 9, 4:51 pm–Dec 11, 5:22 pm	4th	Scorpio
Dec 17, 7:48 pm–Dec 20, 2:43 am	1st	Pisces
Dec 20, 2:43 am–Dec 22, 1:25 pm	2nd	Aries
Dec 27, 3:06 pm–Dec 30, 2:45 am	2nd	Cancer

Dates to Destroy Weeds and Pests

From		To		Sign	Qtr.
Jan 9	11:35 pm	Jan 12	4:44 am	Leo	3rd
Jan 12	4:44 am	Jan 14	8:28 am	Virgo	3rd
Jan 18	2:29 pm	Jan 20	5:40 pm	Sagittarius	4th
Jan 22	9:53 pm	Jan 23	2:39 am	Aquarius	4th
Feb 7	4:54 pm	Feb 8	12:32 pm	Leo	3rd
Feb 8	12:32 pm	Feb 10	2:54 pm	Virgo	3rd
Feb 14	7:56 pm	Feb 17	12:03 am	Sagittarius	4th
Feb 19	5:28 am	Feb 21	12:31 pm	Aquarius	4th
Mar 8	4:39 am	Mar 8	11:50 pm	Virgo	3rd
Mar 13	2:54 am	Mar 14	9:25 pm	Sagittarius	3rd
Mar 14	9:25 pm	Mar 15	6:24 am	Sagittarius	4th
Mar 17	12:11 pm	Mar 19	8:05 pm	Aquarius	4th
Mar 22	5:57 am	Mar 22	10:37 am	Aries	4th
Apr 9	11:12 am	Apr 11	1:02 pm	Sagittarius	3rd
Apr 13	5:48 pm	Apr 16	1:38 am	Aquarius	4th
Apr 18	11:59 am	Apr 21	12:05 am	Aries	4th
May 6	9:39 pm	May 8	10:00 pm	Sagittarius	3rd
May 11	1:03 am	May 12	5:47 pm	Aquarius	3rd
May 12	5:47 pm	May 13	7:42 am	Aquarius	4th
May 15	5:45 pm	May 18	6:03 am	Aries	4th
May 20	7:05 pm	May 20	7:47 pm	Gemini	4th
Jun 4	7:12 am	Jun 5	8:31 am	Sagittarius	3rd
Jun 7	10:17 am	Jun 9	3:22 pm	Aquarius	3rd
Jun 12	12:21 am	Jun 14	12:22 pm	Aries	4th
Jun 17	1:24 am	Jun 19	11:02 am	Gemini	4th
Jul 4	8:26 pm	Jul 7	12:29 am	Aquarius	3rd
Jul 9	8:14 am	Jul 10	9:48 pm	Aries	3rd
Jul 10	9:48 pm	Jul 11	7:30 pm	Aries	4th
Jul 14	8:26 am	Jul 16	8:31 pm	Gemini	4th
Aug 1	11:27 pm	Aug 3	9:58 am	Aquarius	3rd
Aug 5	4:59 pm	Aug 8	3:28 am	Aries	3rd
Aug 10	4:11 pm	Aug 13	4:27 am	Gemini	4th
Aug 15	2:05 pm	Aug 17	11:54 am	Leo	4th
Sep 2	1:37 am	Sep 4	11:41 am	Aries	3rd
Sep 7	12:10 am	Sep 8	9:15 am	Gemini	3rd
Sep 8	9:15 am	Sep 9	12:49 pm	Gemini	4th
Sep 11	11:00 pm	Sep 14	5:30 am	Leo	4th
Sep 14	5:30 am	Sep 15	10:11 pm	Virgo	4th
Sep 29	11:19 pm	Oct 1	7:26 pm	Aries	3rd
Oct 4	7:47 am	Oct 6	8:45 pm	Gemini	3rd
Oct 9	7:55 am	Oct 11	3:23 pm	Leo	4th
Oct 11	3:23 pm	Oct 13	7:02 pm	Virgo	4th
Oct 31	2:40 pm	Nov 3	3:43 am	Gemini	3rd
Nov 5	2:39 pm	Nov 6	7:36 pm	Leo	3rd
Nov 6	7:36 pm	Nov 7	11:35 pm	Leo	4th
Nov 7	11:35 pm	Nov 10	4:35 am	Virgo	4th
Nov 28	9:46 am	Nov 30	8:55 am	Gemini	3rd
Dec 2	8:57 pm	Dec 5	6:51 am	Leo	3rd
Dec 5	6:51 am	Dec 6	10:31 am	Virgo	3rd
Dec 6	10:31 am	Dec 7	1:35 pm	Virgo	4th
Dec 11	5:22 pm	Dec 13	3:42 am	Sagittarius	4th
Dec 30	2:45 am	Jan 1, 2013	12:35 pm	Leo	3rd

Time Zone Map

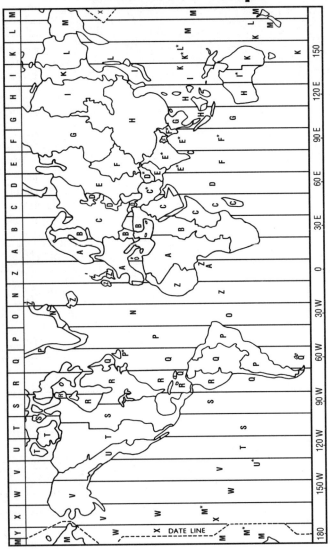

Time Zone Conversions

(R) EST—Used in book
(S) CST—Subtract 1 hour
(T) MST—Subtract 2 hours
(U) PST—Subtract 3 hours
(V) Subtract 4 hours
(V*) Subtract 4½ hours
(U*) Subtract 3½ hours
(W) Subtract 5 hours
(X) Subtract 6 hours
(Y) Subtract 7 hours
(Q) Add 1 hour
(P) Add 2 hours
(P*) Add 2½ hours
(O) Add 3 hours
(N) Add 4 hours
(Z) Add 5 hours
(A) Add 6 hours
(B) Add 7 hours
(C) Add 8 hours
(C*) Add 8½ hours

(D) Add 9 hours
(D*) Add 9½ hours
(E) Add 10 hours
(E*) Add 10½ hours
(F) Add 11 hours
(F*) Add 11½ hours
(G) Add 12 hours
(H) Add 13 hours
(I) Add 14 hours
(I*) Add 14½ hours
(K) Add 15 hours
(K*) Add 15½ hours
(L) Add 16 hours
(L*) Add 16½ hours
(M) Add 17 hours
(M*) Add 18 hours
(P*) Add 2½ hours

Important!

All times given in the *Moon Sign Book* are set in Eastern Time. The conversions shown here are for standard times only. Use the time zone conversions map and table to calculate the difference in your time zone. You must make the adjustment for your time zone and adjust for Daylight Saving Time where applicable.

Weather, Economic & Lunar Forecasts

Forecasting the Weather

By Kris Brandt Riske

Astrometeorology—astrological weather forecasting—reveals seasonal and weekly weather trends based on the cardinal ingresses (Summer and Winter Solstices, and Spring and Autumn Equinoxes) and the four monthly lunar phases. The planetary alignments and the longitudes and latitudes they influence have the strongest effect, but the zodiacal signs are also involved in creating weather conditions.

The components of a thunderstorm, for example, are heat, wind, and electricity. A Mars-Jupiter configuration generates the necessary heat and Mercury adds wind and electricity. A severe thunderstorm, and those that produce tornados, usually involve Mercury, Mars, Uranus, or Neptune. The zodiacal signs add their energy to the planetary mix to increase or decrease the chance of weather phenomena and their severity.

In general, the fire signs (Aries, Leo, Sagittarius) indicate heat and dryness, both of which peak when Mars, the planet with a similar nature, is in these signs. Water signs (Cancer, Scorpio, Pisces) are conducive to precipitation, and air signs (Gemini, Libra, Aquarius) to cool temperatures and wind. Earth signs (Taurus, Virgo, Capricorn) vary from wet to dry, heat to cold. The signs and their prevailing weather conditions are listed here:

Aries: Heat, dry, wind
Taurus: Moderate temperatures, precipitation
Gemini: Cool temperatures, wind, dry
Cancer: Cold, steady precipitation
Leo: Heat, dry, lightning
Virgo: Cold, dry, windy
Libra: Cool, windy, fair
Scorpio: Extreme temperatures, abundant precipitation
Sagittarius: Warm, fair, moderate wind
Capricorn: Cold, wet, damp
Aquarius: Cold, dry, high pressure, lightning
Pisces: Wet, cool, low pressure

Take note of the Moon's sign at each lunar phase. It reveals the prevailing weather conditions for the next six to seven days. The same is true of Mercury and Venus. These two influential weather planets transit the entire zodiac each year, unless retrograde patterns add their influence.

Planetary Influences

People relied on astrology to forecast weather for thousands of years. They were able to predict drought, floods, and temperature variations through interpreting planetary alignments. In recent years there has been a renewed interest in astrometeorology. A weather forecast can be composed for any date—tomorrow, next week, or a thousand years in the future. According to astrometeorology, each planet governs certain weather phenomena. When certain planets are aligned with other planets, weather—precipitation, cloudy or clear skies, tornados, hurricanes, and other conditions— are generated.

Sun and Moon

The Sun governs the constitution of the weather and, like the Moon, it serves as a trigger for other planetary configurations that result in weather events. When the Sun is prominent in a cardinal ingress or lunar phase chart, the area is often warm and sunny. The Moon can bring or withhold moisture, depending upon its sign placement.

Mercury

Mercury is also a triggering planet, but its main influence is wind direction and velocity. In its stationary periods, Mercury reflects high winds, and its influence is always prominent in major weather events, such as hurricanes and tornadoes, when it tends to lower the temperature.

Venus

Venus governs moisture, clouds, and humidity. It brings warming trends that produce sunny, pleasant weather if in positive aspect to other planets. In some signs—Libra, Virgo, Gemini, Sagittarius—Venus is drier. It is at its wettest when placed in Cancer, Scorpio, Pisces, or Taurus.

Mars

Mars is associated with heat, drought, and wind, and can raise the temperature to record-setting levels when in a fire sign (Aries, Leo, Sagittarius). Mars is also the planet that provides the spark that generates thunderstorms and is prominent in tornado and hurricane configurations.

Jupiter

Jupiter, a fair-weather planet, tends toward higher temperatures when in Aries, Leo, or Sagittarius. It is associated with high-pressure systems and is a contributing factor at times to dryness. Storms are often amplified by Jupiter.

Saturn

Saturn is associated with low-pressure systems, cloudy to overcast skies, and excessive precipitation. Temperatures drop when Saturn is involved. Major winter storms always have a strong Saturn influence, as do storms that produce a slow, steady downpour for hours or days.

Uranus

Like Jupiter, Uranus indicates high-pressure systems. It reflects descending cold air and, when prominent, is responsible for a jet stream that extends far south. Uranus can bring drought in winter, and it is involved in thunderstorms, tornados, and hurricanes.

Neptune

Neptune is the wettest planet. It signals low-pressure systems and is dominant when hurricanes are in the forecast. When Neptune is strongly placed, flood danger is high. It's often associated with winter thaws. Temperatures, humidity, and cloudiness increase where Neptune influences weather.

Pluto

Pluto is associated with weather extremes, as well as unseasonably warm temperatures and drought. It reflects the high winds involved in major hurricanes, storms, and tornadoes.

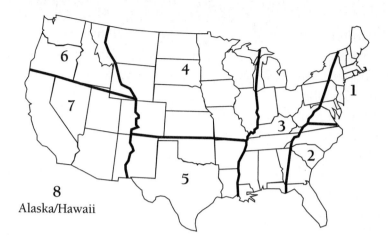

8
Alaska/Hawaii

Weather Forecast for 2012

By Kris Brandt Riske

Winter

Zone 1 can expect a winter with above-average precipitation and seasonal temperatures, while zone 2 will see significant storms and chilly temperatures in coastal areas. Inland and throughout most of Florida, zone 2 will be seasonal, but with periods of cold weather and potential for ice storms and freezing rain in the mid-Atlantic states. Temperatures in eastern and central areas of zone 3 will be unseasonably cold with average moisture, and the north-eastern part of the zone will be very cold.

Low-pressure systems will bring precipitation and cold temperatures to zones 4 and 5. These will form and be centered in north-central areas of zone 4, coming from Canada, and will reach maximum intensity in the central areas of the Plains states (southern zone 4 and northern zone 5) as storm fronts move through the region. Precipitation will be abundant at times.

The northwestern area of zone 4 and eastern areas of zones 6 and 7 will see significant precipitation from storms entering the continental United States from the northwest (the western part of zone 6, which will see significant storms and cold temperatures). Storm fronts will most often move from central zone 6 southeastward to eastern zone 7 and western zone 5. Western areas of zone 7 will have warm temperatures with below-average precipitation.

Alaska will be seasonal with average precipitation. Western parts of the state will see abundant downfall; temperatures will be colder in eastern areas and more seasonal in central regions. Hawaii's weather will be generally seasonal, with increasing clouds and precipitation in eastern areas.

January 1–8, 2nd Quarter Moon

Zone 1: Overcast skies bring precipitation to the zone, where temperatures are below seasonal.

Zone 2: Central and southern areas are mostly fair, windy, and seasonal; northern areas are cloudy with precipitation.

Zone 3: Western and central skies are variably cloudy with temperatures seasonal to above; eastern parts of the zone are cloudy and colder with precipitation.

Zone 4: A front from the northwest brings precipitation, some abundant, that moves across western and central parts of the zone; temperatures are seasonal to below but colder east.

Zone 5: Temperatures are seasonal to below, and western areas are stormy later in the week, with precipitation accompanied by high winds moving into central parts of the zone.

Zone 6: Western areas are windy with precipitation that moves across the zone; some areas see high winds, and temperatures are colder to the west.

Zone 7: Western areas are variably cloudy with more clouds and scattered precipitation in northern coastal areas, moving across northern parts of the zone; temperatures are seasonal to below. Potential stormy conditions could bring high winds.

Zone 8: Central and eastern Alaska see precipitation, western areas are fair to partly cloudy, and temperatures are seasonal to below. Eastern parts of Hawaii see precipitation, but the state is mostly fair to partly cloudy, windy, and seasonal.

January 9–15, Full Moon

Zone 1: Temperatures are seasonal to below with precipitation, some abundant in the north.

Zone 2: Much of the zone sees precipitation, and southern areas have potential for strong thunderstorms, while central parts of the zone could see freezing rain; temperatures are seasonal to below.

Zone 3: Western and central areas are mostly fair, eastern areas see precipitation, and temperatures are seasonal to below.

Zone 4: Western areas see a warming trend, a low-pressure area brings precipitation to the western and central Plains, and eastern areas are variably cloudy and cold.

Zone 5: Areas to the west are fair to partly cloudy and seasonal, central areas are cloudy with precipitation, and eastern areas are fair and cold.

Zone 6: Precipitation in western areas moves across the zone, bringing the heaviest downfall and high winds to central and eastern parts of the zone; temperatures are seasonal to below.

Zone 7: Precipitation in western areas moves across the zone as the week progresses, bringing abundant downfall to northern areas; desert areas are windy and warm with variable clouds.

Zone 8: Western areas of Alaska see precipitation later in the week, and the state is windy and seasonal. Hawaii is mostly fair and seasonal.

January 16–22, 4th Quarter Moon

Zone 1: Weather in this zone is variably cloudy and cold, with a chance for precipitation.

Zone 2: Skies are fair and temperatures are seasonal to above.

Zone 3: Much of the zone is cloudy and windy with precipitation, and temperatures are seasonal to below.

Zone 4: Western and southern parts of the zone see precipitation that moves into central areas of the eastern Plains, and eastern areas see precipitation later in the week; temperatures are seasonal but colder west.

Zone 5: Western and central areas are cloudy with precipitation, with the heaviest downfall in central parts of the zone; temperatures are seasonal, and eastern areas are windy later in the week.

Zone 6: Western areas are cloudy with precipitation, and other parts of the zone are mostly fair and windy with a chance for precipitation; temperatures are seasonal to below; northern coastal areas see increasing clouds and precipitation later in the week.

Zone 7: Skies are variably cloudy west and central, with a chance for precipitation east; temperatures are seasonal to below.

Zone 8: Central Alaska is cold and windy, and other areas are more seasonal with precipitation east. Much of Hawaii is windy with temperatures seasonal to below and a chance for precipitation in central parts of the state.

January 23–29, New Moon

Zone 1: Cloudy skies bring precipitation, some abundant.

Zone 2: The zone is variably cloudy and seasonal with scattered precipitation north; central areas are windy.

Zone 3: Central areas are cold and windy under variably cloudy skies, and eastern areas see precipitation.

Zone 4: Western parts of the zone see precipitation that moves into the western and central Plains; temperatures are seasonal to below and cold in the Plains.

Zone 5: Temperatures are seasonal to below, western skies are fair, and central and eastern areas of the zone are windy and cold with precipitation.

Zone 6: Western skies clear as a front moves into central and eastern areas, bringing precipitation under overcast skies with below-average temperatures.

Zone 7: Eastern temperatures are above normal early in the week until cloudy skies and precipitation move across the zone, lowering temperatures.

Zone 8: Alaska is windy, especially western and central areas, which see precipitation. Hawaii is windy, fair, and seasonal.

January 30–February 6, 2nd Quarter Moon

Zone 1: The zone is cloudy and windy with temperatures seasonal to below.

Zone 2: Skies are fair to partly cloudy and windy with scattered precipitation south; temperatures are seasonal.

Zone 3: Eastern areas have a chance for precipitation, and the zone is seasonal and fair to partly cloudy.

Zone 4: Western areas are windy, seasonal, and partly cloudy; central and eastern areas are mostly fair and cold.

Zone 5: Western parts of the zone are partly cloudy, and central and eastern areas are windy and cold.

Zone 6: Skies are variably cloudy with precipitation east.

Zone 7: Western and central parts of the zone are variably cloudy, and eastern areas are windy with precipitation.

Zone 8: Central Alaska is stormy and very windy, while western and eastern areas are more seasonal. Hawaii is windy as a front brings showers across much of the state; temperatures are seasonal to below.

February 7–13, Full Moon

Zone 1: The zone is seasonal, windy, and cloudy with a chance for precipitation.

Zone 2: Much of the zone is cloudy and windy, especially northern areas; southern areas see scattered thunderstorms.

Zone 3: The zone is fair to partly cloudy with scattered thunderstorms, some strong, in southern areas; eastern parts of the zone are overcast with precipitation; temperatures are seasonal.

Zone 4: Precipitation in western areas moves into the western Plains later in the week, while central and eastern areas are variably cloudy with seasonal temperatures.

Zone 5: Western parts of the zone are cloudy, stormy, and cold; central areas are windy with precipitation, and eastern locations are mostly fair.

Zone 6: Western and central areas are cloudy, and eastern areas are windy; temperatures are seasonal.

Zone 7: Variable clouds and wind are in the forecast for western and central areas, and temperatures are seasonal to above in the desert areas.

Zone 8: Alaska is variably cloudy, seasonal, and windy, with precipitation in central areas. Hawaii is windy with scattered showers and thunderstorms and temperatures seasonal to above.

February 14–20, 4th Quarter Moon

Zone 1: Skies are cloudy and windy with scattered precipitation.

Zone 2: Southern areas see precipitation and more clouds than northern parts of the zone, which are partly cloudy and windy.

Zone 3: Western and central parts of the zone see showers and scattered thunderstorms, increasing in southern areas; northern areas are fair to partly cloudy, and eastern areas are windy with a chance for precipitation.

Zone 4: Much of the zone is overcast with precipitation; western and central Plains are stormy, and eastern areas are partly cloudy; temperatures are seasonal to below.

Zone 5: Western areas are fair and windy, while central and eastern parts of the zone are cloudy with precipitation and potential for strong thunderstorms; temperatures are seasonal to below.

Zone 6: Much of the zone sees precipitation, with the heaviest downfall in central areas; temperatures are seasonal.

Zone 7: Precipitation and high winds in western areas move into central parts of the zone, and eastern areas are cloudy and windy with a chance for precipitation, with some areas seeing abundant downfall; temperatures are seasonal to above in the desert.

Zone 8: Alaska is variably cloudy and seasonal with precipitation west and windy conditions in central areas. Hawaii is mostly fair and seasonal, with western areas of the state seeing possibly abundant precipitation.

February 21–28, New Moon

Zone 1: The zone is cloudy, windy, and seasonal with possibly abundant precipitation.

Zone 2: Northern areas are cloudy, central and southern areas see scattered thunderstorms, and the zone is windy and seasonal.

Zone 3: Western and central areas are windy with potential for strong thunderstorms in southern areas; eastern areas are cloudy with scattered precipitation; temperatures are seasonal.

Zone 4: Overcast skies are in the forecast for western and central parts of the zone, eastern areas are mostly fair to partly cloudy and windy, and temperatures are seasonal to below.

Zone 5: The zone is variably cloudy and seasonal; there is potential for severe weather central and east with locally heavy precipitation.

Zone 6: Much of the zone is cloudy and windy with precipitation; temperatures are seasonal to below.

Zone 7: The zone is windy and seasonal, with cloudy skies and precipitation in central and eastern areas.

Zone 8: Central and eastern areas of Alaska are windy with precipitation, and western parts of the state are mostly fair with a chance for precipitation. Hawaii is cloudy with showers, some locally heavy.

February 29–March 7, 2nd Quarter Moon

Zone 1: The zone is variably cloudy with scattered precipitation and temperatures seasonal to below.

Zone 2: Central and southern parts of the zone have potential for strong thunderstorms with tornadoes, while northern areas are windy and seasonal.

Zone 3: Western and central areas have potential for severe thunderstorms with tornado potential, and the zone is windy with temperatures seasonal to above.

Zone 4: Western areas are cloudy and stormy; the rest of the zone is variably cloudy and windy; temperatures are seasonal but cooler east.

Zone 5: The zone is seasonal and fair to partly cloudy with a chance for precipitation.

Zone 6: Much of the zone is cloudy with precipitation, some abundant in western and central areas, and seasonal temperatures.

Zone 7: Western and central parts of the zone are cloudy with scattered precipitation, while eastern areas are partly cloudy; temperatures are seasonal to above.

Zone 8: Central and eastern Alaska see overcast skies and possibly abundant precipitation, which then moves into eastern areas. Hawaii is cloudy and seasonal with precipitation.

March 8–13, Full Moon

Zone 1: Conditions are windy in northern areas, and the zone is cloudy with possibly abundant precipitation.

Zone 2: Northern and central areas see variable clouds, and southern parts of the zone see scattered thunderstorms, some possibly strong.

Zone 3: Scattered strong thunderstorms with tornado potential are possible in central areas, eastern parts of the zone see scattered precipitation, and temperatures are seasonal.

Zone 4: Much of the zone is cloudy with precipitation, and some parts of the zone see abundant precipitation and high winds; northeastern areas are mostly fair.

Zone 5: Western skies are cloudy, much of the zone sees precipitation, and central eastern areas have potential for strong thunderstorms and tornadoes.

Zone 6: The zone is variably cloudy with seasonal temperatures; western and central areas see scattered precipitation, eastern areas are mostly fair, and western areas are windy.

Zone 7: Eastern areas are mostly fair and windy, and western and central areas are variably cloudy with scattered precipitation.

Zone 8: Eastern Alaska sees possibly abundant precipitation and high winds, and western and central parts of the state are fair to partly cloudy. Hawaii is cloudy with scattered precipitation and locally heavy downpours.

March 14–21, 4th Quarter Moon

Zone 1: Skies are windy and overcast with precipitation; temperatures are seasonal to below.

Zone 2: Northern areas are cloudy with a chance for precipitation, and central and southern areas see scattered showers and thunderstorms.

Zone 3: The zone is variably cloudy with seasonal temperatures, and eastern areas are windy with scattered precipitation.

Zone 4: Central areas are stormy, and other parts of the zone are variably cloudy; temperatures are seasonal to below.

Zone 5: Skies are cloudy across much of the zone with potential for thunderstorms with high winds and tornadoes in central and eastern areas; temperatures are seasonal to below.

Zone 6: Western skies are windy and cloudy, and eastern and central areas are mostly fair.

Zone 7: Northern coastal areas see precipitation, and western parts of the zone are cloudy, while central and eastern areas are fair; eastern temperatures are unseasonably warm with a chance for scattered precipitation.

Zone 8: Western and central Alaska sees precipitation, and eastern areas are fair; temperatures are seasonal. In Hawaii, showers accompany windy conditions and seasonal temperatures.

Spring

Wind and cold weather are the dominant weather features in zone 1, with southern areas also seeing above-normal precipitation. Coastal areas of zone 2 are windy with above-normal precipitation, cool temperatures, and increased potential for tornadoes. To the west in zone 3, precipitation will be abundant in Ohio and southward, while most of the western zone is at high risk for tornadoes and increased precipitation.

The Plains states of western and central zones 4 and 5 also have above-normal potential for strong thunderstorms with high winds and tornadoes, and states from Montana southward to Texas will see abundant precipitation at times. The more northern areas of zone 4 will be unseasonably cold at times.

Central areas of zones 6 and 7 will see abundant precipitation (primarily at higher elevations) and windy, cold conditions. Precipitation will, in general, be normal to above in both of these zones. However, the southern coastal areas will have periods of high temperatures with more dryness.

Eastern Alaska can expect significant precipitation this spring with flood potential, and most areas of the state will have average precipitation with temperatures seasonal to below. Hawaii will be seasonal and windy, with some areas receiving below-normal precipitation.

March 22–29, New Moon

Zone 1: Skies are fair to partly cloudy with possible precipitation.
Zone 2: Much of the zone sees precipitation with thunderstorms south; skies are variably cloudy and temperatures are seasonal.
Zone 3: The zone is fair and warm, with higher temperatures west and precipitation east.
Zone 4: Western areas are windy with precipitation, western Plains are cloudy with precipitation, and eastern areas are windy and variably cloudy with a chance for precipitation; temperatures are seasonal to above.

Zone 5: Western skies are windy and fair, central areas are cloudy with scattered precipitation, and eastern areas are fair to partly cloudy with a chance for precipitation; temperatures are seasonal.

Zone 6: Western and central areas are stormy, and eastern parts of the zone are partly cloudy.

Zone 7: Northern coastal areas are windy with precipitation, as are northern areas of the central part of the zone; eastern areas are fair to partly cloudy.

Zone 8: Much of Alaska is windy with precipitation and temperatures seasonal to below. Hawaii sees temperatures seasonal to above with wind and cloudy skies, precipitation west, and fair to partly cloudy skies central and east.

March 30–April 5, 2nd Quarter Moon

Zone 1: Much of the zone is cloudy with precipitation, some abundant in northern areas, and temperatures are seasonal.

Zone 2: The zone is fair and seasonal.

Zone 3: Western areas are windy with potential for strong thunderstorms with tornadoes, and central and eastern areas are mostly fair.

Zone 4: The zone is windy and mostly fair to partly cloudy, with more clouds and precipitation in central areas; temperatures are seasonal to below.

Zone 5: Wind accompanies fair to partly cloudy skies and seasonal temperatures across much of the zone; western areas see scattered precipitation, and eastern areas are humid with potential for strong thunderstorms.

Zone 6: Western areas are windy, and much of the zone sees precipitation and seasonal temperatures.

Zone 7: The zone is variably cloudy with scattered precipitation in northern coastal areas, while temperatures range from seasonal to above in desert areas.

Zone 8: Central and western Alaska see precipitation, and eastern areas are fair and windy. Hawaii is seasonal with variable clouds and showers central and east.

April 6–12, Full Moon

Zone 1: The zone is windy with possibly abundant precipitation north, and southern areas are mostly fair and seasonal.

Zone 2: The zone is fair and seasonal.

Zone 3: Western areas are windy with thunderstorms, some strong with tornado potential, while central and eastern parts of the zone are mostly fair.

Zone 4: Cloudy skies and precipitation accompany a low-pressure center in western parts of the zone, while other areas have a chance for severe thunderstorms with tornado potential; temperatures are seasonal to above.

Zone 5: The zone is fair west and variably cloudy and humid in other areas with potential for severe thunderstorms and tornadoes; temperatures are seasonal to above.

Zone 6: Much of the zone sees precipitation with seasonal temperatures; central areas are very windy.

Zone 7: Western skies are variably cloudy with a chance for precipitation, while a high-pressure center boosts desert temperatures; northeastern areas have a chance for showers.

Zone 8: Central Alaska is stormy, and western and eastern areas are fair to partly cloudy; temperatures are seasonal. Hawaii is variably cloudy and seasonal with precipitation in eastern areas.

April 13–20, 4th Quarter Moon

Zone 1: The zone is cloudy with precipitation centered in the north, which is overcast with significant downpour in some areas; temperatures are seasonal.

Zone 2: Northern areas see scattered precipitation, and strong thunderstorms are possible central and south; zonal temperatures are seasonal.

Zone 3: Much of the zone sees precipitation, with thunderstorms with tornado potential in western and central areas.

Zone 4: Western skies are fair, with increasing clouds and precipitation central and east; strong thunderstorms with tornado potential are possible.

Zone 5: Central and eastern areas are variably cloudy with strong thunderstorms with tornado potential east, while western areas are fair.

Zone 6: The zone is seasonal with precipitation.

Zone 7: Much of the zone sees precipitation, some significant in coastal areas, and eastern areas are partly cloudy with a chance for showers; temperatures are seasonal.

Zone 8: Central and eastern Alaska are cloudy with precipitation, and western areas are fair. Hawaii is cloudy with abundant precipitation in some western areas, after which the state sees a warming trend.

April 21–28, New Moon

Zone 1: Skies are cloudy, windy, and seasonal with precipitation.

Zone 2: Much of the zone sees precipitation, some abundant, and weather is damp with seasonal temperatures.

Zone 3: Temperatures are seasonal; western and central areas are cloudy with thunderstorms, and eastern areas see precipitation, some abundant.

Zone 4: The zone is seasonal and windy with strong storms west, thunderstorms with tornado potential east, and mostly fair central.

Zone 5: Western areas are fair and seasonal, while central areas are windy with a chance for thunderstorms, and eastern parts of the zone are partly cloudy.

Zone 6: Western and central parts of the zone are partly cloudy, and eastern areas could see strong storms with high winds before skies clear and temperatures warm.

Zone 7: Skies are cloudy west and central with precipitation in northern areas, while eastern areas are variably cloudy; temperatures are seasonal, but above normal in the desert.

Zone 8: Western Alaska is stormy, and precipitation moves into central parts of the state; eastern areas are fair and windy. Hawaii is variably cloudy and seasonal with showers.

April 29–May 4, 2nd Quarter Moon

Zone 1: Northern areas are cloudy with heavy downfalls later in the week, southern areas see scattered showers, and temperatures are seasonal to below.

Zone 2: The zone is humid and variably cloudy with temperatures seasonal to above and scattered thunderstorms, some strong, in central areas.

Zone 3: Western and central areas are windy with strong thunderstorms and tornado potential, eastern areas see possibly abundant precipitation later in the week, and temperatures are seasonal.

Zone 4: The zone is variably cloudy with precipitation west, wind central and east with potential for strong thunderstorms, and seasonal temperatures.

Zone 5: Western areas see precipitation, and central and eastern areas are cloudy with precipitation and strong thunderstorms possible later in the week; temperatures are seasonal.

Zone 6: Much of the zone is windy with precipitation, some locally heavy.

Zone 7: Northern coastal areas see precipitation, while the rest of the zone is variably cloudy and windy with temperatures seasonal to above and a chance for precipitation.

Zone 8: Alaska is variably cloudy and seasonal with precipitation in central areas. Hawaii is humid with showers and thunderstorms and temperatures seasonal to above.

May 5–11, Full Moon

Zone 1: The zone is cloudy, windy, and cool with precipitation, some abundant.

Zone 2: The zone is humid with precipitation, some locally heavy; skies are cloudy and cool north, with temperatures seasonal to above central and south.

Zone 3: Western and central areas are humid with showers and thunderstorms, eastern areas are cloudy with precipitation, and temperatures are seasonal to above, but cooler east.

Zone 4: Northwestern areas see some abundant precipitation, as do mountain areas and the western Plains; central and eastern areas are variably cloudy with possible strong thunderstorms; much of the zone is windy, and temperatures are seasonal to above.

Zone 5: Western areas see precipitation, central and eastern parts of the zone are fair to partly cloudy, eastern parts of the zone could have strong thunderstorms, and temperatures are seasonal to above.

Zone 6: Western and central areas are windy with possibly abundant precipitation; eastern areas are fair to partly cloudy.

Zone 7: Western and north central parts of the zone are windy with precipitation, while eastern areas are variably cloudy; temperatures are seasonal to above.

Zone 8: Eastern Alaska sees precipitation, and western and central areas are windy with possible locally heavy precipitation.

Hawaii is humid and partly cloudy with temperatures seasonal to above.

May 12–19, 4th Quarter Moon

Zone 1: The zone is variably cloudy, windy, and seasonal, with precipitation north.

Zone 2: Central and southern areas are cloudy with showers and thunderstorms, and northern areas are partly cloudy; temperatures are seasonal to below.

Zone 3: Western and central areas are humid, central and eastern areas see thunderstorms, and temperatures are seasonal to below.

Zone 4: Skies are fair to partly cloudy west and east with a chance for showers west; central parts of the zone see thunderstorms, some strong with tornado potential and high winds; temperatures are seasonal to above.

Zone 5: The zone is windy with thunderstorms and tornado potential central and east.

Zone 6: Western skies are fair, and central and eastern parts of the zone are cloudy with precipitation, some abundant; temperatures are seasonal.

Zone 7: Northern areas see precipitation from cloudy skies, and other areas are fair to partly cloudy with a chance for showers.

Zone 8: Alaska is seasonal and windy with precipitation west and central and fair skies east. Hawaii is fair with temperatures seasonal to above.

May 20–27, New Moon

Zone 1: The zone is variably cloudy, windy, and seasonal, with precipitation in southern areas.

Zone 2: The zone is humid and variably cloudy, with possibly abundant precipitation in many areas.

Zone 3: The zone is variably cloudy and windy west with scattered thunderstorms; eastern areas are humid with precipitation, some abundant from strong thunderstorms and possible tornadoes; temperatures are seasonal to above.

Zone 4: Much of the zone is fair and seasonal, but eastern areas are cooler with showers.

Zone 5: The zone is fair and seasonal with a chance of thunderstorms in eastern areas.

Zone 6: Western and central parts of the zone are cloudy with precipitation, and eastern areas are mostly fair but with increasing clouds later in the week; temperatures are seasonal to below.

Zone 7: Western and northern parts of central areas are cloudy, and eastern areas are partly cloudy; temperatures are seasonal.

Zone 8: Central Alaska sees precipitation, and the rest of the state is fair to partly cloudy; temperatures are seasonal. Hawaii is humid, partly cloudy, and seasonal.

May 28–June 3, 2nd Quarter Moon

Zone 1: The zone is mostly fair with temperatures seasonal to above and a chance for thunderstorms.

Zone 2: Central and southern areas are partly cloudy with a chance for showers, and northern areas see more clouds with precipitation; temperatures are seasonal to above.

Zone 3: The zone is variably cloudy with thunderstorms west and central, some strong with tornado potential; humidity rises and temperatures are seasonal to above, but cooler and cloudy with showers east.

Zone 4: Western areas are partly cloudy, central and eastern areas see thunderstorms (some strong with tornado potential), and temperatures are seasonal to above.

Zone 5: The zone is partly cloudy and humid with strong thunderstorms and tornado potential east; temperatures are seasonal to above.

Zone 6: Western areas are cloudy with showers, eastern areas see showers, and much of the zone is windy with temperatures that are seasonal.

Zone 7: The zone is windy with showers east and in northern coastal areas; temperatures are seasonal to above.

Zone 8: Alaska is mostly fair, but cloudy with precipitation west. Hawaii is variably cloudy and humid with showers, and temperatures are seasonal to above.

June 4–10, Full Moon

Zone 1: Southern areas see thunderstorms, northern areas are fair to partly cloudy and windy, and temperatures range from seasonal to above.

Zone 2: Much of the zone is fair to partly cloudy with temperatures seasonal to above and showers and thunderstorms in northern areas.

Zone 3: The zone is humid and fair to partly cloudy with temperatures seasonal to above and showers in eastern areas.

Zone 4: Much of the zone is hot and dry with a chance for thunderstorms, but northeastern areas see some clouds along with wind and cooler temperatures.

Zone 5: The zone is hot and dry with a chance for thunderstorms central and east.

Zone 6: Western areas are cloudy with showers, central areas are windy with thunderstorms, and eastern areas are windy with a chance for thunderstorms; temperatures are seasonal.

Zone 7: Northern coastal areas are cloudy with showers, central areas see scattered thunderstorms, and eastern areas are windy; temperatures are seasonal to above.

Zone 8: Alaska is windy and seasonal with variable clouds and scattered precipitation. Western and central Hawaii are windy with showers.

June 11–18, 4th Quarter Moon

Zone 1: Temperatures are seasonal to above with scattered showers and thunderstorms.

Zone 2: Northern areas are fair to partly cloudy with showers, and central and southern areas see more clouds along with rising humidity, showers, and thunderstorms; temperatures are seasonal to above.

Zone 3: Western and central areas are fair and hot with a chance for showers, and eastern areas are cloudy with precipitation; the zone is humid with temperatures seasonal to above.

Zone 4: Western skies are fair, central and eastern areas see scattered thunderstorms, and temperatures are seasonal to above.

Zone 5: The zone is mostly fair with temperatures seasonal to above and scattered thunderstorms east.

Zone 6: Western skies are cloudy with scattered showers, central and eastern areas are variably cloudy with scattered thunderstorms, and temperatures are seasonal to above.

Zone 7: Northern coastal areas are cloudy with showers, while the rest of the zone is fair to partly cloudy with temperatures seasonal to above; scattered thunderstorms are possible in central and northeastern areas.

Zone 8: Alaska is seasonal and generally fair to partly cloudy. Hawaii is partly cloudy and seasonal, but a warming trend is indicated later in the week.

Summer

Zone 1 will be prone to severe storms, including hurricanes, this summer, as well as unseasonably cool temperatures and wind. Temperatures will range higher in zone 2, along with below-average precipitation. Temperatures in zone 3 will be about average, but with periods of excessive heat, which will trigger thunderstorms followed by cooler temperatures.

The central Plains states in zones 4 and 5 will experience periods of abundant precipitation, as will the eastern parts of zone 5 and the Mississippi River Valley. Western areas of these zones can expect normal precipitation levels and temperatures seasonal to cool. Northwestern areas of zone 4 will also be prone to strong storms.

Precipitation will range from normal to slightly below normal in zone 6, and temperatures will be seasonal to above. Although western and central parts of zone 7 will see precipitation, these areas can also expect periods of high temperatures. Eastern areas of zone 7 can expect significant storms with high winds and seasonal temperatures.

Central Alaska will be cooler than normal with periodic major storms, while western parts of the state will be seasonal with average precipitation, and eastern areas will see more clouds and windy conditions along with cooler temperatures. Summer in Hawaii will be generally seasonal, but with potential for strong thunderstorms and locally heavy precipitation.

June 19–25, New Moon

Zone 1: The zone is humid with possibly abundant precipitation—the heaviest downfall comes in northern areas; temperatures are seasonal to above and then cooler.

Zone 2: Humidity and temperatures are seasonal to above, triggering scattered showers and thunderstorms under variably cloudy skies.

Zone 3: Western skies are clear, central parts of the zone are windy with scattered showers and thunderstorms, eastern areas could see abundant precipitation, and the zone is humid with temperatures seasonal to above.

Zone 4: The zone is humid and variably cloudy with scattered showers and thunderstorms in central areas; zonal temperatures are seasonal.

Zone 5: Humidity, windy conditions, partly cloudy skies, and temperatures seasonal to above prevail, with scattered thunderstorms east.

Zone 6: Western areas are cool with precipitation, while central and eastern areas see increasing clouds with showers and possible locally heavy precipitation east; temperatures are seasonal.

Zone 7: Northern coastal areas see precipitation, and the rest of the zone is seasonal and variably cloudy with scattered precipitation.

Zone 8: Central and eastern Alaska are windy with precipitation, and western areas are fair; temperatures are seasonal. Hawaii is humid and cloudy with precipitation, some locally heavy.

June 26–July 2, 2nd Quarter Moon

Zone 1: The zone is windy, variably cloudy, and seasonal with scattered showers.

Zone 2: Central and southern areas could see abundant precipitation from cloudy skies, while northern areas are windy and partly cloudy; temperatures are seasonal.

Zone 3: Temperatures are seasonal to above, central areas are cloudy with some heavy precipitation, and eastern areas are fair and windy; temperatures and humidity are seasonal to above.

Zone 4: Western skies are fair, while central and eastern areas see scattered thunderstorms, some strong with locally heavy precipitation; humidity rises and temperatures are seasonal to above.

Zone 5: Skies are fair west and central, and eastern areas see scattered thunderstorms, some strong with high winds and tornado potential; humidity rises and temperatures are seasonal to above.

Zone 6: The zone is seasonal, variably cloudy, and windy with showers west and a chance for showers central and east.

Zone 7: Western and central areas are windy, and the zone is variably cloudy with a chance for showers; temperatures are seasonal to above.

Zone 8: Alaska is variably cloudy and windy, fair west, stormy east, and seasonal. Eastern Hawaii is windy and cloudy with showers, and western and central parts of the state are fair and seasonal.

July 3–9, Full Moon

Zone 1: The zone is partly cloudy and humid with scattered showers and temperatures seasonal to above.

Zone 2: Temperatures are seasonal to above with humidity, wind, showers, and thunderstorms.

Zone 3: Western parts of the zone are cloudy with potential for abundant precipitation, possibly from a tropical storm. Thunderstorms, some strong, are possible in central and eastern areas, and the zone is humid and seasonal, but cooler west.

Zone 4: Western areas see showers, the Plains are humid with a chance for showers in central areas, and eastern areas are cloudy with a chance of locally heavy precipitation.

Zone 5: Western areas are windy with potential for strong thunderstorms; central and eastern areas are humid with showers and thunderstorms, possibly from a tropical storm.

Zone 6: Western areas are partly cloudy and cooler with scattered thunderstorms, and central and eastern areas are windy with showers and thunderstorms in eastern parts of the zone; temperatures are seasonal to above.

Zone 7: Northern coastal areas are partly cloudy with scattered showers, and eastern areas are humid with a chance for thunderstorms; temperatures are seasonal to above, and much of the zone is windy.

Zone 8: Alaska is mostly fair to partly cloudy and windy with precipitation in eastern areas; temperatures are seasonal to below. Hawaii is partly cloudy, seasonal, and windy with some showers.

July 10–18, 4th Quarter Moon

Zone 1: The zone is humid with showers and thunderstorms, some strong with locally heavy precipitation; temperatures are seasonal to above.

Zone 2: Temperatures are seasonal to above, and the zone is humid with thunderstorms, some strong with tornado potential.

Zone 3: The zone is humid with temperatures seasonal to above and thunderstorms, some strong with tornado potential.

Zone 4: Western parts of the zone see scattered thunderstorms, central areas are windy and partly cloudy with scattered showers, and eastern areas are cloudy with showers and thunderstorms, some strong with tornado potential.

Zone 5: The zone sees scattered thunderstorms, some strong with tornado potential, and central areas see more clouds, possibly from a tropical storm.

Zone 6: The zone is partly cloudy with scattered showers and seasonal temperatures.

Zone 7: Western and central areas are cloudy with potential for abundant precipitation, and eastern areas have a chance for showers; temperatures are seasonal to above.

Zone 8: Much of Alaska sees precipitation under variably cloudy skies and seasonal temperatures, with the heaviest downfall in western areas. Hawaii is humid with temperatures seasonal to above and showers and thunderstorms.

July 19–25, New Moon

Zone 1: The zone is seasonal and variably cloudy with scattered precipitation south and showers north.

Zone 2: Central and southern areas could see strong thunderstorms with tornado potential, and northern areas have a chance for showers; temperatures are seasonal to above.

Zone 3: Western and central areas have potential for strong thunderstorms with tornadoes, and conditions are humid and windy—a tropical storm or hurricane is possible; eastern areas are partly cloudy with scattered showers.

Zone 4: Western areas are windy, and central and eastern parts of the zone are humid with partly cloudy skies and scattered showers; temperatures are seasonal.

Zone 5: The zone is partly cloudy with scattered showers and seasonal temperatures.

Zone 6: Temperatures are seasonal and skies are cloudy with showers, bringing abundant precipitation to some western and central parts of the zone.

Zone 7: Western and central areas see showers and thunderstorms, some strong, and eastern areas see scattered showers; conditions are humid with temperatures seasonal to above.

Zone 8: Western Alaska is cloudy with abundant precipitation in some areas; central areas see showers, and eastern parts of the state are mostly fair; temperatures are seasonal. Hawaii is fair and seasonal with scattered showers.

July 26–31, 2nd Quarter Moon

Zone 1: The zone is windy with scattered thunderstorms and temperatures seasonal to below.

Zone 2: Central and southern areas are windy with a chance for scattered precipitation, and northern areas are variably cloudy and dry; temperatures are seasonal.

Zone 3: Western and central areas are windy with showers, eastern areas are partly cloudy, and temperatures are seasonal.

Zone 4: Western areas have potential for heavy precipitation with strong thunderstorms, and the Plains are windy, with more clouds in central areas; temperatures are seasonal.

Zone 5: Western areas see abundant precipitation, and central and eastern parts of the zone are mostly fair and dry with a chance for precipitation central.

Zone 6: Conditions in western parts of the zone are windy and cool with precipitation, central areas see scattered precipitation, eastern areas are windy with a chance for showers; temperatures are seasonal to below.

Zone 7: Skies are fair to partly cloudy in western and central areas with a chance for precipitation, eastern areas see scattered thunderstorms, and temperatures are seasonal to above.

Zone 8: Alaska is variably cloudy with scattered precipitation in central areas, and temperatures are seasonal to below. Hawaii is windy with temperatures seasonal to above and scattered thunderstorms, some strong.

August 1–8, Full Moon

Zone 1: Northern areas of the zone are cloudy with potential for abundant precipitation, possibly from a tropical storm or hurricane, and southern areas are windy with precipitation; temperatures are seasonal.

Zone 2: The zone is variably cloudy and windy with thunderstorms, some strong, possibly from a tropical storm or hurricane.

Zone 3: The zone is humid with temperatures seasonal to above and generally partly cloudy; eastern areas have a chance for strong thunderstorms with tornado potential.

Zone 4: The zone is variably cloudy and windy with scattered precipitation, and eastern areas are humid with heavier precipitation later in the week; temperatures are seasonal to above.

Zone 5: Western areas are windy, and the zone sees scattered thunderstorms and showers under variably cloudy skies; temperatures are seasonal to above.

Zone 6: The zone is variably cloudy, breezy, and seasonal with a chance for precipitation.

Zone 7: Northern coastal areas are cloudy with precipitation, possibly abundant, and the rest of the zone is partly cloudy with scattered thunderstorms and high humidity east.

Zone 8: Western Alaska is cloudy with precipitation, and other areas are partly cloudy; temperatures are seasonal. Hawaii is humid and partly cloudy, but with more clouds and scattered showers west.

August 9–16, 4th Quarter Moon

Zone 1: The zone is variably cloudy, humid, and seasonal.

Zone 2: Much of the zone sees potentially strong thunderstorms, especially south, where there are more clouds and precipitation, possibly from a tropical storm.

Zone 3: Abundant precipitation, possibly from a tropical storm, is possible in western parts of the zone, which are cloudy and windy, as are central areas; eastern areas are partly cloudy, humid, and seasonal.

Zone 4: Eastern areas see abundant precipitation and more clouds than the rest of the zone, which is fair to partly cloudy; temperatures are seasonal to above.

Zone 5: Western areas are fair to partly cloudy with scattered precipitation, and eastern areas see more clouds with precipitation later in the week.

Zone 6: Western areas are stormy, central and eastern areas have a chance for precipitation, and temperatures are seasonal.

Zone 7: Temperatures are seasonal to above with precipitation in northern coastal parts of the zone and a chance for precipitation in western and central areas; eastern areas are humid with a chance for thunderstorms.

Zone 8: Eastern Alaska is stormy, and the rest of the state is fair to partly cloudy with temperatures seasonal to below. Hawaii is mostly fair and seasonal, with showers in eastern areas.

August 17–23, New Moon
Zone 1: The zone is windy and variably cloudy with scattered precipitation and temperatures seasonal to above.

Zone 2: The zone is windy and humid with scattered precipitation north and south and strong thunderstorms in central areas.

Zone 3: Western areas are stormy with strong thunderstorms, and much of the rest of the zone is fair to partly cloudy with a chance for precipitation.

Zone 4: Western areas see precipitation with high winds, central parts of the zone could see potentially strong thunderstorms, and eastern areas are cloudy and stormy with strong thunderstorms; the zone is humid with temperatures seasonal to above.

Zone 5: Abundant precipitation and high winds are possible in some western areas, central parts of the zone see showers later in the week, central and eastern areas are humid, and temperatures are seasonal to above.

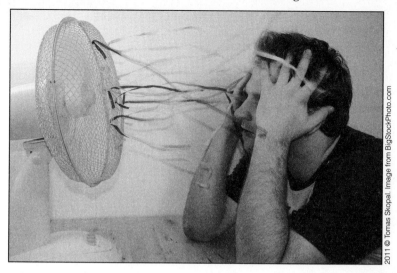

Zone 6: The zone is fair to partly cloudy with temperatures seasonal to above.

Zone 7: Much of the zone is fair to partly cloudy, eastern areas are humid with a chance for thunderstorms, and temperatures are seasonal to above.

Zone 8: Alaska is variably cloudy, windy west with precipitation, and mostly fair in other areas with seasonal temperatures. Hawaii is fair to partly cloudy and seasonal with scattered showers.

August 24–30, 2nd Quarter Moon

Zone 1: The zone is seasonal and humid with showers, some locally heavy.

Zone 2: Northern areas are partly cloudy, and the zone is humid with temperatures seasonal to above; southern areas are mostly fair, but with precipitation and possible severe thunderstorms followed by cooler temperatures later in the week; a tropical storm is possible.

Zone 3: The zone is humid and variably cloudy with temperatures seasonal to above and a chance for showers and thunderstorms.

Zone 4: Scattered showers and thunderstorms; the zone is variably cloudy with temperatures seasonal to above.

Zone 5: The zone is variably cloudy with temperatures seasonal to above and potential for scattered thunderstorms, especially in western areas.

Zone 6: Western and central areas see precipitation, some abundant with flood potential, and eastern areas are fair to partly cloudy with precipitation later in the week; temperatures are seasonal.

Zone 7: Northern coastal areas could see abundant precipitation, and the rest of the zone is fair to partly cloudy with scattered showers and thunderstorms; temperatures are seasonal to above.

Zone 8: Western and central Alaska are windy and cloudy with precipitation, eastern areas are partly cloudy, and temperatures are seasonal to below. Hawaii is variably cloudy and humid with showers and thunderstorms and temperatures seasonal to above.

August 31–September 7, Full Moon

Zone 1: The zone is cloudy with abundant precipitation and potential severe thunderstorms, possibly from a tropical storm or hurricane; temperatures are seasonal to below.

Zone 2: Northern areas see precipitation, central and southern areas are humid with a chance for thunderstorms, and temperatures are seasonal to above.

Zone 3: Western and central parts of the zone see strong thunderstorms with tornado potential, eastern areas see showers, and the zone is humid.

Zone 4: Much of the zone sees showers with a chance for thunderstorms central and east, and conditions are humid with temperatures seasonal to above.

Zone 5: The zone is partly cloudy with scattered showers and thunderstorms, humid in central and eastern areas, and temperatures seasonal to above.

Zone 6: The zone is variably cloudy with more clouds and precipitation west; temperatures are seasonal.

Zone 7: Western and central areas see scattered showers with variably cloudy skies, and eastern parts of the zone have a chance for thunderstorms; temperatures are seasonal to above.

Zone 8: Alaska is windy with precipitation west and central, fair east, and temperatures seasonal to below. Hawaii is windy with scattered thunderstorms and temperatures seasonal to above.

September 8–14, 4th Quarter Moon

Zone 1: Northern areas are cloudy with precipitation, southern areas are fair to partly cloudy, and temperatures are seasonal.

Zone 2: The zone is variably cloudy with humidity and scattered thunderstorms and locally heavy precipitation central and south; temperatures are seasonal to above.

Zone 3: Western areas are windy, and western and central areas see scattered thunderstorms, some possibly strong; skies are fair to partly cloudy, and temperatures are seasonal to above.

Zone 4: The zone is fair to partly cloudy, western areas are windy, and eastern parts of the zone could see frost.

Zone 5: Skies are fair to partly cloudy, western and central areas are windy, eastern areas are humid with a chance for thunderstorms, and temperatures are seasonal to above.

Zone 6: Western areas see precipitation and then clearing skies, temperatures are seasonal to above, and the zone is generally fair to partly cloudy and windy.

Zone 7: The zone is fair to partly cloudy with a chance for precipitation in northern coastal and eastern areas, and temperatures are seasonal to above.

Zone 8: Western and central Alaska are cloudy with precipitation, eastern areas are mostly fair, and temperatures are seasonal. Hawaii is seasonal with variable clouds and scattered showers, and central and eastern areas are windy.

September 15–21, New Moon

Zone 1: The zone sees seasonal temperatures with precipitation and thunderstorms.

Zone 2: Northern areas see precipitation, while central and southern areas have potential for strong thunderstorms with tornadoes; temperatures and humidity rise.

Zone 3: Western areas sees showers and thunderstorms, eastern parts of the zone see precipitation, and skies are variably cloudy with seasonal temperatures.

Zone 4: Western parts of the zone are windy with precipitation, central areas have potential for thunderstorms and tornadoes, eastern areas are cloudy with precipitation, and temperatures are seasonal to below.

Zone 5: The zone is partly cloudy and seasonal with a chance for scattered thunderstorms, and central areas see more clouds.

Zone 6: The zone is very windy with precipitation and temperatures seasonal to below.

Zone 7: Much of the zone is windy with precipitation, which is heaviest in eastern areas later in the week; temperatures are seasonal to above.

Zone 8: Alaska is windy west and central with precipitation, some abundant, and eastern areas are mostly fair; temperatures are seasonal to below. Hawaii is windy with precipitation west and central, and temperatures are seasonal.

Autumn

Coastal areas of zones 1 and 2 can expect precipitation to range from average to above average, with hurricane potential in northern areas of zone 1. These zones will also be prone to an increased level of severe thunderstorms with tornado potential in early autumn and winter storms later in the season. Northeastern areas of zone 3 will experience much the same weather, and western and central parts of this zone will also see abundant precipitation and strong thunderstorms with tornado potential at times. Temperatures will dip quite low at times in zone 3 and central areas of zone 2.

The Plains states of zones 4 and 5, as well as northeastern areas of zone 4, will at times see abundant precipitation, strong low-pressure systems, and cool temperatures. A southerly flow of moisture will elevate temperatures and humidity, aiding in the development of storm systems. These areas can also expect periods of below-average temperatures, as can the western Plains, which will also see abundant precipitation as a result of low-pressure systems. Heaviest downfall throughout these zones is likely to occur in the central parts of the zones.

The northwestern coastal part of zone 6 will experience cold temperatures and abundant precipitation, while central and eastern areas will be more seasonal. Temperatures will tend to be above normal in western parts of zone 7, and this area will also be prone to high winds, which could equate to severe fire weather. Central areas of zone 7 will see more clouds and precipitation, and temperatures in eastern parts of this zone will be above normal, especially in desert areas.

Central Alaska can expect an increased number of cloudy and windy days with average precipitation and temperatures ranging from seasonal to below. Western Alaska will see abundant precipitation at times with seasonal temperatures, while eastern parts of the state will be generally seasonal. Hawaii will be generally seasonal, although precipitation may be below average.

September 22–28, 2nd Quarter Moon
Zone 1: The zone is windy and seasonal with precipitation.
Zone 2: Skies throughout the zone are variably cloudy and windy with a chance for precipitation.
Zone 3: The zone is windy, western areas are cloudy with a chance for precipitation, and the rest of the zone is fair to partly cloudy and humid with a chance for precipitation later in the week.

Zone 4: Western areas are windy with precipitation, and the zone is variably cloudy and seasonal.

Zone 5: The zone is mostly fair to partly cloudy and windy with a chance for precipitation in central areas later in the week; temperatures are seasonal to above.

Zone 6: Temperatures are seasonal to below, and the zone is windy with precipitation.

Zone 7: The zone is fair to partly cloudy with precipitation east; temperatures are seasonal to above.

Zone 8: Alaska is variably cloudy with precipitation in central areas; temperatures are seasonal. Hawaii is seasonal with showers, some locally heavy.

September 29–October 7, Full Moon

Zone 1: The zone is fair to partly cloudy with more clouds, wind, and precipitation in southern areas later in the week; temperatures are seasonal.

Zone 2: Central and southern areas see scattered thunderstorms, while northern areas see more clouds with precipitation; temperatures are seasonal to below.

Zone 3: Western areas see significant precipitation and high winds, including potential for thunderstorms, tornadoes, and flooding, possibly from a tropical storm or hurricane; central and eastern areas are cloudy with precipitation, and temperatures are seasonal to below.

Zone 4: Western areas are mostly fair, and other parts of the zone are variably cloudy with precipitation, which is abundant in some locations; eastern areas are stormy.

Zone 5: Western and central parts of the zone are mostly fair, and eastern areas are windy with potential for strong thunderstorms with tornadoes.

Zone 6: The zone is windy with precipitation, which is abundant central and east, and temperatures are seasonal to below.

Zone 7: Skies are windy and cloudy west and central with precipitation, and eastern skies are partly cloudy; temperatures are seasonal to above.

Zone 8: Alaska is variably cloudy with precipitation and wind in eastern areas, and temperatures are seasonal. Hawaii is fair to partly cloudy and seasonal.

October 8–14, 4th Quarter Moon

Zone 1: The zone is windy and seasonal with precipitation, some abundant.

Zone 2: Temperatures are seasonal to below, and the zone is windy and variably cloudy.

Zone 3: Skies are fair to partly cloudy and temperatures are seasonal to above but cooler with more clouds east.

Zone 4: A low-pressure system in the western Plains brings abundant precipitation, along with temperatures seasonal to below.

Zone 5: The zone is windy and variably cloudy with precipitation central and east; temperatures are seasonal to below.

Zone 6: Temperatures are seasonal to below, and the zone is variably cloudy with scattered precipitation east.

Zone 7: Northern coastal areas are windy and cold with a chance for precipitation, and the rest of the zone is partly cloudy with more clouds and scattered precipitation east.

Zone 8: Central and eastern Alaska see precipitation, western parts of the state are partly cloudy, and temperatures are seasonal to below. Hawaii is variably cloudy and seasonal with precipitation east.

October 15–20, New Moon

Zone 1: The zone is windy with temperatures seasonal to below, southern areas are fair to partly cloudy, and northern areas see precipitation later in the week.

Zone 2: Northern areas are fair to windy, central and southern parts of the zone are cloudy with precipitation, and temperatures are seasonal to below.

Zone 3: Western areas are windy with thunderstorms, and the zone is seasonal to below and variably cloudy with more clouds and precipitation east.

Zone 4: The zone is seasonal, windy west, partly cloudy central, and windy east with a chance for thunderstorms.

Zone 5: Central and eastern areas are windy with a chance for thunderstorms, which could be locally heavy in central parts of the zone; western areas are very windy.

Zone 6: Western and central parts of the zone are fair to partly cloudy, eastern areas see increasing clouds with precipitation later in the week, and the zone is seasonal.

Zone 7: The zone is windy and seasonal, and very windy east with a chance for precipitation.

Zone 8: Western Alaska is windy with precipitation that moves into central areas, and eastern parts of the state are fair to partly cloudy and windy; temperatures are seasonal. Western and central Hawaii are windy and cooler with scattered precipitation, and eastern areas are mostly fair.

October 21–28, 2nd Quarter Moon

Zone 1: Northern areas are fair to partly cloudy, southern areas see precipitation with high winds, and temperatures are seasonal to below.

Zone 2: Strong thunderstorms with tornado potential are possible in central and southern areas, and northern areas are windy with precipitation; temperatures are seasonal to below.

Zone 3: Temperatures are seasonal to below, much of the zone sees precipitation, and eastern areas are very windy.

Zone 4: Western and central parts of the zone are windy with thunderstorms (some possibly strong with locally heavy downfall), eastern areas see showers, and temperatures are seasonal.

Zone 5: Strong thunderstorms with tornado potential are possible across much of the zone with abundant precipitation and high winds in eastern areas; temperatures are seasonal to below.

Zone 6: The zone is variably cloudy with temperatures seasonal to below and a chance for precipitation in eastern areas.

Zone 7: Western and central parts of the zone are windy with scattered precipitation, eastern areas see more clouds with precipitation, and temperatures are seasonal.

Zone 8: Precipitation moves across much of Alaska, which is windy with temperatures seasonal to below. Hawaii is fair to partly cloudy and seasonal.

October 29–November 5, Full Moon

Zone 1: The zone is variably cloudy, windy, and seasonal with precipitation in northern areas.

Zone 2: Thunderstorms, some strong with tornado potential, are possible in central and southern parts of the zone under variably cloudy skies and temperatures seasonal to above.

Zone 3: Strong thunderstorms are possible in central areas; the zone is variably cloudy and seasonal with more clouds east.

Zone 4: Western parts of the zone see precipitation as a front moves in, central parts of the zone are windy with abundant precipitation, eastern areas are fair to partly cloudy, and temperatures are seasonal to below.

Zone 5: Western areas are partly cloudy with precipitation later in the week, temperatures are seasonal, and central and eastern areas are windy with precipitation, some abundant.

Zone 6: Precipitation moves across the zone as the week unfolds, and temperatures are seasonal to below.

Zone 7: Much of the zone sees precipitation, skies are variably cloudy, and eastern areas are very windy.

Zone 8: Western Alaska is windy with scattered precipitation, central areas are stormy, eastern areas see precipitation, and temperatures are seasonal. Hawaii is seasonal and much of the state sees showers, which are heaviest in eastern areas.

November 6–12, 4th Quarter Moon

Zone 1: The zone has seasonal temperatures and partly cloudy skies with scattered precipitation.

Zone 2: Much of the zone is windy and variably cloudy with precipitation, some abundant in southern areas, possibly from a late-season tropical storm.

Zone 3: Much of the zone is cloudy with precipitation, and western and southern areas could see locally heavy downfall from thunderstorms; temperatures are seasonal.

Zone 4: The zone is fair to partly cloudy, windy, and seasonal, with scattered precipitation east.

Zone 5: Temperatures are seasonal to above under fair to partly cloudy skies, and eastern areas see showers and strong thunderstorms with tornado potential later in the week.

Zone 6: Western and central parts of the zone are fair to partly cloudy and temperatures are seasonal, while eastern areas are cloudy with precipitation.

Zone 7: Much of the zone is windy, western and central areas are mostly fair, eastern areas are cloudy with precipitation, and temperatures are seasonal to above.

Zone 8: Central Alaska is windy with precipitation, western and eastern areas are partly cloudy, and temperatures are seasonal. Hawaii is windy, seasonal, and partly cloudy with scattered possible precipitation.

November 13–19, New Moon

Zone 1: Southern areas are cloudy with precipitation, some locally heavy; northern areas are partly cloudy; and temperatures are seasonal.

Zone 2: Much of the zone sees precipitation, possibly abundant in northern areas; central and southern areas could experience strong thunderstorms with tornado potential; and temperatures are seasonal.

Zone 3: Western areas see precipitation with potential for thunderstorms and tornadoes, central parts of the zone are partly cloudy with a chance for precipitation, eastern areas are cloudy and windy with precipitation, and temperatures are seasonal.

Zone 4: Much of the zone (especially the eastern Plains) sees scattered precipitation, and temperatures are seasonal.

Zone 5: The zone is variably cloudy and seasonal with scattered precipitation west and central and precipitation in eastern areas.

Zone 6: Western areas are partly cloudy, central areas are cloudy with precipitation, and eastern parts of the zone are stormy with high winds; temperatures are seasonal to below.

Zone 7: The zone is variably cloudy, windy, and seasonal; central areas see precipitation, and eastern parts of the zone are stormy.

Zone 8: Alaska is seasonal with precipitation central and east and fair skies west. Hawaii is seasonal with showers.

November 20–27, 2nd Quarter Moon

Zone 1: The zone is variably cloudy and windy with precipitation and temperatures seasonal to below.

Zone 2: Northern areas are partly cloudy, and southern and central areas could see strong thunderstorms with tornado potential and abundant downfall; temperatures are seasonal.

Zone 3: Western areas see high winds and precipitation, central and eastern areas are fair to partly cloudy, and zonal temperatures are seasonal.

Zone 4: Western parts of the zone see scattered precipitation, while central and eastern areas are windy with precipitation—conditions could be stormy at week's end; temperatures are seasonal to below.

Zone 5: Western and central areas are partly cloudy with a chance for precipitation, eastern areas could see strong thunderstorms with tornado potential, and temperatures are seasonal.

Zone 6: Temperatures are seasonal to below with precipitation across much of the zone; abundant downfall is possible in western and central areas.

Zone 7: Western parts of the zone are very windy with abundant precipitation in some areas, central areas see precipitation, and eastern areas are fair to partly cloudy with scattered precipitation.

Zone 8: Alaska sees temperatures seasonal to below with precipitation in central areas, some abundant; western and eastern parts of the state are partly cloudy. Hawaii is seasonal with showers.

November 28–December 5, Full Moon

Zone 1: The zone is windy with precipitation and temperatures seasonal to below.

Zone 2: Northern areas are cloudy, central and southern areas are partly cloudy with thunderstorms, and temperatures are seasonal.

Zone 3: Western and central parts of the zone are fair to partly cloudy, eastern areas are cloudy with precipitation, and temperatures are seasonal to below.

Zone 4: Western areas are stormy with high winds, central and eastern areas are partly cloudy, and zonal temperatures are seasonal to below.

Zone 5: Much of the zone is windy with precipitation west and central and temperatures seasonal to below.

Zone 6: The zone is mostly fair to partly cloudy and seasonal with a chance for precipitation in central areas.

Zone 7: Seasonal temperatures accompany partly cloudy skies.

Zone 8: Alaska is seasonal and much of the state sees precipitation. Hawaii is seasonal with showers.

December 6–12, 4th Quarter Moon

Zone 1: The zone is windy and cloudy with abundant precipitation north; temperatures are seasonal to below.

Zone 2: Much of the zone sees precipitation with temperatures seasonal to below, and an ice storm or freezing rain is possible.

Zone 3: Western and central areas are windy with precipitation, and temperatures are seasonal.

Zone 4: Western skies are fair to partly cloudy with precipitation later in the week, eastern areas are windy with precipitation, and temperatures are seasonal to below.

Zone 5: Western areas are fair, eastern areas are cloudy with precipitation, and temperatures are seasonal to below.

Zone 6: The zone is variably cloudy with a chance for precipitation, especially central and east, where weather is windy and cold.

Zone 7: Much of the zone is very windy with precipitation, and temperatures are seasonal to below.

Zone 8: Western and central Alaska see precipitation, with abundant downfall in central parts of the state, and eastern areas are windy; temperatures are seasonal. Hawaii is windy and seasonal with showers.

December 13–19, New Moon

Zone 1: The zone is cold and fair to partly cloudy with a chance for precipitation.

Zone 2: Northern areas are fair to partly cloudy, central and southern areas see more clouds with precipitation, and temperatures are seasonal to below.

Zone 3: Much of the zone sees precipitation with variable clouds and overcast skies in central areas; zonal temperatures are seasonal to below.

Zone 4: Western areas are windy with precipitation, some abundant; strong thunderstorms with tornado potential are possible in central and southern parts of the zone; temperatures are seasonal to above.

Zone 5: The zone is windy with precipitation in western areas, and possible thunderstorms with tornado potential in central and eastern areas; temperatures are seasonal to above.

Zone 6: The zone is windy with precipitation and temperatures seasonal to below.

Zone 7: Temperatures are seasonal to below and the zone is windy with precipitation.

Zone 8: Central and eastern Alaska are windy as a front moves through bringing precipitation, while western parts of the state are fair to partly cloudy; temperatures are seasonal. Hawaii is seasonal with showers, some locally heavy in central parts of the state.

December 20–27, 2nd Quarter Moon

Zone 1: The zone is cold with some stormy conditions later on in the week.

Zone 2: Northern areas are cold with precipitation, and southern areas are variably cloudy with scattered precipitation.

Zone 3: The zone is cloudy and seasonal with scattered precipitation, and storms are possible in eastern areas later in the week.

Zone 4: Much of the zone sees possibly abundant precipitation, and temperatures are seasonal.

Zone 5: Temperatures are seasonal and much of the zone sees precipitation with the possibility for strong thunderstorms with tornado potential.

Zone 6: Western and central areas are fair to partly cloudy, central and eastern areas are windy, eastern parts of the zone see precipitation, and temperatures are seasonal to below.

Zone 7: Temperatures are seasonal to below, western areas are fair to partly cloudy and windy, and eastern areas see precipitation, some abundant.

Zone 8: Alaska is variably cloudy and seasonal with precipitation in eastern areas. Hawaii is fair to partly cloudy and seasonal with scattered precipitation central and east.

December 28–January 4, Full Moon

Zone 1: The zone is windy with precipitation and temperatures seasonal to below.

Zone 2: Northern areas are cloudy with precipitation, central and southern areas are windy with variable clouds and thunderstorms, and temperatures are seasonal.

Zone 3: Western areas see more clouds, and much of the zone is windy with precipitation; temperatures are seasonal.

Zone 4: The zone is variably cloudy with temperatures seasonal to below and precipitation in eastern areas.

Zone 5: Temperatures are seasonal and the zone is variably cloudy with more clouds central and east with precipitation, some abundant.

Zone 6: Much of the zone sees precipitation, and temperatures are seasonal to below.

Zone 7: The zone is cloudy with precipitation, high winds in eastern areas, and temperatures seasonal to below.

Zone 8: Alaska is variably cloudy with precipitation in western and central areas and temperatures seasonal to below. Hawaii is windy and cool with showers and thunderstorms, some strong.

About the Author

Kris Brandt Riske is the executive director and a professional member of the American Federation of Astrologers (AFA), the oldest U.S. astrological organization, founded in 1938; and a member of National Council for Geocosmic Research (NCGR). She has a master's degree in journalism and a certificate of achievement in weather forecasting from Penn State.

Kris is the author of several books, including: Llewellyn's Complete Book of Astrology: The Easy Way to Learn Astrology; Mapping Your Money; Mapping Your Future; *and coauthor of* Mapping Your Travels and Relocation; *and* Astrometeorology: Planetary Powers in Weather Forecasting. *Her newest book is* Llewellyn's Complete Book of Predictive Astrology. *She also writes for astrology publications and does the annual weather forecast for* Llewellyn's Moon Sign Book.

In addition to astrometeorology, she specializes in predictive astrology. Kris is an avid NASCAR fan, although she'd rather be a driver than a spectator. In 2011 she fulfilled her dream when she drove a stock car for twelve fast laps. She posts a weather forecast for each of the thirty-six race weekends (qualifying and race day) for NASCAR drivers and fans. Visit her at www.pitstopforecasting.com. Kris also enjoys gardening, reading, jazz, and her three cats.

Economic Forecast for 2012

By Dorothy J. Kovach

As the year begins, the economy is still struggling and people are mad as hell—will they keep taking it? This national unrest is not very good news for political leaders. One of the problems associated with the timing of Obama's inauguration was that he chose to have the ceremony a full hour early. This placed the portion of the chart that rules the electorate (you and me) in the agitated sign of Aries. For those new to astrology, Aries is the most action-oriented of the signs. It's the original "I want what I want, when I want it" sign. But we cannot place the blame for our economic woes on our elected leaders alone. First Americans stopped caring where our products were made. Then we fooled ourselves into thinking our technical jobs were special and would always stay on American soil—but that wasn't the case. Still, we didn't give the issue much thought. We then became so addicted to cheap imported goods that we arrived at a sorry state: if you want to buy American-made goods, there is little left to buy. Finally, the money has run out. Our jobs are gone, and we see the politicians in their Armani suits, seemingly in bed with the big-money lobbies. In short, disenchantment is on the rise.

It is no surprise that Americans are angry. For the first half of the year, our nation's natal chart will be in what is known as an eighth house profected year. Profection is an important method of direction whereby we move a chart ahead by one house per year, with the next house becoming the starting point. Thus a subsequent house becomes the main feature each year. Starting with July 4, 1776, and working our way to the present, we circle back to the original chart every twelve years. The eighth house has to do with crisis and death. Historically, it can be a bad year for presidents. The last eighth house year was 1999, when President Clinton was impeached. The one prior to that was in 1987, when we had the Iran Contra hearings. Before that, in 1975, we saw Nixon resign.

While embarrassing for the presidents mentioned, an eighth house profected year can be deadly too. 1963 we saw assassination bring an end to the Camelot that was John F. Kennedy's administration. Thus, for the first half of the year, we can expect Barack Obama to be gravely criticized, and not just on economic matters. Hopefully, he will be very careful in all his dealings so as to survive this unlucky alignment. When our national chart has so many factors indicating deep dissatisfaction among citizens, it can't be good news for incumbents of either party, much less the president should he decide to run for reelection in this climate.

Regardless of who is to blame for the economic downturn, we will have to roll up our sleeves and work together to pay the piper. After all, it's not just the politicians who have been lax. For almost three solid decades, Americans watched passively as jobs were sent abroad, from call stations to factories, and we did not call on our lawmakers to take account. In return, we were inundated with cheap goods made in China at insanely cheap prices. Lulled into inactivity by one or another technological gadget, we looked the other way. After all, with interest rates so low and credit so easy, Americans could get loans to buy anything they wanted. From credit cards to car loans, everything was easy terms. Collateral was an outmoded concept in the new "manufactured in China" world, where anybody could buy a huge house, or even two. "Hey, if the banks want to give the money away, I would be a fool not to take it," was how one fellow put it. The general feeling was that real estate always appreciates, so it's a no-risk investment. Alas, that is not the case.

Given the amount of debt our nation has accumulated, we will probably never be able to dig our way out of it in our lifetime, even with our currency debased, making dollars cheaper. And don't expect great economic strides to be made within our central government. With a Republican House and a Democratic Executive Branch, we can expect a good deal of gridlock in Washington, D.C.

However, the economy doesn't have to stay in such a state. We do not have to be divided, but each of us does need to be willing to work hard in order to improve our sluggish economy. Unless we can wake up our inner entrepreneur and kickstart things, don't expect much relief from double-digit unemployment. It may be frustrating down on Main Street, but now that the middle class has been decimated, this once-great nation is comprised of two separate and unequal worlds: one that exists for the very rich, and another for everybody else. But for wise investors or traders (which are two different devils), there is always a silver lining in congressional clouds.

Combust Planets:
The Market Can Get Sunburned Too

Like moths hypnotized in the candle's flame, planets are dragged down to their deaths when they get too close to the Sun. No matter how they try, businesses that come under the influence of such a planet are crushed under an inevitable weight that drags the entire sector down. The ancients called this condition combustion, and it is just as destructive as real fire.

A planet is said to be combust when it is within 8.5 degrees of the Sun.[1] When this influence comes into play, it is as if the "force" has left us altogether. This is especially true for those who are born with Gemini, Cancer, or Virgo rising, because the Moon and Mercury are melded into the Sun several times a year.

Combustion is one of the most overlooked of the celestial influences. Ignore it at your own peril though, because it has the ability to rob us of our money, health, and peace of mind. When planets are combust, there is no doubt in our mind that the glass is not only half empty, but that it has a leak. The attitude in the affected markets is one of general despair. When combustion happens, the sector represented by the combust planet suffers a minideath, which analysts often do not see coming.

Wise investors always keep an eye on our purchases when combustion is happening in the heavens, because knowing when this loser mentality is going to take over can help you avoid the inevitable slump. Combustion causes a bad attitude that sometimes has no basis in reality. Knowing when a planet is combust (and thus the sectors it rules) can spell the difference between profit and loss, because what looks good may turn out to be junk, and what looks bad may not be so bad after all. Much like baking bread, using combustion periods for finances is all about

---

1. Note that different astrologers may use different degrees for combust influences, especially in regard to different planets. We use 8.5 degrees as a general rule of thumb; don't be surprised to see combust periods listed elsewhere as longer or shorter in duration.

2011 © Susanne Karlsson. Image from BigStockPhoto.com

timing and patience—knowing when combustion is going to "punch down" a stock and when it is likely to rise back up.

In markets, the combustion factor can make or break an investment. Since our objective is to make money, our motto should always be "Buy Low, Sell High." Thus, if we keep an eye on the rhythms within the market place, we are best served (if other factors corroborate) to wait until a planet representing a sector—say, Mercury for the tech sector—is separating more than 8.5 degrees from the Sun, after the sector had been "punched down" for a while during combustion. This is the time we should buy into that sector; in most cases, negative sentiment has left the affected stocks highly undervalued. This is exactly the time to pounce on the stock. Mass emotion drives markets, but emotion is rarely accurate. Knowing when planets are going combust and when they are coming out of that combustion allows us to profit while the rest of the herd blindly runs off the cliff of despair.

Moon

Nowhere can we observe combustion more clearly than by watching the Moon as she gets swallowed up in the light of the Sun and reborn anew each month. Just because it is a common activity doesn't mean we should overlook the power of the Moon going combust. She brings to us all light of the other planets. Much celestial lore is based around her death to the Sun. As many an astrological business planner will tell you, we always want to start new projects after the Moon has come out of her monthly darkness. We never want to start new projects (especially if we wish them to be profitable) any time after the Moon reaches fullness.

The stock market is the best place to watch this phenomenon. Statistically, volume and prices increase as the Moon reaches fullness. Once she becomes full, the market will be more likely to become bearish. If we buy stocks or other financial instruments during the Moon's waning darkness, we should be going short, that is, betting against the stock to go up. Avoid buying stocks once the Moon reaches her balsamic stage, and wait until she has light before resuming.

The Moon will be combust from January 22–24, February 21–24, March 20–23, April 19–23, May 18–22, June 17–21, July 17–21, August 17–21, September 13–17, October 13–17, November 14–18, and December 14–18.

Mercury

When Mercury is combust, it is as if the planet is under the thumb of a great force, squashing its energies. When making long-term investments, it is always wise to know when the combustion is about to take place, because we can be more gullible when planets are combust. We are more willing to believe only what we want to hear rather than the cold hard facts. It can be a great time for salesmen, however, especially the unscrupulous

kinds, the smooth talkers who exude confidence and usually turn out to be confidence men. We might want be very careful about long-term investing, especially in technology, during these times. (A combust period weakens the negative influence of Mercury retrograde; retrograde combust periods do not have the above effects and thus are not listed.)

Mercury will be combust from January 28–February 13, May 21–June 3, and September 1–17.

Venus

Business is a Venus commodity. Thus, when Venus is darkened, we lose our sense of proportion and all our investments suffer. Venus rules retail, beauty products, and (above all) money. Look for bad retail sales during Venus combust times. When Venus is heading into combustion, it's a good time to trim our holdings of speculative items. But if you're feeling the need to gamble, this is almost always a great period for gold and its trickle-down friend, silver. Warning to art lovers, especially those who may have recently inherited valuable artworks: When Venus is combust, her endeavors are sacrificed to the demands of the business world. This means that should you decide to auction during this time, you will more likely than not be disappointed with the results. On the other hand, this is a time for us regular folks to find a Rembrandt at the flea market!

Venus will be combust from June 2–12.

Mars

With terms like "in the red" or "volatility" being synonymous with being in the market, many astrological traders consider Mars to be the king of the stock market. Historically, when Mars goes combust, it puts a real downer on the market. Add just one more negative celestial factor to this mix and you end up with the great stock market crash of 1929. However, the good news is that Mars manages to completely skirt the Sun and will not be combust at all in 2012! This is great news; given the existing Uranus/Pluto square in operation all year, tempers are short. Mars being free from the Sun means energy is not bottled up and instead flows freely. This is fabulous news for investors, because it implies that we will have less chance for financial crashes, technical or otherwise.

Mars has no combust periods in 2012.

Jupiter

When Jupiter is combust, we make mistakes because we think everybody is lucky except us. We think the whole world is doing something, but we were left out of the good stuff. It is a time when people just don't see reality. They think too big. It is a great time for gold and silver sales. It is also good for alcohol sales, because people are feeling either very sorry for themselves or very unlucky. When Jupiter is combust, we can expect to see a decline in places that cater to gambling, such as Las Vegas, which gets a double whammy thanks to the dip in gambling and sports. People are less charitable during these times, and tensions can rise on the worldwide military stage.

Jupiter will be combust May 1–21.

Saturn

One might think that once the Sun swallowed up the grim reaper Saturn, we would have sunny skies and a great sense of confidence; unfortunately, just like life, this is not how it works out. When the Sun combusts Saturn, it's like the qualities of Saturn are enhanced, and fear becomes incredibly strong. When Saturn is combust, we feel as though the light of the Sun has blocked out all sense of reason. At no time is the old adage about the market hating uncertainty more true. Business in general tends to stagnate. Confidence lags because nobody seems to know when the next shoe will drop. It is not uncommon for people to work doubly hard; however, like rats on the wheel, they often get nowhere. It is the epitome of what economic pundit John Maudlin calls the "muddle along" economy. Investments made at this time also seem to go nowhere. Stocks tend to suffer, as do gold prices. Ah, but there is a silver lining: the dollar tends to do well when Saturn is combust.

Saturn will go combust October 16–November 4.

Uranus

When the planet of rocketry and all manner of gadgets and modern wizardry is burned to a crisp, one would think our tech industry would go down like a blazing meteorite—but that is far from the case. Perhaps it is because we cannot see Uranus, perhaps it is because both Uranus and the Sun drive electricity, but in recent years, Uranus combust has often signaled a nice breakout for tech stocks. In 2011, for example, Apple took off. Even tech laggard Microsoft managed a substantial upswing during our last Uranus combustion.

However, there is a downside to this marvelous event a lot of times, and we should prepare ourselves for a bubble effect. What goes up, must come down. Thus wise astro-traders keep an eye out a whole month after this combustion for the correction to follow. Look for high-tech government contractors to do well because of increased geopolitical tensions, which may mount during this time. Then be prepared to be nimble for the next month, and always keeping a close watch on holdings, ready to reallocate at any time.

Uranus will be combust March 22–April 4.

Neptune

Highly nebulous, Neptune loves to fuzzy up the edges, donning rose-colored glasses so things appear to be something entirely different than what they really are. We see only what we want to see and believe only what we want to believe. Oddly enough, when Neptune is combust, we are forced to take those glasses off and face reality. Whatever undertakings we commence at this time will eventually force us to face reality. When Neptune is enclosed in the Sun's rays, it is as if we finally get a crack at the truth after years of self-delusion. Neptune is also associated with drugs, oil, alcohol, tobacco, and everything under the sea. Back in 2006, with gas prices soaring, and peak oil the talk of the town, the oil companies (especially BP) told us that there was plenty of oil out there, we just had to dig deeper. It was so "easy" that BP was able to convince the federal government to waive environmental impact reports! Watch for fraud to be unleashed during this time as well.

Neptune will be combust from February 12–29.

Pluto

Even though its erratic orbit has forced it out of the astronomer's pantheon, Pluto still reigns over all magnetic power down here on Earth. Thus, it represents a force vastly greater than us. It has to do with very large secret organizations. Pluto has been linked to the idea of regeneration and transformation. We can liken the effects of the combust Pluto to the time before the caterpillar becomes the beautiful butterfly. Its nature is secretive and penetrating. Pluto has been connected with deep energies that hover just beneath the surface, silently ready to explode. This is why Pluto was connected to all things sexual in nature.

In business, it has to do with the "too big to fail" powerhouse companies that verge on the fascistic control of the world by means of owning the governments they secretly run. It is not surprising that Pluto has been linked to oil exploration and military contractors. When Pluto is combust, it seems to create a vast magnetic force on the planet, which often results in greater seismic activity, even in places not usually known for earthquakes. If you live in a seismically active area, make sure you have your emergency preparedness kit ready before a Pluto combust period.

Pluto will be combust December 22, 2011–January 9, 2012.

Combust Planets for 2012

	Dec 11	Jan 12	Feb	Mar	Apr	May	Jun	Jul	Aug	Sep	Oct	Nov	Dec
☽		■	■	■	■	■	■	■	■	■	■	■	■
☿			■			■				■			
♀							■						
♂													
♃						■							
♄											■		
♅				■									
♆			■										
♇	■												

Companies Can Also Go Combust

We can have every other factor going for us, but if a money planet is going bad, we will lose money. This is why it's always good to hire a business astrologer before investing your hard-earned money. Had an astrologer been called in early 2010, he or she could have told the savvy investor to either short buy, sell, or at the very least *don't buy* British Petroleum (BP) stock, because it was about to hit a major combustion in its NYSE Listing chart. That influence came in April 2010, and it drove profits down. A company's NYSE listing chart can be a complex thing, so it is best to consult a professional if you wish to use combust planets in your financial planning this way. Consulting a professional astrologer may seem like a big step, but let's look at another example of the power of combustion.

Another example of a combust company is that of the mighty Apple. Way back in 1997, Apple's Mercury was heading into combustion. Believe it or not, Steve Jobs had such cash-flow problems with the initial public offering (IPO) of Apple stock that he was forced to borrow money from Microsoft to survive. In 2012 the tables are turned; it will be Microsoft that will face a combust ruler in its chart, and it will take a double whammy to its stock. Look for a major shakeup in this mega-corporation, which may need to become more innovative to keep up with the rest of the technology community.

Jupiter and Saturn

While the Moon lights our path through life, it is the ways of Jupiter and Saturn that control the ups and downs of the markets. Jupiter brings us abundance and all those good things in life, from food to bull markets. Speculators dream of a world where only Jupiter was in command. After all, then the markets would only go in one direction: up! However, it would be a world where every single square foot of the Earth would be devoted to commerce, and not a tree would be left standing. The massive ghost towns built during the mid-2000s are a reminder of what happens when too much of a good thing goes bust. This is why we need Saturn—to bring us back down to reality.

Jupiter will be in Taurus for the first half of the year. Taurus likes stable industries that make steady and predictable gains. Since the Moon finds her exaltation here, food will do well in this climate. When Jupiter is in reliable Taurus, people prefer value over growth industries. Thus, look for those value stocks that give dividends to perform well in the first half of the year. Jupiter will enter Gemini the second week of June. Gemini favors the computer industry and, with it, the makers of all technological products, like software, mobile phones, and the often-overlooked intelligence industry. In addition, the combination of Jupiter in Gemini and Uranus in Aries may bring those much-talked-about innovations needed to spark new life into the auto industry.

As always, there would be no backing in markets were it not for Saturn. In 2012, Saturn will be in the sign of harmony, Libra. This is one of the strongest placements for Saturn, the place known as exaltation. This may be good for value, but it is not necessarily good for growth. Saturn placed here demands truth above all else. This is why Libra is composed of the scales of justice. Libra is the law, and so when Saturn is here, he enforces that the rules are carried out. This is not necessarily a good sign for markets whose only purpose is to make investors rich, because this brings the much dreaded *R* word, *regulation*, into markets. Luckily for traders, when Saturn is in Libra and Jupiter is in Taurus, they do not see eye to eye. Therefore, we may not see actual regulation—just talk without action—until June.

Saturn in Libra also favors the technological and automotive industries. Saturn will slow down in early February, which may slow down markets; it does so again at the end of June, when the investors will seek value. Look for those businesses that spend a good portion of their money on research and development to thrive when Saturn enters Scorpio in early October. Fraudsters and underworld figures, beware! Long-term investigations could culminate this fall, which may make for some stunning preelection arrests.

The Financial Quarters

First Quarter, Winter Solstice (December 22, 2011) to Spring Equinox (March 20, 2012)

Although our secular year begins on January 1, the actual celestial beginning of first quarter takes place a fortnight earlier, on the Winter Solstice, at the very nanosecond that the Sun enters the last of the cardinal signs, Capricorn.

There may be a plaintive sigh of relief echoing down the halls of Wall Street with markets turning in a good performance as the year begins. Unfortunately, there is still plenty of pain down on Main Street as we dig ourselves out of the mess left from the last few years. In many ways, it still seems like we're caught between the rock of fewer jobs and that hard place of debt. There are some signs of hope and perhaps things are starting to turn around. Some are even hoping their prayers have been answered. Of course, many are skeptical that this is all a mirage, but for the first time in what feels like a month of Sundays, there seems to be a lot of optimism that this recovery might actually have legs. With the numbers starting to roll in from the holiday spending season, could we be on the verge of a real recovery? Of course, time will tell, but it appears that there is much to be grateful for as the beginning of the first quarter rolls out, with several positive indications on the Standard & Poor's (S&P 500).

The secret message of the first quarter of 2012 is "If you envision it and are willing to do the work, it can happen." That is why it's important for us to think positively and really get out there and seek what we want. Yes, money is tight, and that does not look to be ending anytime soon, and we have many debts that need to be paid off. However, we are still skeptical of government and wonder whose side our leadership is really on. Those ready to make major changes will do better than those who refuse to adapt.

Although real estate is still just barely treading water in far too many places, we may be seeing a glimmer of light at the end of that long, dark tunnel. The housing market may see a slight gain. Remember, we are a generally unhappy electorate this year, but getting angry is not the answer. Our forefathers imbued this nation with the unique ability to achieve whatever goal we have in mind. Wallowing in what might have been will only bring us down like quicksand. The successful investors know how to swim upstream.

Second Quarter, Spring Equinox (March 20) to Summer Solstice (June 20)

Wise investors want to know if this recovery is for real. Let's hope so, because the dreaded Saturn's placement in the government's monetary sector might imply that the Federal Reserve may be unable to use any more of their magic tricks to force feed the economy into recovery, like Quantitative Easing (QE1 & QE). Let's hope that the entire government largess has not left our treasury as empty as old Mother Hubbard's cupboard. After all, we cannot fix a solvency problem with liquidity.

On the other hand, speculators seem ready to invest, and that is a great thing. We may even see some sparks returning to the sector that represents real estate. Prices may have finally dropped low enough to attract foreign investors. One of our greatest (though often overlooked) assets, the farming industry, may be set to have great yields.

On the international scene, people may be rather restless. Given Mars' location, inflation may be on the rise, especially in developing countries. Look for the worldwide tech industry to bring smiles to even the grumpiest of traders.

However, all this great optimism on the markets still does not translate into a happy populace. Unfortunately, abundance for the farm industry may not necessarily mean lower food prices for the consumer. A weaker dollar may instigate higher prices at both the supermarket and the gas pump. Unfortunately, it's going to be tough to get out of debt, no matter what we do. Until the electorate wakes up and forces all levels of government to remember they serve the people and not the special interests, we will have to get used to official 9+ percent unemployment, when the real figure is closer to 20 percent. When the national debt stands at a whopping $14,27,107,875,134.48,[2] even if you paid your bills and owe nothing, thanks to the proliferate government spending, every man, woman—and even the tiniest little baby— is in debt to the tune of $45,272.19. And this number increases every single day!

Third Quarter, Summer Solstice (June 20) to Autumn Equinox (September 22)

Regardless of what they tell you, things are not quite what they seem to be. Remember, when Jupiter is with the South Node, all that glitters is not gold. When Jupiter and the South Node travel together, confidence men and swindlers abound. Make sure that you know exactly what you are buying before signing on the dotted line. In many ways, the summer season reflects the old Chinese curse, "May you be born in interesting times." Those holding gold may be glad. The odds are that major challenges will combine to bring a sense of trauma to our shores. Will more uncertainty bring more bullishness to the yellow metal? Stay

---

2. http://www.brillig.com/debt_clock/. Data as of January 13, 2011.

tuned as we enter a worrisome period on the markets. Geopolitical rumblings might trickle down to markets. With the Moon in
the house of death and in the watery sign of Cancer, there may be
troubles concerning water. If you live in hurricane country, this
may be a dangerous quarter.

With the representative of the American people placed in one
of the most dangerous sectors of the chart, we will need to be
very careful in all our financial dealings and, more importantly,
with our children. Plan accordingly, because anything can happen with this configuration. We are clearly in harm's way. There
has not been a quarter that has screamed "Danger!" with so much
force in a long time. When astrologers see such a configuration,
they cringe, because it places people in the gravest of situations.
We really need to heed the old scout motto and be prepared.
There are rough waters ahead. We may need to reach out to others. It wouldn't be the first time our president reached out to our
open enemies. In dangerous times, it is not always a good idea
to take on a lot of risk. There may be some bumps this summer.
Still, there will be many reasons to be grateful for our friends.

Elected officials will do well to cross party lines to find solutions. August seems to be especially important. We may see some corrections in tech areas, as well as some travel restrictions. Perhaps gas will go up during the worrisome month.

Fourth Quarter, Autumn Equinox (September 22) to Winter Solstice (December 21)

At last we can take a deep breath and go forward. For years now, we've been growing more and more impatient with a future of diminishing promise. Are there really promising green shoots for everybody this time around, or are we seeing the red shoots of inflation? We do not want promises; we want action. Even though officials tell us that the economy is getting better, it's just not true for far too many of Americans. We are still being forced to deal with the repercussions of betting the house by both the private sector and the public one.

Given that the greatest investment Americans make is not in the stock market nor in bonds but in our houses, and with many still underwater and facing foreclosure, home is not the place of warmth and security we would like it to be. This is an election season, and how the election turns out could be very important for the future of all Americans. Do not be hasty with your vote. There are those who, under the guise of "reform," would like to remove your right to directly choose your own senator. Do not be fooled. Corruption does not stop at Washington DC—lobbies and special-interest groups are also at the state level. Get the facts before you decide.

About the Author

Dorothy J. Kovach is a traditional astrologer and writer based in Northern California. Her specialty is horary astrology. She was a contributing editor for the **Horary Practitioner.** *Her work has been featured in www.msnbc.com, www.star-IQ.com, and various print media. For the past decade, she has been applying time-tested traditional techniques to the economic markets. Best known for hav-*

ing predicting the end to the 1980s and 1990s bull market, Kovach warned readers to divest holdings on the NASDAQ prior to 9/11; called the oil, commodity, and real estate bull markets; and warned Moon Sign Book readers about the September 2008 market crash. She has been writing the economic forecasts for Llewellyn since 2001. Her clients hail from around the globe. If you would like her help, you can reach her via email at dorothyjkovach@gmail.com or by phone at 01 707-882-2342. Her website is www.worldastrology.net.

New and Full Moon Forecasts

By Sally Cragin

When I speak to groups about astrology, I always ask them, "what is the Moon doing this week? Is it getting bigger, or smaller?" Usually a couple of people get the answer correctly, and this segues into talking about the branch of astrology everyone can understand pretty much right away: the phases of the Moon.

Our words *month*, *Moon*, and *menstrual* come from the same root Greek words, *men* for "month" and *mene* for "Moon." Females can learn a lot about their monthly rhythms by charting their menstrual cycles according to the Moon.

The Moon takes about a month to go from new to first quarter to full to last quarter to new again. Like all celestial objects, it rises in the east and sets in the west and changes its position in the sky depending on the time of year (lower in the sky in the summer months for those of us in North America, for example).

The Moon is primarily composed of volcanic basalt, and if you use binoculars when you look at the Moon during its quarter or full phase, you'll see a stunning number of impact craters. The poor little Moon has been battered and bruised in the billions of years it's kept us company. Those of us who were around in the 1960s remember well Apollo 11's successful landing on the Moon. We have left everything from rocket boosters to photographs to Alan Shepard's golf balls on the Moon! I am still amazed that the United States organized successful lunar missions during the administrations of three president, but I am deeply saddened we have not set up an outpost on the Moon to make further exploration into space.

However, we can all enjoy the Moon, and by understanding its phases, our appreciation will only deepen. One summer, my family was vacationing in Delaware, which has a long, uninterrupted beachfront. Most years we were there, the Moon was waxing or full, but on a recent visit, the Moon was waning and new. During that time, there were also tropical storms, and during high tide that season, the waves surmounted every toy-shovel-dug barrier. Waves crashed over the last berm and spread across the beachface, creating an artificial lagoon. It was a spectacular display of tidal force, and the lifeguards on duty noted that the lunar phase contributed to the unusual height of the waves. That's just one example of the Moon's power made manifest on Earth.

So what is the Moon doing in our lives? Basically, counting out the months, as each phase takes about a week and a complete "lunar month" (as opposed to a calendar month) is about 29 days.

When the Moon is new we don't see it, or we see it as a tiny sliver in the shape of a backward *C*. The New Moon is a time of starts, commencements, germination, and eruption. If you are planning a project that will take a long time to unfold, the New

Moon is a good time to start. Folklore also has "customs" that accompany the New Moon, such as jingling the change in your pocket for good luck when you first see the New Moon.

The first quarter Moon signifies a turning point for actions or projects that began around the New Moon. From here through the Full Moon, you may as well go full steam ahead. The first quarter Moon has a large dark circle, with smaller scattered dark spots beneath it. One of these spots is the "Mare Serenitatis," or the Sea of Tranquility; "Tranquillity Base," the landing spot of the Apollo 11 spacecraft can be found (if not directly seen!) in the southwestern corner of that plain.

The gibbous Moon is when the Moon is well past first quarter and on its way to the Full Moon phase, but not there yet. Thus, we see more of the Moon revealed, as the darkness on the left side of the satellite diminishes with each passing evening. This is when many people say they can "feel" the Full Moon, or ask if the Full Moon has already happened. Activities to focus on during this phase are taking your life from first or second gear into third or fourth!

The Full Moon is the Moon no one can miss, and due to our perspective, it looks gigantic when it rises, thanks to the scale between landscape and Moon (it doesn't actually get smaller once it goes up the sky, but because of the lack of comparison landmarks, it just seems that way!). Most people are sensitive to the Full Moon the night or two before it's actually full. When I have clients who are born on the Full Moon, I usually try to find a diplomatic way of saying to them, "You groove on chaos, right?" Seriously, though, the Full Moon can find us at our best, as long as we can stay focused. It's also excellent for creative endeavors. Music writer Lisa Robinson noted in her diaries about Led Zepplin drummer Bonzo, "When Bonzo was sober, he was a sweetheart—articulate and a gentleman. Drunk, and particularly during a Full Moon—a nightmare."

The waning Moon cycle begins after the Full Moon. You'll see the Moon diminishing in size as Earth's shadow increases from right to left. The fourth quarter Moon comes a week before the New Moon. (This is also often called the last quarter Moon.) During this time, you'll want to review progress on projects begun on or around the New Moon, or that may have had some kind of "climax" around the Full Moon. This phase is about getting results, and it's also the time when you may lose interest in a project that isn't panning out. If there's someone you've been trying to connect with—for a meeting, or coffee, or business—and if neither of you can make a meeting work on the calendar, try to reschedule your meeting for after the Full Moon and before the time of the last quarter.

The Moon is in its balsamic stage between last quarter and New Moon. I always suggest cleaning or removing as useful activities after the last quarter phase. For some reason, it's easier to throw things away when the Moon is waning; on some level we all want to simplify our lives, which is hard to do when you're surrounded by clutter.

The dark Moon is the day before the New Moon. It's an accident-prone time, and decisions made during a dark Moon (versus the New Moon) can be reversed, denied, or go unrecognized. There's a very popular play that high school groups performed frequently in the 1960s and 1970s called "Dark of the Moon." It anticipated the "goth" fixation of the 1980s and beyond and featured characters called "Conjure Witch." When I performed in it at Lunenburg (MA) High School in 1978, I played the Dark Witch and had to say a lot of mumbo jumbo. Needless to say, the play was a tragic tale based on the folk tale/song of Barbara Allen, and I'd love to see it again! In any event, the dark Moon may not be the time to draw lines in the sand or make your investments. Sleep on big decisions and wait until the New Moon.

The Moon in Various Elements

I've given you highlights on the big lunar phases, but remember that the Moon is in constant motion, changing signs every 2.5 days or so. Here are some guidelines for evaluating the best course of action on a particular day, based on the four elements.

When the Moon is in a **fire sign—Aries, Leo, or Sagittarius**—start projects, or move them to the next level. Cooking, barbequeing, performing, arguing (or advocating) are all useful activities. Don't expect people to have long attention spans or to listen while you're talking. They may just be waiting for their turn to talk. This is also a time when arguments could flare up over nothing. Passions run high, as could thoughtlessness. You may find yourself dressing in haste or showing up to the big meeting wearing clothes in a brighter hue than you would ordinarily select.

When the Moon is in an **earth sign—Taurus, Virgo, or Capricorn**—practical matters rule. Banking, acquiring, handling debt, managing others, or managing items (such as inventory or stocks on hand) will put you in tune with this Moon. This is usually a fine time for shopping, cleaning, organizing, and being "businesslike." You might feel like dressing more conservatively during this Moon.

When the Moon is in an **air sign—Gemini, Libra, or Aquarius**—try to be social and reach out to others, especially if you need to "ask" for something. Talking/writing and intellectual activities can flow more easily now. Air-sign Moons are excellent for gathering old friends together or plotting out fun activities. It's easy to overdo activities now, whether it's too much time in front of a computer, too many drinks, or too many plans for a short amount of time. It's also easy to be absentminded. You could find yourself picking clothes that clash in terms of pattern, color, or cut.

2011 © Erik Reis. Image from BigStockPhoto.com

When the Moon is in a **water sign—Cancer**, **Scorpio**, **or Pisces**—emotional response is key. "Going with the flow" is a goal, but it will be hard for some to figure out where that "flow" is (or how to turn off the spigot). Watersports and swimming, poetry, singing, and having an emotional response to the arts are all likely with this Moon. Exaggerating or gossip can also be a temptation and "saying too much" (also "eating too much") could be a theme. When you get dressed during this Moon, you'll probably choose your most comfortable, least structured garments.

When the Moon changes signs, it ceases making angles to other planets. During this time, the Moon is considered "void-of-course" (VOC). This interval can last anywhere from minutes to hours. During this period, do NOT sign papers, finalize contracts, or make lasting agreements. DO use your imagination to find creative solutions, expect alternate routes to an outcome. This is a "freefall" time for all. See page 75 for more on the void-of-course Moon and 2012 dates and times.

Navigating the Lunar Phases, Sign by Sign

The calendar of New and Full Moon dates that follows provides some specific assistance for the signs, but I'd like to include a sign-by-sign narrative for the coming year as well, according to your natal Sun sign. After all, the Sun-Moon relationship is what creates Moon phases in the first place!

Aries: You rule the first house of the self and what people perceive. This sign is the "baby" of the zodiac, but with your Mars rulership, you're a baby who can throw a heck of a tantrum! When the Moon is in a fire sign, you could be charged up and ready to go or easily vexed—or both. Your Full Moon comes on September 30.

Taurus: The second house of security and banking is your place, but with Venus as your ruling planet, you have a strong aesthetic sense. Everyone else thinks you're stubborn, but you think of yourself as principled and sensible. So why do people have a problem with that? When the Moon is in an earth sign, you insist on getting your way—you'll succeed if you're charming and strategic. Your Full Moon comes on October 29.

Gemini: The third house belongs to you, ruling siblings, short messages, and short journeys. Your planet is Mercury, which makes you curious and learned. When the Moon is in an air sign, you have a hundred ideas, a thousand phone calls to make, and a million places you could be, so focus will be an issue. Your Full Moon comes on November 28.

Cancer: The fourth house of hearth and home belongs to you, and the Moon is your ruling planet. So you can and could be "in tune" with the Moon all the time (exhausting, yes?). Your perceptions are extra sharp when the Moon is in a water sign. You have two Full Moons this year: January 9 and December 28.

Leo: Children, parties, and good times are the fifth-house theme, and with the Sun as your ruling planet, you might think twice about riding on a moonbeam. However, the Moon is your friend if you're like the Leos I know (social, curious, and protective). You'll be insightful, funny, and potentially hot-tempered when the Moon is in a fire sign. Your Full Moon comes on February 7.

Virgo: The sixth-house topics of health, work, and service are Virgo themes. Since Mercury rules your sign, you can be a genius when it comes to sussing out people's emotions, motivations, and hopes and fears. When the Moon is in an earth sign, you'll be practical, hardworking, and stubborn. Your Full Moon comes on March 8.

Libra: The seventh house of partnership rules you, which is why some Libras are happy models of codependence! Venus rules you, so you have great taste in friends as well as "stuff." When the Moon is in an air sign, you could be mentally alert and highly decisive, even as you recognize there are no easy answers and myriad options. Your Full Moon comes on April 6.

Scorpio: Pluto rules your sign, and your eighth house covers sex, death, and other people's money. Doesn't that sound like a Hollywood caper film? People think you're intense or mysterious, although you think you're simply careful and sincere. Water-sign Moons find you at your most "Scorpionic" (moody and insightful). Your Full Moon comes on May 6.

Sagittarius: The ninth house is Sagittarius's realm and with Jupiter's rulership, your themes are long journeys, higher education, and justice. You also are ruled by joviality; when you find things are getting "too heavy," see if the Moon is in a water sign. When the Moon is in a fire sign, you could be accident-prone but also highly ambitious and hardworking. Your Full Moon comes on June 4.

Capricorn: Saturn is your ruler, and the tenth house of reputation, career, limits, and responsibilities is your domain. You like to take your time, and the Moon's movements can make you feel rushed, which is never comfortable. However, when the Moon is in an earth sign, you should make a point of saying what you need (even if that's simply solitude), and doing exactly what you need to do. Your Full Moon comes on July 3.

Aquarius: Your eleventh house of hopes and wishes, mass movements, and trends explifies Aquarian values. Uranus is your ruling planet. You're full of interesting ideas. Excitement and unpredictability are your hallmarks—just ask your friends and family! Even if you think you're a stick-in-the-mud, chances are that they don't. When the Moon is in an air sign, the world should watch out! Your Full Moon comes on August 2.

Pisces: Neptune rules Pisces, which oversees the twelfth house of secrets, hidden places, X-rays, and photography. This Moon takes you off to Never Never Land, which can be an excellent place to visit. When the Moon is in a water sign, you'll be perceptive, personable, and possibly psychic. Your instincts could surprise you, but listen to them. Your Full Moon occurs on August 31.

New and Full Moons in 2012

Full Moon in Cancer, January 9

This Full Moon and Saturn are at odds. Tremendously generous folks might be tempted to put the brakes on relationships that veer into overly emotional territory. However, this is an excellent phase for staying at home or focusing on children. It's a banner day for those who do massage, ceramics, and baking. *Moody*: Aries, Libra, Capricorn. *Insightful and satisfied*: Cancer, Pisces, Scorpio, Taurus, Virgo.

New Moon in Aquarius, January 23

Have a crazy new idea? Launch it with a champagne flourish! This New Moon favors acts of rebellion and short, sharp turns. Those who thrive on a predictable routine might find themselves discombobulated. But in the depths of winter, isn't it exciting to feel sparks? *Imaginative*: Aquarius, Libra, Sagittarius, Aries, Gemini. *Trying to find a groove*: Scorpio, Taurus, Leo, Virgo, Capricorn, Pisces, Cancer.

Full Moon in Leo, February 7

This Full Moon favors those who strategize. Pride, loyalty, and a sense of fun come with this Full Moon. Regression is also a theme, particularly among folks with a strong sense of nostalgia for childhood pleasures (sugar cereal and cartoons, anyone?). During this Full Moon, put your ideas and tastes forward. Grit your teeth if you find yourself competing with someone who's equally passionate. *Fierce and forging forward*: Leo, Aries, Sagittarius, Libra, Gemini. *Quietly determined*: Pisces, Virgo, Cancer, Capricorn. *Accident-prone*: Taurus, Scorpio, Aquarius.

New Moon in Pisces, February 21

Wednesday's child could be full of woe, but Pisces Moons tell you to go with the flow. Old friends are more appealing than new acquaintances. Escapism beckons, particularly in the form of music or films. It's a super day for photographers, or for those who uncover "the hidden" (including therapists, archaeologists, and renovaters). *At their best*: Pisces, Scorpio, Taurus, Capricorn, Cancer. *At sixes and sevens*: Virgo, Gemini, Sagittarius.

Full Moon in Virgo, March 8

The March Full Moon brings the first wave of spring fever, which could come with a (useful and commendable) urge to clean this week. Take care of health issues that may have been ignored over the winter. Others may be more persnickety over the small stuff; rather than be irked, see what can be improved by a greater attention to detail. *Frazzled but efficient*: Taurus, Virgo, Capricorn, Scorpio, Cancer. *Impulsive*: Gemini, Sagittarius, Libra, Aquarius, Gemini, Aries, Pisces.

New Moon in Aries, March 22

Spring fever can be a multi-part episode (with comic aspects thanks to Mercury retrograde). This New Moon stirs up dormant ideas. Finding shortcuts brings joy to even the most rigid, by-the-book folks. Think about starting seeds from scratch, churning your own cream into butter, and getting in touch with the process rather than the end result. It's a great time for experimenting. *Adventurous and fun-seeking*: Aries, Leo, Sagittarius, Gemini, Aquarius. *Impulsive and in need of caution*: Libra, Cancer, Capricorn, Taurus, Virgo, Pisces, Scorpio.

Full Moon in Libra, April 6

Venus rules this peaceful Moon, which brings an appreciation of harmony, both in personal relationships and in projects. No one gives in easily, but this is still a time to look at all angles. *Feeling romantic*: Sagittarius, Leo, Libra, Aquarius, Gemini, Taurus, Virgo. *Yearning for more*: Capricorn, Cancer, Scorpio, Aries, Pisces.

New Moon in Taurus, April 21

Taurus rules the second house of banks and personal security, so if you got an extension on your taxes, this weekend will improve your ability to address details with greater depth. This weekend is also excellent for improving your wardrobe, downloading music, or enjoying the theater. However, Taurus can bring out stubbornness in even the meekest folks. *Hard to handle*: Scorpio, Leo, Aries, Sagittarius, Gemini, Aquarius. *At their best*: Taurus, Capricorn, Cancer, Pisces, Virgo, Libra.

Full Moon in Scorpio, May 6

It's too early for gardening in some climates, but raking the surface and turning over topsoil could be satisfying during this Full Moon. Scorpio Moons bring a desire to dig your fingers deep into what can't be seen. It's an excellent weekend for a radically different haircut. *Efficient and analytical*: Scorpio, Pisces, Cancer, Virgo, Capricorn. *Well-meaning but awkward*: Leo, Aquarius, Taurus.

New Moon in Gemini, May 20

Ask the question, no matter how hesitant you feel about hearing all the details. Gemini Moons bring out the talkers, so this weekend is excellent for a mixer. Curious folks will need to know everything. So exactly what did you do Saturday night, hmmm? *Feeling bold*: Gemini, Aquarius, Libra, Leo, Aries. *Feeling awkward*: Virgo, Pisces, Sagittarius. *Amused by others' shenanigans*: Taurus, Scorpio, Capricorn, Cancer.

Full Moon in Sagittarius, June 4

The June Full Moon brings sweetness to those with a sense of humor or a taste for travel. This Moon is ruled by generous Jupiter, and grand gestures could be a commonplace this week. If you've got itchy feet, travel opportunities could arise, and folks living in places you'd love to visit could contact you (or vice-versa). *Craving freedom*: Sagittarius, Leo, Aries, Libra, Aquarius. *Accident-prone*: Pisces, Virgo, Gemini.

New Moon in Gemini, June 19

With Mercury ruling this New Moon, agitation could be a theme. Who's at their best with nervous energy or unexpected socializing? Air and fire folks will be full of ideas, even though Mars in practical Virgo is shouting, "slow down, you missed a spot!" *Pace yourself*: Virgo, Taurus, Capricorn, Pisces, Cancer, Scorpio.

Full Moon in Capricorn, July 3

Earth-sign Moons can prompt us to be practical. Short-term solutions won't do, so looking at how things fit together will be irresistible for some. Folklore says to dig holes for fence posts or pour concrete at this time. Can you set limits and keep them? *Sticking to the rules*: Capricorn, Taurus, Virgo, Pisces, Scorpio. *Senstitive*: Libra, Aries, Cancer. *Easily bored*: Gemini, Sagittarius, Aquarius, Leo.

New Moon in Cancer, July 19

This is a highly sensitive time for all. On top of that, Mercury retrograde makes communication difficult. Can you separate feelings and responses from what's actually going on? For those who bake bread, do massage, or play with clay, today and tomorrow is a time for inventiveness and risk-taking. *Accident-prone*: Capricorn, Aries, Libra. *Having revelations*: Cancer, Pisces, Scorpio, Taurus, Virgo.

Full Moon in Aquarius, August 1

During this Aquarius Full Moon, the best solutions are the most unlikely, and fantasy could seem like reality—in a good way! This Full Moon brings out the schemers and dreamers, so if you need a push to take the next step on the job, stick with the optimists. *Trusting*: Aquarius, Libra, Gemini, Aries, Sagittarius. *Suspicious*: Taurus, Leo, Scorpio.

New Moon in Leo, August 17

"The mouse that roared" is the theme for this New Moon. Those who are usually shy or timid must speak up, even if they immediately say, "whoops! Sorry!" Today and tomorrow are great for developing a marketing or advertising plan for yourself, a friend, your business, or a cause. Actors, musical performers, and those who work with children will be at their best. *Amusing*: Leo, Sagittarius, Aries, Libra, Gemini. *Ready to laugh*: Capricorn, Cancer, Virgo, Pisces.

Full Moon in Pisces, August 31

This is 2012's Blue Moon (second Full Moon in a month). What would you do only once in a Blue Moon? Do it now, and the Pisces Moon—which favors artistic expression, free-range paranoia, and secrets kept—will encourage you. It's a super day for photography or making images. *In tune with the Moon*: Pisces, Scorpio, Cancer, Capricorn, Taurus. *Accident-prone*: Virgo, Gemini, Sagittarius.

New Moon in Virgo, September 15

Health and exercise should be addressed during this New Moon. Are you drinking enough liquids? Are you using that gym membership? If you use herbs, read up on plants you haven't sampled

2011 © Kurhan. Image from BigStockPhoto.com

yet, as a Virgo Moon brings curiosity to all. *Caretakers*: Virgo, Taurus, Capricorn, Scorpio, Cancer. *In need of TLC*: Gemini, Sagittarius, Pisces.

Full Moon in Aries, September 29

It's another Full Moon weekend, and this one helps us all to shine. Start something you can finish quickly and make the most of any opportunity to barbeque (some regions will still have fresh corn at this time). *Full of pep*: Aries, Leo, Sagittarius, Gemini, Aquarius. *Overwhelmed by choices*: Taurus, Scorpio, Pisces, Virgo, Capricorn, Cancer, Libra.

New Moon in Libra, October 15

Air-sign Moons are always sociable, so look for opportunities to mix with diverse groups or to be in touch with more people than usual. You should also try to compromise where you can—Libra Moons are about finding middle ground. For folks who are literal-minded, this could be a gray area, so look for guidance from open-minded acquaintances. *Taking a chance*: Taurus, Leo, Libra, Sagittarius, Aquarius, Gemini. *Waiting for others to act*: Virgo, Pisces, Scorpio. *Doubting their abilities*: Capricorn, Aries, Cancer.

Full Moon in Taurus, October 29

The previous Full Moon was ruled by Venus, and it may have brought new people into your life. Venus rules this Full Moon also, so if relationships are getting more tender and deep, you're in tune with the Moon. However, this Full Moon means some folks will draw a line in the sand and dare you to cross it. *Tightly wound*: Taurus, Capricorn, Virgo, Scorpio, Cancer, Aries, Pisces. *Feeling the groove*: Aquarius, Libra, Gemini, Leo, Sagittarius.

New Moon in Scorpio, November 13

"In dreams begin responsibilities" wrote poet Delmore Schwarz, and this New Moon is excellent for meditation or big plans that streamline a process. Scorpio Moons can be emotional for some; if you have a possessive side, it may come out. *Picking up on the subtleties*: Scorpio, Pisces, Cancer, Taurus, Leo, Aquarius. *Not getting the drift*: Capricorn, Virgo, Aries, Sagittarius, Libra, Gemini.

Full Moon in Gemini, November 28

The Gemini Full Moon finds all in a chatty mood, so exaggeration and overexplaining could be the rule of the day. Are you the kind of person who tells people more than they need to know? This Moon is urging you to tell all, but your better angels are advising you to keep quiet. *Pepped up and ready to go*: Gemini, Libra, Aquarius, Leo, Aries. *Amused by others' antics*: Taurus, Capricorn, Scorpio, Cancer.

New Moon in Sagittarius, December 13

From now through the Christmas/Yule week, activity increases and your sense of "doing it all" increases. Today and tomorrow are excellent for planning a long journey or thinking of humorous ripostes. If you're a stand-up comedian, this is when you can slay that audience deader than Marley's ghost. *On happy trails*: Sagittarius, Capricorn, Leo, Aries, Libra, Aquarius. *Riding on bumpy roads*: Virgo, Pisces, Taurus, Cancer, Scorpio, Aries.

Full Moon in Cancer, December 28

This Cancer Full Moon is a home-based day. This can mean finding homes for all your presents, or appreciating friends and family members for their reliability. Today and tomorrow can bring out enormous domestic urges in some—baking or making your abode seem more cozy is an excellent use of your time. However, Cancer can bring out the confessional side in some. *Sharing secrets*: Cancer, Pisces, Scorpio, Aries, Libra, Virgo, Taurus, Capricorn. *Lending an ear*: Gemini, Sagittarius, Leo, Aquarius.

About the Author

Sally Cragin, as Symboline Dai, writes "Moon Signs" for the **Boston Phoenix** *newspaper chain. She is the author of* **The Astrological Elements,** *from Llewellyn. Sally is available for private consultations and can be reached at www.moonsigns.net/.*

2012
Moon Sign Book
Articles

Return to Now: Finding My Center In the Garden

by Clea Danaan

Winter

The forecast calls for a high of sixteen degrees with no more snow. My two-year-old daughter and I huddled cozily in the house when the snow was falling, but now we long to get out. She needs to move and I need to breathe. I learn that the Denver Botanic Gardens has a free day for Colorado residents. I invite friends to meet us there; they all shake their heads with a little you-must-be-nuts smile. We bundle up, load the car, and drive across town.

Most of the snow has been plowed off the roads, but it still pads the world with nearly a foot of cold white. Where I grew up, in the Pacific Northwest, snow is a state of emergency. It falls heavy and wet and shuts down the plow-deficient city. Here the snow is squeaky and dry, not good for building snowmen but fairly easy to drive on. Here the dryness makes the cold brisk instead of chilling, especially when the Sun is out.

My daughter babbles in her two-year-old chatter the entire drive. She's a very busy child. I haven't really been able to set her down since the moment she was born. She still wakes up several times a night, and when she is awake, she doesn't stop moving, exploring, or talking. The cold barely phases her. She narrates our trip across town as I enjoy the relative lack of traffic.

The sweater-clad woman in the gardens' ticket booth doesn't know it's a free day; we must be the only people here besides employees. I point to the sign on her window and she lets us through the gate. The pathways of the gardens have been plowed but still sport a dry, packed path of white. Beneath my corduroys, the fronts of my thighs begin to sting in the chill. The rest of me is warm. My daughter is off and crunching across the snow. We have the gardens to ourselves, and the crisp, dry quiet beckons us past sleeping perennials poking gray stems through snow.

I take a deep breath of cold and feel myself expand. The Botanic Gardens cover several acres and feature one outdoor room after another, each showcasing a different type of plant or style. We pass through the chill silence of xeriscaped perennials, herbs, grassland flowers, and a wintry woodland. The calm gives me space to simply be and to experience the winter garden as it unfolds before us.

The Sun slips from behind clouds to bounce against the ice crystals and blind me, then skips back to gray. The whole Botanic Gardens to ourselves! I am the proverbial kid in a candy shop. My daughter scoops up snow with one mittened hand and licks it like frozen cotton candy. I have to call to her repeatedly to keep up as we walk the paths of the garden, white and still as an ice palace. She sees no point in walking on when she discovers a nice pile of pristine eating snow.

Walking along the frozen paths of the garden, I can hear—and see—my own breath. My heart pumps warm blood steadily, calm and dependable as the day. This moment is as ephemeral as the snow, which will be gone in a few days, never to fall in exactly the same way again. And when the snow melts or sublimates (turns directly into water vapor from its solid state), then the garden too will soon transform. Against the shade of brown and gray will pop crocuses in purple, white, and yellow. Bumblebee queens will emerge from their sleep, pregnant and hungry, and visit each cup of nectar with the urgency of a mother repopulating the world. The barest peek of chartreuse will unfurl as leaf buds fold into spring.

For now, though, it is still and cold and white. I soak in the calm. My nose stings. I follow my daughter's lead and let a bit of snow melt on my tongue. It tastes of mountains and clouds with a hint of soil. I feel my shoulders relax. The moment folds over me and fills me to overflowing, where everything feels perfect.

Spring

In May, my newly planted grapes are just twigs poking up from clay soil. I planted them bare-root, a gamble even in the best of soils. Sometimes bare-root plants take, sometimes they don't. The previous year's grape roots never quite made it, and I had to wait a year for the nursery to send replacements. I plant them in early spring with a prayer and a heap of compost, then wait anxiously for the first buds.

But then my brother telephones from my mom's house. Dad died last night. I go home for my father's service and help Mom sort through things. The grape vines and the rest of the garden rank low on my list of concerns. Mom wants the whole base-ment cleared out. While my daughter plays with Grandma, my husband and I pack up almost thirty boxes of books to sell or donate to the library. I ask Mom if she wants to keep Dad's rusted and worn garden tools. She pauses but shakes her head. A home-steader when I was a child, Dad hadn't gardened in years—they moved too frequently, and then his age and an undetected illness took over. We set aside a hand spade and bring the rest to the Salvation Army.

At the farmers' market, I buy organic herbs and flower seed-lings and a big bag of potting soil. I fill some abandoned pots I find under the stairs with soil and plants, and line the stairs up to the apartment with a potted garden. I want Mom to feel joy and connection when she comes home to an empty house. The plants make her smile.

We can only stay a week. Her container garden is a way for me to stay with her as we say goodbye to Dad in our own ways.

Whenever I return home after time away, I head straight to my garden. It brings me back to my Colorado home in a way nothing else can. This time we return at night. I feel disconnected—from the garden, the light, my family, my home, even my body. Flying does that to me. Saying goodbye to my father makes the strange sense of off-ness even more acute.

Dragging the hose around my garden in the warm spring dark, I revisit my plants. I squat beside my grapes. I can't see them well in the dark, but I gently finger the vines. Furry little leaf buds decorate the sticks. I smile into the night, and despite the relative warmth, chills run down my neck. I dedicate my vines to Dad. Each spring when the fuzzy pink buds emerge, I will send a prayer of remembrance to my father, who taught me to garden. I feel returned to myself and my place in all things.

Summer

Squash blossom time finds my nine-month-old son exploring the yard on his hands and knees. His sister (now four) did this, too, lifting her knees off the scratchy patio and the pokey grass toward the garden. My son picks up mulch, inspects it, tosses it away with a shake of his fat little hand. He watches the chickens, drool dripping off his bottom lip. I follow closely, letting him have his experience but nervous about the risk of him swallowing rocks or choking on wood chips.

I see the yard through two sets of eyes: a mother wary of dangers, and a baby feeling grass and wind and stones for the first time. My son loves shapes and is very aware of his auditory landscape. He adores wind chimes, the solar-powered lamps lining the path, large rocks, and squawking chickens. He is fully immersed in his senses. He and the summer garden pull me into my own. I hear the wind through the corn, see the honeybees alighting from blossom to blossom, smell the sharp and heady tang of a tomato plant on my hands. This is summer: life exploding, exploring, rejoicing.

On truly hot days, when the zucchini leaves droop and the corn husks curl, I dream of snow and know that I will soon long for this sweet heat. I bring myself back to the now, the dry hot burst of sun, the verdant green all around, and the sweet soft baby who soon will learn to walk into his boyhood years.

I am told many times by older mothers whose children are grown how much they miss this time of their child's life. I understand the sadness of letting go of loved ones. I miss the relationship I had with my father when I was young. I miss the relationship that my son will never have with him. But I have learned to let go of the regret, if not the sorrow, and to aspire to live in the moment. To live in my senses. In this moment, my baby is a baby and I am here with him, following his amble through the garden.

I sit on the path between two garden beds and look, listen, feel, taste. I munch on some peas and a few chives, then scoop up a handful of dirt to smell. A bumblebee shimmies inside a tomato flower. I find my mind wandering into plans for new plantings. I frown at the weeds taking over. The boards lining my beds are

warped and I want to replace them. I need more manure. More peat moss. More time.

But the bee reminds me: one flower at a time. This moment here is a gift. Sit. Be with the garden, with the baby, with life. I rub a leaf between my fingers. Pea leaves feel waxy with a soft dust covering. Tomato leaves crush easily, releasing their scent. Carrot tops tickle. The piece of myself I had forgotten in the rush of life emerges slowly, like the Moon after an eclipse. Time unfolds, and rather than fighting its inevitable march, I am once again part of it.

Autumn

Now the fall peas emerge. Unfolding chartreuse against black compost are fairy-sized promises of cool-weather sweetness. The spring and summer vegetables have either set fruit or shriveled in the hot sunshine, and the new peas are sentinels of the season to come: cooler, calmer, more receptive yin than aggressive yang. They offer hope, an antidote to frustration over squirrel-ravaged squash, chicken-pecked Brussels sprouts, and corn that somehow failed to fertilize itself.

I guard my green babies well. My chickens love more than anything to scratch in fresh dirt in search of bugs, and a newly planted bed stands no chance. I erect stakes and wrap the beds in bird netting. When the hens ignore my defenses, I spray them with the hose. They squawk and run in circles, then strut back to the freshly spread compost when I'm not looking.

I have heard gardening likened to warfare. A pacifist, I usually scoff at such a metaphor, but some days I must admit I feel like an embittered soldier taking losses right and left. Am I a glutton for punishment, knowing that much of what I plant in my garden will be ravaged by the weather, chickens, squirrels, and bugs? Should I not just give up and buy my eggs, peas, and corn at the supermarket? My garden is not large enough to grow all the food I need, so most of our food comes from the store anyway. So why, year after year, season after season, do I keep planting, keep feeding my chicks, keep dreaming of the garden to come?

I suppose it is the calm, the reflection of myself, the reminder that I am not just my ego. The garden connects me to life, to death, and to life again. I return to some inner Self that can so easily be lost in the whirlwind of daily life, of emotions and tasks and dreams of the future. When I press seeds into soil, turn the compost, pluck a cherry tomato, or water the carrots, I find a calm and centered place inside me. It is the same calm I feel in the winter Botanic Garden, the same centeredness I see in my baby's face as he plays in the hot sunshine, the calm of letting go of my father on a budding spring evening.

As the days cool, my daughter and I study space together. We're embarking on a new journey: kindergarten home school. As she learns about the planets and the solar system, I marvel anew at the vastness of the universe. Inside the bubble that is me—mother, gardener, writer, daughter, friend—I rarely hold in my consciousness the sense of being a tiny speck of life in the overwhelming hugeness of space. How can I when my senses are here and now, on Earth? The only direct sense of the universe I have is on an autumn night, after I've put the kids to bed and locked up the chickens, and I stand out in my garden and stare up. Stare out. At stars billions of light years away, whose light takes thousands of years to reach me. My sense of perception has no way to grasp this fact. I feel dizzy. As the Moon rises over our house, I look back at the night garden, curling toward the calm of winter. Here is my universe, more precious for its miraculous existence here on this ball of rock we call home. Here is where I literally ground, where I find my center in the spinning of life and death and stars. Here, with the corn and the yarrow, the swallowtails and hens.

. . . .

When I return to the now and really sit in this moment, everything feels perfect. Sometimes it is the joy of watching my children interact with the unfolding world, and sometimes the perfection of letting go, of uneclipsed sadness, or of a harvest at the end of the growing season. The garden reminds me that some plants don't make it, but every fall there is something to reap and share and rejoice in. This is our place in all things.

To stand in the midst of a garden at any time of year is to soak in a miasma of attention and cyclical growth. The garden does not call it winter or spring, it just fulfills its mysterious injunction to grow. When I attune with this basic truth, I remember to care better for myself, my own growth and attention. I remember what is real. For what am I but growth and attention? Like the garden, I am the growth unfurling in the mystery of life. The garden brings me back to my home, to my feet on the ground, to myself.

About the Author

Clea Danaan is the award-winning author of Sacred Land *and* Voices of the Earth *(both Llewellyn),* Zen and the Art of Raising Chickens *(Leaping Hare, 2010), and* Magical Bride *(Wyrdwood e-book, available at her website). These days she's absorbed with Earth-based gifted homeschooling and permaculture. Read more of her work at cleadanaan.blogspot.com or visit her at www.CleaDanaan.com.*

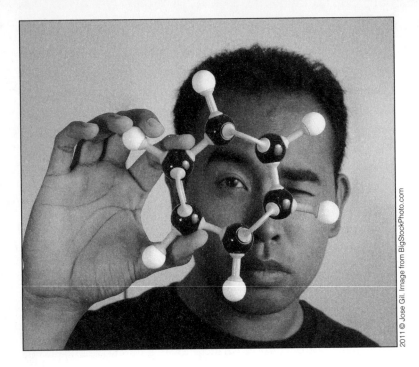

Growing Plants to Improve Indoor Air Quality

By Alice DeVille

Today's home and office buildings have become so energy efficient that very little outdoor air circulation occurs within their walls at any time of the year. Windows in many newer structures cannot be opened at all. Although that is not the case in most residences, homeowners have been extremely diligent about installing airtight windows and doors in houses to cut down on energy costs. Residents opt for the highest-rated insulation package to keep out drafts and maximize the savings in the operation of heating and cooling systems. While that's great for the environment, the result is that homes and offices harbor trapped pollutants and chemicals that can make you ill. Over the last thirty years, the indoor environment has become much more sealed off and filled with synthetic materials that leach chemicals called VOCs—volatile organic compounds. Recognizing which of the many possible VOCs are in the air is a daunting task; VOCs are in every manufactured substance, from caulking to computers.

Among the most notorious culprits are benzene, trichloroethylene (TCE), and formaldehyde, which are found in common products in industrial and household settings. Benzene is a solvent present in numerous items, such as inks, oils, paints, plastics, rubber, gasoline, detergents, pharmaceuticals, and dyes, as well as explosives. This substance has been known to irritate skin and eyes. Acute inhalation of benzene causes dizziness, nausea, headaches, respiratory diseases, liver and kidney damage, irregular heartbeat, and lymphatic system diseases. External contact with skin may cause dermatitis, drying, patchiness, swelling, inflammation, and blistering.

Dry cleaning services overwhelmingly use TCE, which can also be found in paints, lacquers, adhesives, inks, and varnishes. Repeated exposure to TCE contributes to toxic air quality and might lead to a high incidence of carcinomas and liver damage.

Most indoor environments have considerable levels of formaldehyde, commonly found in the particle board or pressed wood products that manufacturers use in office furniture, shelving, and foam insulation. The most publicized form of this substance is urea-formaldehyde, whose resins appear in many paper products, grocery bags, facial tissues, paper towels, and cleaning products. Side effects of prolonged exposure to formaldehyde include headaches; irritation of the mucous membranes of the eyes, nose, throat; contact dermatitis; and asthmatic conditions. Some readers may have worked in structures that were tested and diagnosed with "Sick Building Syndrome" after significant numbers of employees became ill and missed work. This diagnosis calls for remedial action to restore indoor air to a healthy state.

To combat the escalating effects of exposure to these chemicals and to raise air quality levels in our indoor spaces, environmental experts recommend the use of plants that mitigate the toxicity. In most buildings identified with sick symptoms, management employs office plant services to strategically place a variety of toxin-absorbing plants in the workplace. Likewise, homeowners who suspect high levels of impure air can hire environmental firms to test the air quality and take action to rid the home of pollutants. Common indoor plants are one of the most effective ways of combating the stagnant, unhealthy air that lingers in our environment. For detailed information about studies that address clean air and the use of plants, contact NASA, the Associated Landscape Contractors of America, and/or the National Cancer Institute.

Live Trees and Plants for Health and Beauty

If your goal is to purify your indoor environment's air and maintain healthy humidity levels, the following passages highlight tips for growing a selection of houseplants that reduce indoor air pollution and absorb harmful gases. Plants will also produce negative ions—much as air purifying machines do—and will effectively remove dust particles, mold spores, and bacteria.

For best air-cleansing results, place two or three plants in each average-size room; add another plant or two for larger rooms. Cluster plants in bigger rooms according to specified growing conditions for maximum benefit. Horticultural experts recommend having fifteen to twenty plants strategically located in a two-thousand-square-foot home. Be sure to find a space for at least one live plant in each sleeping area. You'll find that these plants help to eliminate formaldehyde, benzene, carbon monoxide, TCE, and most toxins that lurk in building and household materials.

Gerbera Daisies will grow indoors and out. They love the sunshine and come in bright, cheerful shades of red, yellow, orange, and pink. Deadhead their spent blossoms, keep the soil moist but well-drained, and fill a sunny corner with these beauties. Mature clumps are the best bloomers and give you the option to move your plants outdoors next spring to fill your deck boxes with amazing color.

Weeping Fig, also known as **Ficus**, is a tree with shiny leaves that needs bright light and adequate space. Ficus grows best in an established location, doesn't like to be moved, requires less water in winter, and actually prefers the pot-bound state. If the air is too dry, leaves turn yellow and drop. Feed quarterly.

Bamboo Palm and **Butterfly Palm** are medium-to-large plants that look like trees, especially the bamboo variety, which can grow over 5 feet tall. Its canopylike growth is especially attractive when used to fill a corner. Realtors often use them strategically in sale properties to attract buyers. They like light, but not direct sunshine. The bamboo variety requires little watering, but if brown leaves appear, you haven't watered enough. The graceful butterfly palm has a fountainlike form and needs evenly moistened soil. Mist it with water, keep it clear of drafts, and clean the leaves to keep it dust-free. An excellent air purifier, butterfly palm removes formaldehyde and xylene from the atmosphere.

Golden Pothos is a cascading plant that looks attractive on a shelf or ledge. This plant does well in all but direct sunlight and needs watering only when the soil becomes dry. Some gardeners place this plant at the base of a tall indoor tree, such as corn plant, a member of the Dracaena family. Pothos are very robust and last a long time with proper care.

Jade plants remind me of little trees. They have thick, fleshy leaves on thick, fleshy stems with clusters of small white flowers; over time they may grow a massive trunk. Jade prefers moderate light levels. Placing this houseplant in an east-facing or west-facing window or within 2 to 3 feet of a south-facing window gives it the required three to five hours of bright, direct sunlight each day. If the stems become spindly, your plant doesn't get enough light.

2011 © Elena Elisseeva. Image from BigStockPhoto.com

Dracaena plants, good for reducing all toxins, are African in origin and come in many varieties and sizes. Some Dracaena, such as the *Marginata*, *Variegated*, and *Janet Craig* resemble small trees, reaching a height of approximately 5 feet. Characteristics vary in that *Marginata* (also referred to as "tri-color") has creamy white stripes edged in red; *Janet Craig* has dark-green lance leaves banded in white or yellow; and *Variegated* has long, 24-inch leaves with a green center stripe. These plants love good light and evenly moist soil, but they don't tolerate water on the leaves, which causes spotting. Dracena are excellent decorative plants that grow best in large pots. They add dramatic accents to your tabletop, desk, or favorite niche.

. . . .

Houseplants are especially beneficial in winter, when they emit water vapor and help to maintain humidity levels. Environmental horticulturists also favor Boston Fern, Peace Lilies, Schefflera, and Snake Plant to purify your space. Test your healthy green thumb and discover how plants make a difference in the air you breathe.

For Further Reading

Accessed August 2010

Articlesbase. "How Indoor Plants Clean Indoor Air." http://www
.articlesbase.com/health-articles/how-indoor-plants-clean-indoor-
air-295997.html.

Kramer, Jack. *Complete Houseplants.* Upper Saddle River, NJ: CRE-
ATIVE HOMEOWNER® A Division of Federal Marketing Corp.,
2008.

Hogan, Elizabeth L., ed. *Sunset House Plants A to Z.* Menlo Park, CA:
Lane Publishing Company, 1989.

Zone 10. "NASA Study: House Plants Clean Air." http://www.zone10
.com/nasa-study-house-plants-clean-air.html.

About the Author

*Alice DeVille is an internationally known astrologer, writer, and
metaphysical consultant. Early in her government career, she worked
on the Environmental Air Quality staff. Her extensive knowledge
of both indoor and outdoor gardening has been acquired over many
years, beginning with her parents' plant-filled home and her personal
enjoyment of decorating with beautiful, healthy houseplants. She
has developed a growing interest in container gardening, using a
variety of pots and planters to nurture indoor spaces and purify the
air. Alice incorporates design and Feng Shui in selecting ideal plant
locations. In her busy northern Virginia practice, Alice specializes in
relationships, business advice and counsel, real estate, government
affairs, and career and change management. She has developed
and presented more than 160 workshops and seminars related
to her fields of expertise. Star IQ, Astral Hearts, The Meta Arts,
Inner Self Magazne, ShareItLiveIt, and numerous other websites
and publications feature her articles. Quotes from her work on
relationships appear in books, publications, training materials,
calendars, planners, audio tapes, and Oprah's website. Alice is
available for writing books and articles for publishers, newspapers,
or magazines, and for conducting workshops and radio or TV
interviews. Contact Alice at DeVilleAA@aol.com.*

How Does Your Roof Grow?

by Janice Sharkey

Green roofs may sound like a new-fangled idea, but they have actually been around for a long time. The Vikings covered their earthen houses with grass to insulate and protect them from intruders just as much as from the elements. Eighteenth-century Norwegians created sod roofs to absorb run off from rain. Today it seems we have come full circle to realize that the kind of roof we keep over our heads can hold many rewards. It is only in the last few centuries we have built upward, as if never knowing when to stop. We also rejected ancient green wisdom for modern alternatives such as slate, tile, or glass. It's not that these materials are not suitable, for they have served their function well and continue to keep our houses dry; but what is now dawning on many of us is that they are not the most energy-efficient way to build in the twenty-first century, with the cloud of climate change upon us.

A green roof on a building is partially or completely covered in vegetation that is planted over a waterproof membrane. It may also include additional layers, such as a root barrier and a drainage or irrigation system. The use of the word *green* refers to the eco trend on environmentally friendly anything. Living roofs serve several purposes for a building, such as absorbing rainwater, providing insulation, creating a habitat for wildlife, and helping to lower urban air temperatures and combat the heat island effect in cities. Chicago is now recognized as a leader in building green roofs; the U.S. city is realizing many benefits from its 600 green roofs, which all add up to a wonderful green oasis within an urban terrain.

There are two types of green roof: intensive and extensive. An intensive roof is thicker and can support a wider variety of plants. These are usually seen on top of large corporate buildings or tower blocks, and they require a great deal of maintenance. Then there are extensive green roofs, which are covered in a thinner layer of vegetation and are lighter than intensive green roofs, mainly because they are lying on top of out-buildings such as sheds, garages, stables, even hutches.

Choosing to have a living roof has many ecological benefits. A living roof absorbs rainwater, which is beneficial in regions like Scotland, which can have its fair share of precipitation. This allows the moisture to be later released through evaporation and is kinder to the climate. A green roof helps insulate a building, allowing for a reduction in energy bills. Studies have revealed that green roofs in urban areas can help lower urban air temperatures and combat the heat-island effect.

Another benefit is that green roofing offers a living ecosystem to wildlife. With more urban areas being built upon, there seems to be ever-less greenery in our world. By making use of the roof as a planting space, a biodiverse roof oasis can be built, ready and waiting for wildlife to share. We can enjoy watching nature return to our urban space, helping us to relax and be in touch with the larger local ecology. It is a well-known fact that observing nature helps us to unwind and reconnect to our natural world. We get a chance to see the seasons change and improve a previously boring view like a garage roof, all the while knowing that we are lessening our impact on this planet.

Brown Roofs

Brown roofs differ from green roofs in that they typically make use of local species and materials. For this reason, brown roofs are also called biodiverse roofs. This can make them more economical, using recycled local materials and reducing the carbon footprint. Often they are constructed to meet a particular ecological need within the locale, for example, providing a local nature reserve within an industrial estate or creating a habitat for a particular local species.

Overused or abandoned industrial sites, what are called "brownfields," can be converted to create valuable ecosystems to support rare species of plants, animals, and invertebrates.

Wildlife Roofs

Closely related to brown roofs are wildlife roofs. These roofs are becoming more popular with one aim in mind: conservation. As more and more land is built upon and less and less natural habitat is to be found for rare species, one way to counteract this trend is to address specific habitat needs with a biodiverse roof. Usually it will be designed for one of two reasons: to copy the habitat of a limited number of species, such as butterfly or bird, or to create a range of habitats to maximize the array of species that may inhabit the roof.

Installing a wildlife roof is often considered when the budget for a green roof is squeezed. Wildlife and biodiverse roofs are sometimes assumed to be less costly to install due to the use of recycled materials, but in practice they usually end up costing about the same as a true green roof. Planting will be aimed at attracting and sustaining the species being conserved.

Earth Houses

A cave could be considered an earth house in its barest form. Our ancestors sought shelter within the rocks against the elements. In Norse culture, earthen houses had a blanket of grass for a roof and would lie unnoticed within the undulating landscape and be capable of maintaining a balanced heat, withstanding fierce gales of wind, and remaining secure from enemy sight.

Modern earth houses are built with some of these ideas in mind, but they also draw upon ecologically progressive architecture. They are shaped organically with predominantly round, curved rooms that embrace the theme of unity with the earth. Using the underlying heat residues within the soil gives advantages of insulation and retains a more balanced air temperature, thus saving CO_2. An added benefit is the feeling of security in an earth house, which can withstand wind storms and even earthquakes. The land seems unscarred by the eco-house, as it sits under a blanket of grass. There is even less likelihood of fire.

Roof planting is done by excavation of materials and dug-in planting to create a diverse plethora of color and flora. The cost is economical compared to conventional brick-and-mortar buildings. Often many materials are locally sourced, like recycled tires, or the home is built using ancient and affordable techniques.

Building Your Own Green Roof

To construct a successful living roof relies on good design. Roofs do come is various shapes and sizes. Has it got a slope or is it a flat roof? This will determine what you put down as a foundation. You have to incorporate adequate water retention and drainage too. Obviously, sloped roofs will have greater drainage at the top as opposed to a flat roof, where pooling can occur if drainage matting is not in place.

So let us imagine you are building an extensive living roof over a garage that has a flat surface. A retro green roof added to an existing build should not be more than 4–6 inches deep and have low-growing, drought-tolerant, lightweight plants. You need to check that the building can take the weight you intend to add.

First, you will need a strong waterproof membrane such as butyl pond liner. (If there is less than 3 degrees of slope, use drainage matting.) Over the waterproof membrane should go water-retention matting. Water-retention matting is a lightweight, relatively inexpensive fleece that helps the plants have enough water to stay healthy. Next comes a layer of Enviromat or your own equivalent of a planting turf to put over the top. On a slope of 10 degrees or more, irrigation should be available as a precaution against water loss in some areas.

Planting

You will need the help of a local greenhouse or horticulturist to determine the right species for your type and location of green roof. Since species that work well in one zone won't do well in another, here is just a guide to the different classes of plants you may decide to grow on your green roof.

Wildflower turf is a wonderfully lightweight turf that is unlike normal grass turf. Soil levels are minimal, thus keeping the roof's weight low. It is low maintenance, as it only needs to be cut once a year. These plants thrive on a lack of fertility and many are drought tolerant, such as yarrow or ribwort plantain. The variety of plants attract a wide range of wildlife. Very little is needed to maintain this instant wildlife garden, apart from removing the odd gate-crasher seed dropped from a bird's beak or blown onto the roof. The mat covering over the roof will be an excellent insulator for the building.

Special **grasses** specific to the needs of your roof will need to be chosen. These grasses are usually tough and create a dense mat of turf rather than long seed stems. The main purpose of the grass is to absorb and insulate, as well as provide a habitat with food for local wildlife.

Sedums are often the first option when thinking about planting on any green roof because they are resistant to wind, frost, and drought. This group of flowering plants are able to absorb rain, making them drought resistant, but they do not like sitting in rain puddles, so some form of drainage must also be incorporated into the planting design. There are so many sedums to choose from that can provide color almost all year round: from red to green, pink to yellow, and alpine forms that put out florets of color. The low-growing succulent leaves of sedum, otherwise known as stonecrop, can be seen in rockeries everywhere. Most of them are evergreen and they are amongst the easiest of plants to grow, flourishing in dry and often poor soils where very little else can grow. They are also easy to propagate; if you want to economize, why not multiply your plant volume with a few bought plants and watch them spread to fill the roof space in no time? Varieties to grow depend upon the size of roof to be covered, as there are large-spreading sedums and compact varieties. Creating a patchwork of color makes the roof stunning, so why not intersperse different colors of sedum species? Sedums do best in full sunlight, but they will still produce a reasonable display in partial shade.

. . . .

Creating an urban oasis with a living roof is within everyone's grasp. As Austrian artist, architect, and philosopher Freidersreich Hundertwassen said, "When one creates green roofs, one doesn't need to fear the so-called paving of the landscape: the houses themselves become part of the landscape."

For Further Reading

Dunnett, Nigel, and Noël Kingsbury. *Planting Green Roofs and Living Walls*, 2nd edition. Portland, OR: Timber Press, 2008.

Green Roof Centre. *Green Roof Pocket Guide*. Sheffield University.

Brickell, C., ed. *The RHS New Encyclopedia of Plants and Flowers*, 3rd edition. London: Dorling Kindersley, 1999.

About the Author

Janice Sharkey is a freelance writer living in Scotland, UK. She is a year-round gardener who now has a green roof positioned outside her kitchen so she can enjoy the garden even when doing housework.

EcoSavvy Gardening: Creating Your Ecosystem

by Misty Kuceris

Years ago while traveling through Southern California, I was amazed to see all the lush green golf courses offering natives and tourists a retreat from their cares in life. While enjoying the natural desert, I encountered a U.S. Fish and Wildlife employee. We discussed the loss of habitat caused by the amount of water used to maintain the golf courses. Moisture was being trapped in the air and changing the ecosystem. Some native vegetation was actually having trouble growing in the more moist environment.

The stark realization that what we plant could actually cause changes in our ecosystem continues to be a prime motivation for me, now a horticultural specialist, to work with home owners in improving their yards—or as I prefer to call them, their little ecosystems. The prime approach is EcoSavvy Gardening, a term coined in Virginia by Green Spring Gardens and the Fairfax County Park Authority.

EcoSavvy gardening is not a new concept, and you may know it by one of its other names: garden ecology, sustainable gardening, GreenScaping, or biodynamics. It is an approach to gardening in which you understand that your little plot of land is just a molecule in the whole cosmos of the planet. Your land is an ecosystem, where the balance of various elements supports the land and becomes self-sufficient. Rather than taking from Earth, you embrace her by replacing nutrients and working with natural ecological factors to better your garden.

The benefits to EcoSavvy gardening are enormous. You use less fertilizer because you enrich the soil naturally. You use fewer pesticides because you create an environment for beneficial insects, which then take the place of invasive pests. You use water more efficiently because you plant trees, shrubs, and vegetation that thrive in your natural climate. You attract more birds, butterflies, and other wildlife into your yard with native species. All this protects the environment because fewer chemicals are released into the various water systems. Plus, once your garden is established, you spend less time and money maintaining the beauty that surrounds your home.

Soil

Soil is the first place to start, no matter where you live. Soil is nature's gift to us. The soil comes from years of decomposition of various minerals and plant materials. East of the Mississippi River in the United States, most of the soil is acidic because of the decomposition of trees and shrubs from various forests. West of the Mississippi River in the United States, the soil leans toward the alkaline side because of various lime deposits and other minerals. By testing the soil, you'll know what nutrients are needed for your plants as well as what nutrients already exist in your soil. This prevents you from over-fertilizing your land. Soil testing is easy; you can either do it yourself by purchasing one of the kits sold in local garden centers, or you can contact your local Cooperative Extension office for a special soil-testing kit, which is usually then sent to a land grant college or university for analysis. The advantage to having an outside source test your soil is that such a test not only indicates the level of pH, phosphorus, and potassium in your garden, but also other elements and minerals that are important to plant growth.

Once you've addressed any specific pH or mineral problems, you can look at improving the soil's overall value. Compost is one of the best nutrient supplements available, and it's not difficult to make. Compost helps sandy soils to hold water and clay soils to drain faster. It increases the number of earthworms and beneficial microorganisms in your soil. These factors, and more, increase the strength of your plants and decrease the need for fertilizers and watering. You can use anything from your garden to make a compost pile—grass clippings, fallen leaves, even twigs. You can also use vegetable scraps and coffee grounds. Dairy products, meats, or oils are not recommended because of the pests they attract. You should also never compost animal waste, as it contains bacterium that you don't want to add to your growing soil.

Grass

Now it's time to look around your property and think lawn. Should you decrease the size of your lawn and increase the size of your garden? Keep the lawn? Perhaps you live in a neighborhood where covenants require a specific amount of lawn. If so, how do you maintain a lawn and still engage in EccoSavvy gardening? One great way to keep everyone happy is to plant native ornamental grasses.

There are two types of ornamental lawn grasses. The cool season grasses, such as fescue and bluegrass, thrive in early spring and late fall but go dormant when warmer weather hits. Since most people like to keep their lawns green during the warm months, they water them. But these grasses don't need as much water as you think: just 1 inch of water per week (including rainfall) will keep the cool season grass green. If you don't know how long to run the sprinkler or irrigation system to get your 1 inch of water, put a cup or rain gauge in the area you're watering and time how long it takes for 1 inch of water to fill into the cup. Reduce that amount of time if you've received rainfall in the last week.

The warm season grasses, such as Bermuda grass or zoysiagrass, don't do much in spring but come to life as soon as the heat hits. Not only are these grasses popular in areas like Arizona or Hawaii, but they are also favored for golf courses. However, these grasses are considered weeds in cool season grass lawns.

Unless you live in a zone with little temperature variation, you'll want to use both grasses in order to keep your lawn interesting for the entire growing season. If you're unsure of the best grasses for your area, contact your Cooperative Extension office.

Grasses need nitrogen to stay green and need to be fertilized during their growing seasons. Remember: warm season grasses grow from late spring to early fall. Cool season grasses grow in spring, go dormant in the hot summer months, and grow again in the fall. When you fertilize, use natural organic fertilizers, such as corn gluten, or slow-release fertilizers.

Trees and Shrubs

The next areas to consider are the gardens and placements for trees and shrubs. This gets back to the soil. Find out which plants support your ecosystem. Determine what type of area you have. You can best determine the type of area you have by asking yourself the following questions:

- Does the Sun shine in that area? If so, at what time of day and for how long? An area that gets a lot of Sun in the morning (usually the east side of your property) may not get much Sun in the afternoon; that would be considered a partial-shade to shade area. An area that gets afternoon Sun (usually the west side of your property) and/or more than six hours of sunshine per day is considered a full-sunshine area.

- What type of drainage do I have? If you're not certain, you can do a simply drainage test. Take a soup can and cut both ends of the can open (don't cut yourself!). Push one of the open ends of the can 2 inches into the soil. Pour 2 inches of water in the top of the can. In one hour, 1 inch of water should have drained away. In two hours, the second inch of the water should have drained away. If there is still water in the can, the drainage is too slow. If the water goes out of the can more quickly than two hours, the drainage is too fast. Either type of drainage indicates that the roots of your plant may not thrive. You'll either need to amend the soil according to your drainage or find plants that work in that type of drainage environment.

- How does the air circulate around my garden? Depending on your location, air circulation can bring either colder or warmer temperatures to your little microclimate. Some areas of your garden might have surprising wind drafts, which might discourage more delicate plants. Again, wind impacts the type of plants you'll want in that area.

- What native plants are available for my area? Native plants are more conducive to your environment. Once established, they thrive with little coddling. Resources are abundant through various native plant societies that exist in your area. To find out more about native plants in your area, look into the websites for the National Wildlife Federation (www.nwf.org) or the Lady Bird Johnson Wildlife Center (www.wildflowers.org).

• What plants support each other? It's important to group plants with similar needs together. If you have a moist area, make certain all the plants in that spot have roots that prefer moisture. If you have a very sunny area, make certain all the plants there are full-Sun plants.

Mulch

Now that you created your garden, it's time to apply mulch. The purpose of mulch is to retain moisture in your garden and prevent weeds from forming. You can use grass clippings, leaves, or old wood chips to mulch your garden. In some areas, you may use pebbles or straw as mulch. While compost is not technically mulch, some people use it as such, especially with new plantings, due to the high nutrient content. Besides saving water, the benefit to most mulch, except pebbles, is that it degrades into the soil and contributes nutrients as it does so. Another benefit is in deterring weeds, so you use fewer chemicals to battle weeds in the garden.

Pests

Too many weeds in your garden can be an invitation for insect pests, which eventually destroy your other plantings. Integrated pest management (IPM) is the best approach to preventing pests. Before you go out and destroy the insect, make certain that it is indeed a harmful insect. There are many beneficial insects that destroy the harmful insects, and you don't want to eliminate those beneficial insects. Companion gardening is another IPM approach. There are certain plants that repel or trap harmful insects. For example, spreading the herb rosemary throughout your garden repels slugs and snails. Planting African marigolds will destroy harmful nematodes.

If you need to spray for pests, consider organic sprays, such as neem, insecticidal soap, permethrin, or pyrethrum. When using pesticides, read the instructions and follow them carefully. One proper application is preferred to two or three sloppy passes.

. . . .

Bringing your garden's soil, grasses, trees and shrubs, mulch, and insect management in line with your natural climate can make a difference in the look of your garden and the effort it takes to keep it in great shape. Through seeing your garden as a molecule of the entire cosmos of the planet, you create an environment that sparks local life. Birds, butterflies, and other creatures will flock to your yard. You'll create an oasis for yourself, migrating creatures, and animals that remain year-round. Through this balance with nature and renewed perspective, you'll find a balance in your soul.

References

Accessed August 2010

Biodynamic Farming and Gardening Association. "What is Biodynamic Agriculture." http://www.biodynamics.com/biodynamics.html.

Christian, A. H., G. K. Evanylo, and R. Green. "Compost: What Is It and What's It to You," Virginia Cooperative Extension, Virginia Tech. http://pubs.ext.vt.edu/452/452-231/452-231.pdf.

Relf, Diane, and Alan McDaniel. "Composting." Virginia Tech, http://pubs.ext.vt.edu/426/426-325/426-325.pdf.

U.S. Environmental Protection Agency (EPA). "GreenScaping: The Easy Way to a Greener, Healthier Yard." http://www.epa.gov/epawaste/conserve/rrr/greenscapes/owners.htm.

Virginia Cooperative Extension, Virginia Tech. "Making Compost from Yard Waste." Alex Niemiera, reviewer. http://pubs.ext.vt.edu/426/426-703/426-703.pdf.

About the Author

Misty Kuceris is a horticultural specialist and astrologer working with individuals, advising them in plant and lawn care. She is a Master Gardener volunteer specializing in the diagnosis of plant diseases and insect indentification. Misty views nature as one of the best forms of meditation and one of the best means for feeling the life flow of energy. She can be reached at misty@EnhanceOneself.com.

Natural Beekeeping

by Calantirniel

Many of us are aware today of the alarming disappearance of bees in recent years, including Colony Collapse Disorder (CCD). The honey bee (*Apis mellifera*) is an absolute agricultural necessity becuase of the number of food-producing plants that require its pollinating abilities. A 2000 Cornell University article states that honey bees were the sole pollinators for $15 billion in U.S. crops. While science struggles to find causes and solutions to this problem, the keen observer will notice the following: beekeepers who practice organic methods experience virtually no colony collapse.

This fact is inspiring an amazing number of hobbyist beekeepers (or bee stewards) worldwide. And the time cannot be better to embrace this hobby! But, how does a "newbee" begin? If you were to look even casually online, you would think it could cost thousands to even start, which is very discouraging. Luckily, there are low-cost alternatives that are also low-maintenance for the would-be apiarist (beekeeper).

Before You Begin

Start by determining if you are the type of person who could keep bees. If you are afraid of them, it may not be a good idea. If you are highly allergic to their stings, keeping bees is heavily discouraged because at some point, you will get stung. I always have a bottle of plantain tincture in my pocket to apply to any stings that have a reaction, and hopefully a hospital is also nearby just in case. Most beekeepers get stung and don't treat the stings other than removing the stingers; they feel that this process of being stung is medicinal, believing it adds years to their lives. Some more radical treatments for multiple sclerosis (MS) use live bee stings to treat symptoms, though that's beyond the scope of this discussion. You'll be keeping bees simply for environmental and gardening benefits, so do avoid being stung as much as possible, even if you are not allergic to bee stings.

Next, look into your local ordinances on beekeeping. Surprisingly, many cities are now changing their laws in favor of beekeepers, knowing the seriousness of the current bee-population decreases. If the ordinance in your city isn't in favor of beekeeping, you and interested others can propose changes to your council or commissioners, and see what needs to be done to follow through. The folks at *Bee Culture Magazine* (www.beeculturemagazine.com) are a good resource for this. If you are a renter, you must obtain permission from the property owner(s), and it is likely a good idea to let neighbors know about your proposed hobby, and that your intention is to be as unobtrusive as possible. While I am not an advocate of government intervention, you may also need to contact or even register with the state Department of Agriculture or other governing division in your state. When you are exploring your state's DoA website, try looking under "crops" and even "livestock" to find your state's policy on bees and beekeeping. You may even find that your state Department of Agriculture has resources for apiarists!

Before going too much further, learn about your geographical area and consider placement of the hive(s). This could be anywhere from backyards to rooftops—just make sure the bees have ideal temperatures and are away from human traffic. The bees will travel/forage an approximate two- to three-mile radius during daylight hours, so make sure they have the space to do so. Also, look for the closest water source to the hive placement—reconsider your placement if that source is your neighbor's hot tub! Either think of a different place for the hive, or create a reliable water source that is much closer to the hive. Determining a spot for your hive is critical to determining if you will be able to keep bees in the first place.

After securing the proper permits and permissions and making sure you have a good location to keep a hive, find some established beekeepers in your area—this is imperative. Beekeeping varies so much for every area because every microclimate has unique needs. For instance, if you wish to keep bees in Southern California, you can begin earlier in the year, but you need to know about recognizing and dealing with Africanized bees. For beekeeping in western Montana, the season is very short (winters are very long and cold), and you need great reserves of honey for over-wintering bees, not to mention knowing how to keep them warm (having wind-blocks to the north and west is ideal). For hives in the woods, bears are a big problem, so electric fences are warranted.

While Google might help you find nearby beekeepers, some beekeepers just do not go online. So, besides your Department of Agriculture, try local colleges and universities that have an agricultural track, as they are bound to have referrals. Also contact some of the commercial exterminators in your area; chances are they do not remove bees but will give you name(s) of people who do, and those folks are almost always beekeepers. You may discover there are beekeeping groups in your area. Go and learn all you can from fellow beekeepers, as they are often enthusiastic to see others wanting to join the fold. Get involved, as this will further expand your reach.

Creating Your Hive(s)

You have basically three options at this point: (1) purchase Langstroth-style commercial equipment (boxes, frames, etc.); (2) make your own Top Bar hive; or (3) make your own Warre hive. Since this article is about saving money, the purchasing option will not be discussed in great detail here, but for those interested in pursuing that track, the companies who sell this equipment are very helpful for "newbee" hobbyists. They may not, however, be organic beekeepers, so be careful of their recommendations and if possible, bring someone who knows about natural beekeeping with you when purchasing.

One of the easiest and least expensive ways to keep bees is in a Top Bar hive (TBH). Rather than having frames all the way around like in commercial hives, bees will instead form a comb that hangs from a top bar that has some "starter" on it for them to work with. The hive itself is a long horizontal box, usually perched on sturdy legs, and divided into three sections (and the bees are good at figuring out where in the box to put the brood, where to put honey storage, etc.). This is also the best style if you do not want to be doing lots of heavy lifting, since some of the ready-made hive boxes can weigh fifty to seventy pounds!

With the Top Bar hive, you make a wooden "holder" for the bar that holds the comb. You can then lift the bar out to inspect the comb right at the hive. You do not need to check this hive as often as one using commercial parts because the bees have the freedom to utilize their space to the greatest advantage, which lessens the likelihood of pests, mites, and so on. The plans are available free online and are relatively easy to follow. You can purchase non-treated wood at most lumber yards to make this style of hive—you may even have some nice scrap wood from another project, saving you even more money! Remember to talk to your local mentors about variations that work better for your climate. In some areas, it is best to have openings on the bottom, but in other areas, openings may be better on the top. Some just have screened bottoms, others have closed or closeable bottoms, and often the bees will make a hard substance, called propolis, to close off something they don't want. Try not to use chemicals/paint to treat the wood of your hive—after it is built, use a mixture of linseed oil with some melted beeswax (preferably from one of your new beekeeper friends) and a tiny bit of lemongrass essential oil if desired.

If you like the ease of the Top Bar Hive (TBH) but prefer the vertical setting that is similar to the ready-made hive boxes, consider the Warre hive. Where the TBH is a horizontal setting, the Warre implements a vertical setting, but still uses top bars in the same manner. The plans are also available free online. The Warre hive will require more wood and is a bit more complicated than the TBH, but some beekeepers love the design and are willing to go the extra mile. The Warre is still more economical than using commercial equipment and is also low maintenance. No matter which hives you decide to implement, read *Beekeeping for All* written by Abbé Warré (1866–1951)—it is most interesting! Again, treat the wood when done with the mixture of linseed oil, melted beeswax, and (optionally) a tiny bit of lemongrass essential oil.

Obtaining Bees

We'll discuss three ways to obtain bees. The first is to allow some scout bees to find your delicious-smelling, inviting hive, which requires some luck! This is one reason for the lemongrass oil: it mimics honey bee's pheromones. Waiting for bees to find your hive is the least expensive option and requires the least effort, but can also have less-than-desirable results.

If you want bees now, you can purchase them—but they are not cheap! There is also a chance that the bees you purchase won't be genetically adapted to your area or be of weaker stock than bees that live close by. Often the queen—the largest, boss-lady bee—is not a part of the hive you order, so the bees do not yet have a relationship with her. The places that sell bees may be far away, and it can be hard on the bees when they are shipped (not to mention shipping personnel being less than enthusiastic about your deliveries). And be careful with your queen—I once heard of a person who accidentally lost her queen, and had to reorder, which was at least $50. Read the directions *to the letter* when releasing the queen from her special box into the hive.

This leaves the third option: catching your own swarm. A swarm is formed when a hive becomes overpopulated. A second queen is born, and one of the queens will lead a number of bees out of the hive to find a new permanent home. Until such a home is found, the bees will latch onto a handy surface (branch, bench, whatnot), piling on top of each other to protect the queen deep inside a solid cluster of bees. Sounds scary! The good news is that when bees are swarming, they are very docile and will not sting. Still, you should prepare for this event by having some clothing that bees won't really be able to permeate. You won't need a complete bee-suit, but do tie your pantlegs to your boots (or wear sweats with a snug band) and wear a buttoned long-sleeved shirt, thick gloves, and a veil. You can purchase a mosquito netting for less than $2 in the hunting/sporting section of your nearest superstore and place it over a baseball cap or other brimmed hat to make your own veil. Dress so that bees cannot get into your clothing and get caught. You'll need a good ladder and branch cutters;

many swarms stay close to ground level, but it's not unusual to find one in a tree. Finally, have a nice box prepared to catch the swarm: use a large corrugated cardboard box (perhaps scratched with some beeswax and a couple of drops of lemongrass). Cut out a "window" for ventilation, then obtain a piece of window-type screen larger than the cut-out window and securely tape it to the inside of the box, leaving no holes whatsoever. Use duct tape to seal up the edges. This will allow the bees to breathe while you transport them to your hive.

When you see a swarm (or receive a call if you can get placed on a list), place the box as close to the swarm cluster as possible and either quickly jerk the item the bees are holding onto (branch) or gently sweep the bulk of the bees into the box—yes, this is why you should be wearing thick gloves! Again, swarming bees are not very aggressive, but use common sense. If you need to cut a branch from a tree, do so, but don't let the swarm drop too far—place the box up close to it (you may need a brave partner). As long as the queen is in there, the bees will go into the box, so place the box on the ground and wait a few minutes for the rest of the bees to get into the box. Then, while gently sweeping any random bees into the box, carefully close the box and secure the top with tape. Carry the box so your hands are not near the window. When you get the swarm to your hive, place the item holding the swarm (if there is one) into the hive and shake it off, then "dump" the rest of the bees into the hive. If there is no branch or item holding the bees, simply tip the box to dump the bees into the hive. Again, try to *make sure* the queen is in the hive. She's larger than all the rest, but you might have to look carefully for her. As long as boss-lady bee is there, all the other bees will eventually go to the hive.

Now What?

The wonderful part about bees is that they can do most things for themselves—all you really need to do is make sure they have a water source nearby. While some people feed their bees sugar water to get a head start on honey production, this is not recommended. Feeding is the first step toward unnatural beekeeping, which invites pests and disease. Since the idea here is to be bee stewards rather than honey producers, allow the bees to forage the way nature intended. Much of their resources at first will be devoted to making comb and then to making honey reserves for the hive to last through winter. When inspecting the comb, make sure you do not wiggle the bar sideways, or the comb could fall off! If this does happen, tie the comb back to the bar, and the bees will reattach it with new comb. Don't count on having any honey the first season, since the winter reserves can be thirty to sixty pounds, depending on the size of the hive and how long and cold winter will be. As winter approaches, learn how to "winterize" your particular type of hive with wool blankets and wind blocks and by keeping the hive closed until the warm season is back. This is where your local beekeeping friends will come in handy, as they will know the dates in your area to do this. Only use sugar water if the bees didn't have time to make enough honey to get

2011 © Vladimir Alexeev. Image from BigStockPhoto.com

through the winter (if you captured the swarm in later summer or fall)—even then, purchasing raw local honey to supplement their stores is a much better option. Research the best way to place the overwintering honey in the hive by asking your local mentors.

Honey Harvest

At some point, the bees will have made more honey than they can use, and that is when you want to harvest! It is ideal to harvest honey when the weather is very warm, as it helps the extraction process. It can be difficult to determine exactly when a comb is ready for honey harvesting, so rely on your mentors for this step. You'll also want to obtain some kind of bee repellent to get the bees off the comb so you don't take them home with you. In general, it is best to harvest during the daytime, on a sunny warm day; this means most of the bees will be out foraging. While bee-keepers with commercial frames might also purchase an expensive manual honey extractor, those with Top Bar or Warre hives can implement an easy extracting system themselves.

Obtain three heavy-duty food buckets from a restaurant, and make sure they are clean inside and out. One bucket will be used for holding the honey-filled comb(s), so there needs to be a hole at the bottom with screening so the comb doesn't pass through. The second bucket is placed inside the first bucket to squeeze down on the comb and press the honey through the screened hole. You'll need weights to accomplish this—you can use bricks, rocks, or even your feet if you want to stand there balancing on two buckets all day! The third bucket, with a hole cut in the lid to match the hole in the bottom of the first bucket, is to catch the screened honey. Using some materials from your local hardware store, you could even add a dispenser at the bottom of the bucket to make filling jars easier. Otherwise you'll need to spoon or scoop your honey, which could get rather messy. You can either purchase jars or recycle jars (keep the lids) throughout the year from other food purchases. Voilà—an inexpensive honey harvest! Raw unprocessed honey is a treat you don't know you're missing until you've had it.

The comb that remains after you press out the honey can be melted down and results in beeswax—perfect for candles and as an ingredient in some cosmetics and herbal healing products (including salves).

When you've removed the combs from the bars, just place the top bars carefully back into the hive. The bees will make new comb, and more honey!

There is so much more to being a "beek" (beekeeper's nickname), and the information here really just scratches the surface—it is my hope your bee steward adventures are rewarding in many ways! Can you not hear their enchanting buzzing-hum calling you?

For Further Reading

Top Bar Hive (TBH) Free Plans and Forum: www.biobees.com.

Warre Hive Free Plans and *Beekeeping for All* eBook: www.thebee space.net.

Morse, R. A., and N. W. Calderone. "The Value of Honey Bees as Pollinators of US Crops in 2000." Cornell University (2000).

About the Author

Calantirniel has been published in over a dozen Llewellyn annuals and has practiced many forms of natural spirituality since the early 1990s. She is a professional astrologer, tarot card reader, dowser, flower essence creator and practitioner, and Usui Reiki Master, and became a ULC Reverend and a certified Master Herbalist in 2007. She has an organic garden, crochets professionally, and is co-creating Tië eldaliéva, the Elven Path, a spiritual practice based upon the Elves' viewpoint in Professor J. R. R. Tolkien's Middle-Earth stories, particularly The Silmarillion. Please visit http://aartiana.wordpress. com for more information.

Waning Moon Yardwork

by Elizabeth Barrette

It's common knowledge that the waxing and waning of the Moon creates a tidal effect in energy. Waxing energy helps things increase or approach, while waning energy helps things decrease or depart. Most garden activities focus on the waxing or Full Moon, hoping to increase growth. However, the waning Moon also supports some important tasks in the garden and lawn. Let's explore ways to take advantage of this energy.

Pruning Plants

Pruning is a "diminishing" task. When we prune trees and bushes, we make them a little smaller or less dense. We usually want to avoid having new growth spurt out. Pruning during the waning Moon helps plants hold onto their new shape, since they have a resting time before a new growth cycle starts. Used thoughtfully, waning Moon pruning can slow growth (so you don't have to trim hedges as often) and influence shape (so fruit trees put out new branches in appropriate places).

Different plants have very different pruning requirements, so consult a guide for the kind of trees or shrubs you grow. In general, you should remove weak growth such as thin branches, those with a bad angle, or ones that cross over each other. Also remove any dead wood. Make the cuts at a moderate angle and, for most purposes, just above a bud. Always use sharp pruning tools that cut neatly.

Mowing the Lawn

Like pruning, mowing is a "diminishing" task. The timing of mowing has a subtle influence on the way grass grows. Mow during the waning Moon to keep grass under control and discourage it from growing too quickly. Then you won't need to mow it as often, which saves both time and gas for the mower. This approach slows the grass in general, also inhibiting its lateral spread. Note that if you are trying to establish a new lawn, do not mow it during the waning Moon—mow instead during the waxing Moon to encourage growth.

Also pay attention to the mowing height. Some grass types do better when left several inches high, while others can be cut almost to ground level. Know your lawn mix and set your mower blades accordingly. Grasses that need more height are less tolerant of restrictions, so mow them just after the Full Moon. Grasses that accept very low height can be cut during the waning crescent.

Composting

Composting is a "breaking down" process that reduces complex materials to their component nutrients. These nutrients then become available to nourish plants. In nature, this process happens very slowly. At home, you can make it happen a lot faster if you know how it works.

A compost pile begins with a mix of wet/green and dry/brown materials, so as to balance nitrogen and carbon. The pile needs an ample supply of air and moisture. Bacteria, fungi, insects, arthropods, worms, and other tiny creatures then shred and digest the organic matter. Eventually you get a quantity of dark, fluffy compost. This detritus ecosystem thrives on entropy.

Pretty much any activity relating to compost will benefit from waning Moon energy. This is a good time to create a new compost pile, as it will break down faster. Check your existing pile to see if it needs maintenance; you may need to water it or turn it over with a pitchfork. This is also a good time to take finished compost out of the pile and spread it on your lawn or garden, as the compost will be encouraged to break down into the existing soil.

Applying Soil Amendments

Some types of soil amendments need to decompose into the surrounding soil in order to work, and the rest need to blend in smoothly. Applying soil amendments is therefore a "breaking down" chore suitable for the waning Moon. If you do this shortly after the Full Moon, the low energy gives the soil a resting time before plants surge into action with the waxing Moon. Soil amendments may be applied with specialized gear or simply sprinkled over the surface and worked in with a sturdy rake, hoe, or shovel.

Choose amendments based on what your soil lacks. Organic matter (which needs to decay) improves soil texture, nutrients, and often water retention. Wood chips are good for clay or sandy soil, balancing the water flow and aeration while adding carbon. Animal manure enriches soil and adds texture; it's high in nitrogen. Bone meal adds phosphorous. Greens add potash and trace minerals. Compost delivers a relatively balanced set of nutrients while making the soil easier to work through. Sulphur lowers the pH in alkaline soil while lime raises the pH in acidic soil.

Tilling and Digging

Various soil-loosening jobs are compatible with the waning Moon. They can be "diminishing" or "breaking down" tasks, depending on the method and the purpose. When you do these during the waning Moon, it is easier for the soil to break apart and harder for fresh weeds to sprout. About halfway between the full and New Moon is the best time for soil-loosening projects.

Use the right method and tools for your needs. Tilling with a tiller chops the soil into small chunks, which is helpful before planting or after harvest. Digging with a shovel can achieve the same effect. Double-digging is a technique for soil improvement that involves shoveling a deep trench and refilling it; this is especially helpful for blending in amendments. All of these processes also destroy live weeds, although new weed seeds may be activated.

Pest Control

Yards and gardens attract many pests, which we then try to deter. These include insects, slugs and snails, rabbits, squirrels, deer, and birds. The smaller ones we may repel or kill; the larger ones usually just get repelled. Either approach is basically a "banishing" effect, another type of work suitable for the waning Moon. For the greatest impact, apply pest control during the last few days of the balsamic crescent.

Ideally, use eco-friendly pest control methods, especially if your garden is a spiritual place for you. Pesticides or repellants for insects usually consist of spray or powder, often based on pyrethrins or other substances that plants produce to protect themselves. Mosquitoes are easier to prevent than to deter: remove sources of stagnant water or stock pools with fish and frogs to discourage mosquito eggs. For slugs and snails, you can get pellets, but these thirsty pests will drown themselves quite enthusiastically in a saucer of ordinary beer. Aluminum pie plates and streamers can scare away small animals and birds. Large animals such as deer may need to be kept out with fencing. In that case, you can help capture the "banishing" effect of the waning Moon by painting a crescent on each post; silver or pearl nail polish works nicely, or use clear if you prefer to be discreet.

Weeding

Like pest control, weeding is a "banishing" activity, but it also shares a "diminishing" quality with pruning—we want the individual weeds to die and not come back, but we also want the overall population of weeds to shrink. Thus an ideal approach is to devote the two weeks of the waning Moon to heavy-duty weeding. This takes advantage of the deepening energy, catching both the duration and the strongest point. During the waxing and Full Moon, just do small amounts of touch-up weeding to keep things from getting out of hand.

Certain techniques in weeding make the process more effective. As much as possible, remove weeds before they can flower or at least before they go to seed. This minimizes the number of seeds that can produce new weed plants. Weeds that haven't set seed may be composted, but if they have seeds, they should be burned. Make sure that you pull up the entire weed, too. Many of them have strong root systems but a weak attachment to the top parts; when you pull, the upper plant just breaks away, leaving behind the roots, which can regrow. Use a dandelion fork or similar weeding tool to extract deep taproots. A trowel or cultivating fork helps to remove wider, fibrous root systems. If weed roots are causing problems for you, work on those immediately before the New Moon. The last days of the waning Moon, and the New Moon, relate closely to "subconscious" or "underground" things.

In addition to pulling weeds, there are other weed-suppressing things you can do during the waning Moon. Mulch discourages weeds from sprouting in your flower bed or garden. Landscaping cloth also helps, especially when topped by mulch. Small noxious weeds such as poison ivy may be quelled by pouring a bucket of wood chips over them and topping that with a concrete block. As a last resort, herbicide spray kills large or obstinate weeds.

Refinement and Stabilization

On a subtler note, the waning Moon is a time to consolidate what you already have rather than expand to something new. Look around your yard and garden to see what needs attention in order to be at its best. If you see ideas for whole new projects, jot them down and use the introspective energy of the waning Moon to consider possibilities before pursuing them in the waxing phase.

A good place to start is storm security. Make sure lawn furniture is fastened down or tethered so it can't blow around. As mentioned in the pruning section, well-groomed trees stand up better to harsh weather without breaking. Wrapping a tree guard around young saplings will help protect them from gnawing mammals and from winter damage.

The inward focus of the waning Moon is also helpful for creating or maintaining boundaries, such as cutting a neat edge of lawn along a sidewalk or straightening the bricks of a flowerbed border. Installing a fence to keep out pests is a two-fold waning Moon project.

Advance Preparation

Because the waning Moon is not ideal for launching new projects, people often overlook its planning potential. Many projects have early steps that need to be set up and then ignored for a while so they can percolate. Think about what steps involve clearing, limiting, or reducing as part of the setup for something yet to come.

For example, starting a garden would generally be considered a waxing Moon task, so as to take advantage of the growth energy. But you can't just plunk a garden into the middle of a lawn; first you have to prepare the soil. Cutting loose and removing the sod or laying black plastic to kill all the plants underneath are preparations best done during the waning Moon. Similarly, if you want

2011 © Scott Leman. Image from BigStockPhoto.com

to transplant a field-grown sapling, you'll get better results if you root-prune it during a waning Moon first. This means using a spade to cut a wide circle around the sapling, without digging it up all the way. Three months to a year later, transplant the sapling during the waxing Moon. Root-pruning by itself can also be used to keep plants to a small size.

You may find it helpful to jot ideas in a garden planner, date-book, or almanac. This makes it easier to make sure you are ready for new projects and growth during the waxing Moon, and for dreaming and reduction tasks during the waning Moon. Keep a list of each and you'll never run out of ideas for what you can do in the yard at any time of the month.

About the Author

Elizabeth Barrette has been involved with the Pagan community for more than twenty-two years. She served as Managing Editor of PanGaia for eight years and Dean of Studies at the Grey School of Wizardry for four years. She has written columns on beginning and intermediate Pagan practice, Pagan culture, and Pagan leadership. Her book Composing Magic: How to Create Magical Spells, Rituals, Blessings, Chants, and Prayers *explains how to combine writing and spirituality. She lives in central Illinois where she has done much networking with Pagans in her area, such as coffeehouse meetings and open sabbats. Her other public activities feature Pagan picnics and science fiction conventions. She enjoys magical crafts, historic religions, and gardening for wildlife. Her other writing fields include speculative fiction, gender studies, and social and environmental issues. One of her Pagan science fiction poems, "Fallen Gardens," was nominated for the Rhysling Award in 2010. Visit her blog, The Wordsmith's Forge (http://ysabetwordsmith.livejournal.com/).*

Harvesting & Preserving By the Moon

by Janice Sharkey

There's no question that home gardening has exploded in popularity in recent years. With rising food prices and a rising need to reconnect with nature, growing your own food can be an ideal two-for-one hobby. It's wonderful to watch once purely ornamental gardens being transformed into berried hedgerows and vegetable patches that can provide for the kitchen table all year round. You might think eating from your garden all year is practically impossible, but think again. The key to success is in preserving the fruits of your labor. Along with this conversion to growing our own fruit and vegetables must come skills in storing and preserving that food. Not only are we saving money in being more self-sufficient, we are also reducing our carbon footprint. As changes within out climate wreak havoc with world food production, we can lessen that effect by being more self-sufficient, even within our small backyard. Collectively, we can have an impact. One way to help us achieve this self-sufficiency is to time our harvesting with the Moon's cycle.

Since ancient times, methods for storing and preserving fruits from garden, field, and forest have been used. Techniques such as fermentation, salting, smoking, boiling, roasting, drying, and freezing have been used to store goods in dry, often dark places until the food is needed. Now, by being aware of the lunar calendar when harvesting and conserving, we are able to reap excellent results.

Harvesting

After all that gardening effort, it pays to harvest at just the right time. If possible, harvest by the light of a waxing Moon, when the succulence is retained and the goodness preserved. Obviously, such crops as lettuce are best picked around a waning Moon, when their crunchy crispness is kept by being picked at dawn with the cool dew upon them. Then they will have maximum crispness and can be kept in the refrigerator.

In their book *The Art of Timing*, Johanna Paungger and Thomas Poppe state that Aries is the best sign in which to store cereals, vegetables, and potatoes. Choosing to harvest fruit and vegetables during a waning Moon helps to preserve the yield longer and makes for produce that is juicier and has the best chance of remaining so until you eat it. This is also true for preserving jams and juices, as not only is the fruit really succulent, the aroma is at its best as well. Therefore, there is less need for adding artificial setting agents or chemical additives, especially for black currant and blueberries. Most of us end up harvesting crops a lot in August, so pick your crop for storage during a waning Moon to preserve the yield longer. (If you can't resist eating your bountiful harvest straight away, however, pick those items during a waxing Moon to savor that flavor and ripeness.)

Harvesting is the most rewarding garden job in the year, whether it is on a grand or modest scale. Searching out potatoes is like claiming buried treasure, while jam-filled cupboards and freezers full of beans are a wonderful sight to behold. To reach this bountiful stage, there are a few basic rules to follow.

Reap your harvest at the best time for ripeness. The exact best time depends on the micro climate of your garden, as the Sun may not reach the individual fruits or vegetables at the same time. Pick ripe specimens first and leave the rest for another day. Keep in mind that some fruits, such as apples and pears, need to be harvested before pests get at them; in that case, store the best fruits and turn any surplus into cider or juice.

While harvesting time for most vegetables is not usually very critical, most fruits are more demanding and only thoroughly enjoyable when perfectly ripened. Melons are improved by chilling first, but many fruits are tastiest warmed by sunshine and eaten straight off the plant. Strawberries should be picked with their stalk on to avoid damage. A few fruits, such as pears, have to be watched until they are nearly ripe, picked a bit early and brought to perfection in a warm, not too dry, dim room. Inspect such fruit daily for ripeness. The best date to pick fruit depends on the cultivar, soil, site, and season but can only be determined by experience. Most fruits store best when picked just under-ripe. They may keep longer picked younger than that, but this is very much at the cost of flavor and sweetness. Fruit will ripen more quickly if extra warmth is supplied, such as that near a wall, window, chimney, vent, or just close to the soil.

Vegetables can usually be picked over a long season and many are easier to store than fruits since they are less prone to rot. Indeed, some vegetables—parsnips, most roots, brassicas, and leeks—are best left in the ground for a light frost to improve fla-

vor; they are protected from a hard frost because they are underground. Some vegetables, such as squashes and the onion family,
require careful drying after harvest. This can be done by laying
out the crops on soil or a bench in the Sun before moving to an
airy, frost-free place until needed. A few vegetable crops, however,
will ripen and go over quickly, so you need to plan your harvest
carefully. Make sure you can use the fresh produce very quickly
and preserve the excess in one efficient swoop.

Potatoes are an easy vegetable, as they offer considerable lee-
way in harvesting time. It is best to dig up your potatoes by the
end of August to avoid losing them to a hard frost. Surplus new
potatoes should be stored buried in a tin of slightly damp sand;
they should last until Christmas. Alternatively, dig up your potatoes and let them dry before putting into a hessian sack and storing in a dark, cool place until needed. Potato harvest is best done
under a Taurus Moon. Root vegetables, such as carrots, also store
well when harvested under Taurus. Avoid harvesting and storing
roots when the Moon is in the water signs of Cancer, Scorpio, or
Pisces (except days when it enters those signs after 3 pm or leaves
before 3 am).

Preserving

When buying plants, choose varieties that are suitable for storing.
Do some research online to find the best varietals for your zone
and preserving method—don't buy a tomato plant that doesn't
can well if canning is your aim.

The simplest way to store produce is to just set it aside in a
cool, dark place, such as a **cellar**. We can maximize the success
of storing our home-grown produce this way if we treat the food
well. To be stored, a crop must be perfect—a blemish or bruise is
where mold starts. There is no point in trying to store anything
that has any real damage; enjoy such produce straight away. Some
fruits keep quite well wrapped in paper or oiled vegetable paper.

Watch out for rodents intent on eating your fruit, or shrivelling fruit due to water loss or a too-hot storage location. Most houses are too hot and garages are too warm, cold, or dry for long-term produce storage. One especially "green" solution is to use an old fridge or freezer as a compact cellar. They are dark, keep the contents at a constant temperature, and protect the food from pests and frost. The lack of ventilation can be solved by cutting small holes in the rubber door or lid seal. When putting crops in such storage, it is usually best to leave them to chill at night in trays or bags, and then load them into the cellar in the morning, when they have dried out but before they are warm again. Similarly, it is helpful to chill and dry off many crops initially by leaving the storage cellar open on cool, dry nights and closing it during the day. Do this for the first week or so when you are storing your produce. Most fruits taste best if you remove them from their cellar a few days before use. Care should be taken not to store early and late varieties together (such as potatoes) where resistance to disease can be lost if decay or mold from the weaker variety infects the other.

For cellar storage, vegetables need to be kept separate from fruits. Shredded newspaper is safer than straw when it gets damp. Always inspect store cupboards often. Be selective and store only what you will use; share the rest with friends and they'll certainly thank you!

One answer for ripe excess vegetables is **freezing**. Freezing may not be the most carbon-efficient method, but it's very easy and keeps beans and peas in prime eating condition. You need to blanch most vegetables before freezing, or they will become tough. Just drop the cleaned and cut vegetables in a big pot of boiling water for a few minutes (find exact times for different vegetables online). Then remove the food pieces and immediately chill them in a pan of ice-cold water. Next dry the pieces on a clean linen towel and freeze them on flat trays. Once frozen, pack the vegetables into bags or boxes and use them throughout the winter months. (If you don't mind a solid block of vegetables, just skip the flat tray step.) Green beans, peas, carrots, and broccoli lend themselves to freezing very well. Nearly any vegetable can be frozen, so be sure to do some quick research on blanching times and freezing methods if you find yourself with excess.

Juicing is the best way to store fruit (other than making your own wine). Canning fruits or making them into preserves is another way to capture the flavor of fruits; however, this is time-consuming and must be done when the Moon is in the third or fourth quarter, preferably in an earth sign, such as Taurus or Capricorn.

You can also **dry fruits**. When picking the fruit, make sure you choose ripe speci-mens. Wash them to remove any debris, cut into pieces, then air dry. Use a food dehydrator, or the oven method: Turn your oven to its lowest setting and spread

2011 © Boles Kubica. Image from BigStockPhoto.com

the cut fruits on a baking tray. Place the tray on the middle shelf for several hours. Leave the oven door open slightly to let mois-ture escape, so the fruit does not cook but becomes dry. Dried fruit can be stored in jars in a cool, dark place.

Jellying and jamming are two ways to preserve fruit in a sug-ary form. The difference is that jelly is made from just fruit juice, while jam contains the seeds, skins, and sometimes fruit pieces. Almost any fruit can be jammed or jellied. Some fruits can be made into jam or jelly on their own, but others require added sugar, lemon juice, and/or pectin. Again, do some quick research to make sure you have everything you need before you start. Remember to sterilize your containers prior to storage. You may either can the jam or jelly, or store it in the freezer (freezer jam). It's worth the work just to taste your own homemade fruit jam! For best results, make and can preserves when the Moon is in the third or fourth quarter in Cancer, Scorpio, or Pisces for nearly the entire day—avoid days when the Moon enters those signs after 3 am or leaves it before 3 pm.

Chutneys, sauces, and pickles are a lot like jams, except they're made from vegetables. You will likely need to add vinegar and salt to them to help the preserving process. Many vegetables (e.g., courgettes, onions, and cucumbers) are combined with fruits (e.g., tomatoes and raisins) to make really tasty chutney. Chutneys can then be used on meats, rices, or crackers. Tomato sauce is one of the most versatile and most popular ways to preserve tomatoes. Recipes abound, so find a basic one and then tweak to your delight—you'll be enjoying the taste of fresh tomatoes long into the winter. Can vegetables and fruit/vegetable combinations with the Moon in the third or fourth quarter, in Cancer, Scorpio, or Taurus for nearly an entire day—avoid days when the Moon enters those signs after 3 am or leaves it before 3 pm.

For Further Reading

Flowerdew, Bob. *Bob Flowerdew's Organic Bible*. London: Kyle Cathie Ltd., 1998.

Paungger, Johanna, and Thomas Poppe. *The Art of Timing*. Saffron Walden, UK: C. W. Daniel Co. Ltd., 2000.

Henry Doubleday Research Association. *Rodale's Illustrated Encyclopedia of Organic Gardening*. Pauline Pears, ed. London: DK Pub., 2002.

About the Author

Janice Sharkey is a keen Moon gardener who loves trying to grow all sorts of fruits but finds the Scottish climate really good for soft fruits like raspberries and black currants. She writes more in the winter and gardens in the summer.

Using Your Moon Sign to Plant Your Garden

by Pam Ciampi

> *Show me your garden and I'll tell who you are.*
>
> —Alfred Austin

The idea of finding out more about yourself by the type of garden you grow is fascinating. While gardening by the Moon can mean many things, one of them is that because your natal Moon rules the principle of growth as well as your deepest personal needs, you can use your natal Moon sign to find the right garden for you.

Fire Moons: Aries, Leo, Sagittarius

If your natal Moon is in a fire sign, your garden will have a definite style, an interesting shape, or lots of color. Because you love excitement and have an impatient nature, you will do best with plants that mature quickly. Routine maintenance is the side of gardening that bores you to tears.

If you have an **Aries Moon**, you have a fiery nature and should make sure your garden contains a lot of brightly colored plants and veggies, especially in the red or orange family. As the first sign of the zodiac, an Aries Moon is impatient to get going and prefers planting time to harvesting time, when their enthusiasm has begun to wane. Not a natural nurturer, an Aries Moon makes a rather sparse garden with large spaces between plantings. But with high marks for being forceful and assertive, the Aries Moon does well with plants that have strong, hot flavors or thorns. This inclination works out best when growing artichokes, garlic, onions, hot chilies, peppers, bougainvillea, or cactus.

You can spot a **Leo Moon** by their extravagant garden and splashy, larger-than-life plantings. Yellow and gold will be the predominant colors with plenty of citrus trees, poppies, lilies, or sunflowers. There will always be at least one exotic plant or special variety, like a rare species of orchid or an heirloom tomato. Because a Leo Moon feels more like a garden king or queen than a garden slave, he or she will often employ someone else to do the heavy lifting. Leo Moon has great pride of ownership and regards their garden as a favored child, so they derive more enjoyment from showing off its delights than from actually getting their hands in the dirt.

Because you value freedom above structure, anyone with a **Sagittarius Moon** will plant a garden that has a wild, overgrown feeling about it. The natural, unplanted look is also handy for keeping maintenance down to a minimum. If you were born under a Sagittarius Moon, order is not your first priority; in fact, you actually cringe at the thought of cutting back or pruning. You much prefer to go with the school of "too much is not enough" by planting as many different varieties as you can get your hands on. A Sagittarius Moon gravitates toward fields of wildflowers, native shrubs and trees, and the color purple—eggplants, irises, or morning glory vines. You can easily recognize the garden of a Sagittarius Moon because the plants will run together with no spaces in between. Some people might see this as just a big mess, but you'll enjoy the wildness of your Sagittarius garden.

Earth Moons: Taurus, Virgo, Capricorn

If your natal Moon is in one of the earth signs, your garden will be well organized and spotlessly maintained. Earth Moons make fertile gardeners who value growth as well as order. Your goal will be to create a fruitful and productive garden space based on sound gardening principles.

Lucky you, if you were born under a **Taurus Moon,** because this placement is famous for being the green goddess of the garden. Born with a magic green wand, your Taurus Moon has the ability to make any garden grow in abundance and with the profusion of the English cottage garden. Although Venus-ruled Taurus makes beauty a number-one concern, the practical side of Taurus is also expert at producing a lush vegetable garden. Because a Taurus Moon loves getting their hands in the dirt and considers routine maintenance a joy not to be missed, your garden will be devoid of weeds and perfectly groomed.

Like the nursery rhyme, "Mary, Mary quite contrary, how does your garden grow?" **Virgo Moons** want to keep everything in their garden "all in a row." This tendency toward perfection leads to a well-organized garden with neat and tidy plants. As a semi-fertile sign, Virgo considers pruning the most important part of gardening. Since one of the ways a Virgo Moon relaxes is by cooking, their interest is mainly in food-bearing vegetables and fruits. Together with Aquarius, Virgo is one of the two Moon signs that are the most interested in "going green." A Virgo Moon probably invented the use of pesticide-free products and the term "organic gardening." If you have a Virgo Moon, the only thing you need to remember is that the perfect garden isn't created in one season.

Because Capricorn is traditionally known as a disadvantaged position for the Moon, having a **Capricorn Moon** is a bit like being the bad fairy in the garden. Because a Capricorn Moon is more interested in structure and managing than in nurturing and tending, this Moon is commonly known as The Black Thumb. Don't let that stop you! If you were born under a Capricorn Moon, your talent in the world of gardens is best used in creating hardscapes or "dry" gardens, such as the Japanese Zen garden using low-water plants, sand, stone, and rocks. And you can bet it was a Capricorn Moon that inspired the "cash for grass" incentive that encourages homeowners to turn their lawns into drought-resistant gardens.

Air Moons: Gemini, Libra, Aquarius

If your Moon is in one of the air signs, you are one of the social/speculative gardeners. With an air Moon sign, ideas or theories about plants and gardening will always trump more practical considerations like time, space, and money. But because they are so social, air Moons throw the best garden parties.

As the most diverse sign of the zodiac, the **Gemini Moon** garden stands out by its variety of different species, colors, shapes, and sizes. As varied as a wildflower bouquet, the one thing you will never see in a Gemini Moon garden is a massing of one kind of plant or flower. What the Gemini Moon lacks in focus, it makes up for with its flair and willingness to welcome all different types of plantings to the garden. As an air sign, the Gemini Moon will invariably bring wind chimes and mobiles into the garden scene.

Whether it's flowers or veggies, you will know a **Libra Moon** by the harmony and beauty of their garden. If you were born under a Libra Moon, you will create a garden where everything works together in a perfect balance of height, color, and purpose. Because Libras consider relationships to be the most important part of life, someone with a Libra Moon must have invented the concept of companion planting—the system of using certain plants that can assist one another to reduce pests and promote growth.

Although an **Aquarius Moon** is not very interested in the actual practice of getting their hands dirty, they are very willing to talk about gardening. As the sign of the future, Aquarian Moons are obsessed with ecology and "going green." Topics that might come up are sustainable gardening, biodiversity, indigenous plants, gray-water recycling, and wind generators. If you were born under an Aquarian Moon, you might not be a hands-on type of gardener, but you are a master at thinking up and introducing new garden theories—all you need is a nice earth Moon person to put them into practice.

Water Moons: Cancer, Scorpio, Pisces

If your natal Moon is in one of the water signs, you are an intuitive type of gardener who is naturally tuned in to the rhythms of the garden. Because all life begins in water, an individual with a water Moon knows what makes the garden grow without having to read a gardening book. A water Moon should always include some kind of water feature (pond, fountain, waterfall, or pool) as part of their garden.

A **Cancer Moon** is the most nurturing Moon type in the zodiac, so if you were born under this Moon sign, you get the garden goddess award for knowing how to make a garden that is lush, fruitful, and abundant. A Cancer Moon knows intuitively when a plant is hungry (fertilize), when it's thirsty (water), when the fruit is ready to be picked, and when the seeds are ready to be sown. If a Cancer Moon has a fault, it is that it doesn't know when to stop tending the garden and leave it to its own devices.

Because Scorpio is a sign dedicated to crisis and transformation, a **Scorpio Moon** is at their best when renovating garden areas that have fallen into disrepair. Your idea of fun is taking a dried-up lot filled with trash and turning it into tropical paradise. Scorpio Moons can't stay away from the dark side, which is why soil preparation, composting, and worm bins are also Scorpio Moon specialties. Since you are addicted to an emergency type of gardening, an stable, ordinary garden might be a challenge. If you try to fix something that isn't broken, you could cause more harm than good.

As the most romantic water sign, a **Pisces Moon** cherishes the perfume of a Moonlit stroll in a garden of night-blooming jasmine or the echo of water falling into a fountain. If you were born under the sign of The Fish, water will be an essential part of your garden. A koi pond, a fountain, a waterfall, or even a wooden barrel filled with lotus flowers can fulfill this need. Because Pisces is associated with different forms of escapism, this Moon sign is also well suited for growing medical marijuana.

. . . .

At the end of our zodiacal journey through the garden, we have discovered that not only is "the garden a mirror of the heart" (Francis Bacon), but also that there is a right type of garden for everyone. All you have to do is use your Moon sign to find out the right one for you.

About the Author

Pam Ciampi is a professional astrologer (C.A.P. ISAR) who began her astrological studies in 1975. Over the years, Pam has read charts for thousands of people all over the world. She teaches and reads horoscopes in San Diego, California. Her website is www.pciampi-astrology.com.

The Power of
the Progressed Moon

by Amy Herring

Your astrological natal chart is a map of the sky with each planet forever frozen in time at the moment of your birth. But of course, the planets continue to move, and their movement through the sky and around your chart will reveal how you are changing and developing throughout your life. A planet's motion across the sky is called a *transit*. If someone were to look up on the night of your birth, they'd see your natal Moon; if they looked up at the sky two weeks later, the Moon would have already moved halfway across the same sky.

The *progressed planets* cannot be tracked by looking up at the sky, but are symbolic and personal cycles. Progressed planets represent our evolutionary growth over time, and they move more slowly than their transiting counterparts. Both transiting and progressed planets illustrate how you grow and change in different, complementary ways.

We can think of the natal planets as seeds that have been planted. The transits we experience to our natal planets might represent the changes in the environment, such as the sunshine or the rain, and perhaps the bugs in the soil. The progressed planets would represent the more subtle, slow changes in the environment, such as the nature of the soil itself. Progressed planets represent developments that seem to come from within as we interact with the "weather" in our lives and mature with experience.

To find the location of a progressed planet, the calculation of a "day for a year" is used, which means a day's actual movement of any *transiting* planet represents a year's *progressed* planet movement. For example, the transiting Moon moves about 12–14 degrees in a day, or about half a sign, as it transits across the sky. Therefore, the *progressed* Moon moves 12–14 degrees, or half of a sign, in a *year*.

To find your personal progressed Moon, simply look at the location of your natal Moon. This is your starting point. Then consider your current age. If you are 22 *years* old, then you'll want to figure out how far the Moon moved 22 *days* after your birth. Consult an old ephemerides table, or one of the several websites and computer programs that can calculate this for you. You'll need your birth date, birth time, and place of birth. Try www.astro.com > Free Horoscopes > Extended Chart Selection for a basic progressed chart, or www.llewellyn.com > Astrology > Reports & Charts to purchase more detailed charts and analyses.

The Meaning of the Progressed Moon

The natal Moon represents your emotional needs and how you can best feel happy, secure, nurtured, and comfortable. The progressed Moon represents how those emotional needs are slowly evolving as you go through life and what additional or different needs you may develop as your progressed Moon moves through a different sign or house than your natal Moon. What makes you feel happy, secure, nurtured, and comfortable today as opposed to two years ago? Ten years ago? The progressed Moon can supply much of the answer to that question.

For example, let's say you have a Capricorn Moon but are experiencing a Gemini Moon progression. This means you have the nature of a natal Capricorn Moon: someone who appreciates a sense of direction and accomplishment, likes to have clear goals, and enjoys solitude. But now you are wearing a Gemini Moon "suit," so you might find yourself more naturally inclined toward Gemini Moon impulses: trying a myriad of different pursuits without just sticking to one, changing your mind more often about what you want as different things catch your eye (much to your own Capricorn Moon chagrin!), and perhaps even feeling more socially inclined than previously.

Because outer life reflects inner life and vice versa, it may not just be that you desire different experiences, but that life brings about more opportunities and situations in which you are more naturally able to express the impulses your progressed Moon sign has to offer. For instance, in our Capricorn Moon with a Gemini progressed Moon example, not only will these new yearnings be coming from inside you, but you might find that events in your life reflect the Gemini experience—you recieve more invitations to come out and socialize, new people coming into your life at a rapid rate, or classes you've been wanting to take present themselves.

The sign and house of your progressed Moon represent the emotional experiences and style you are yearning for at this time in your life. Trying on all the Moon signs as your progressed Moon moves through them will help you integrate your changing emotional needs into your existing emotional bottom line.

Progressed Moon Aspects

As the progressed Moon makes its way around your chart, it will form angles—called aspects—with all of your natal planets as it moves through your houses. When your progressed Moon moves over your natal Mercury (a conjunction), for example, you may find that you are more talkative in general, or that you are having some deep epiphanies, or that you are hungrier for new ideas and feeding your mind, or any other number of things that would encompass a Mercurial experience. The aspects your progressed Moon makes to the rest of your chart are a critical part of understanding how your evolving emotional needs are making themselves felt in your life as represented by your natal chart.

Equally important is the contact your progressed Moon makes with your own natal Moon. The progressed Moon doesn't replace or override your natal Moon; it's more like wearing clothing—trying something new on over your own skin. Sometimes that experience is comfortable and a natural extension of ourselves, as when the aspect is favorable: sextile (60 degrees) or trine (120 degrees). But sometimes that experience draws us far out of our comfort zone, as when the aspect is unfavorable: square (90 degrees), quincunx (150 degrees), or opposition (180 degrees). A conjunct aspect (0 degrees) occurs when the two bodies concerned cross each other, or occupy the same spot in your chart. Depending on the planets, this could be favorable or unfavorable; with the natal Moon and progressed Moon, a conjunction represents a progressed lunar return (see below). The aspects your progressed Moon is making to your natal Moon can give you the most insight about how far you have to stretch yourself to learn the emotional lessons of that life phase.

Perhaps you are in an Aries progressed-Moon period and are experiencing emotional yearnings for being direct and initiatory, for standing your ground and going after what you want. Circumstances that arise in your life may prompt you to action or the need to defend yourself more often than normal. How comfortable you are with these moods and attitudes will be dependent on your typical emotional temperament—your natal Moon. If you have a natal Gemini Moon, this is roughly a sextile aspect, which is positive. This stretch might not be too incapacitating; perhaps you'll just have to add a little extra oomph to the way you express your feelings. If your natal Moon is in Libra, however, this period may be greatly uncomfortable, as Aries and Libra form a unfavorable opposition aspect. The feistiness and forthrightness of Aries is exactly opposed to what you are most comfortable with as a Libra Moon, which is peacefulness, harmony, and fairness.

It is especially helpful to know where your progressed Moon is when you are experiencing a difficult aspect, so that you don't think you've gone crazy, but merely have to step outside of your comfort zone for a while. These passages that stretch us help us to become more well-rounded in our emotional style.

The Progressed Lunar Return

It takes about 28 days for the transiting Moon to make it around the zodiac, so it completes its transit cycle monthly. That means you have a lunar return every 28 days. Which means you have a *progressed* lunar return every 28 years, when your progressed Moon returns to the position it occupied at the time of your birth.

The return of your progressed Moon only occurs twice, maybe three times in a lifetime, and it can be a very significant internal event. The progressed lunar returns at roughly age 28, 56, and 84. At these times, we are invited to take emotional inventory.

Are we where we want to be in life? Not just from a financial or goal-oriented standpoint, but are we happy? Is our life aimed in a direction that appears to be nurturing to who we are on the inside? A progressed lunar return is a time to remember ourselves and make course corrections if need be, so that we can continue on a fulfilling life path.

. . . .

While all progressed planets can be useful in one way or another, most of them move so slowly that they don't bring up issues of change in your life very often, instead forming the basic backdrop of your evolution. But your progressed Moon is constantly in motion, just as you are constantly developing. It moves slowly enough that it's not as simple as a passing mood swing, but quickly enough that it's always doing something meaningful: it's just entered a sign or a house, it's just *left* a sign or a house, it's just made a conjunction to a planet, or is about to square another, etc. Therefore, your progressed Moon is the perfect emotional barometer for what's going on in your inner life at any given time. When you need to get to the heart of any issue, the natal and progressed Moon can tell you the most about what you *want* in your life.

About the Author

A graduate of Steven Forrest's Evolutionary Astrology program, Amy Herring has been a professional astrologer for 15 years. Her book, Astrology of the Moon, *covers the natal and progressed Moon relationship in detail and is available from Llewellyn. Visit her website http://heavenlytruth.com for personal reading options and study resources.*

A Man and His Moon
in the Kitchen

by Jessica Shepherd

I realize I am lucky to have a husband who loves to cook. After all, the stereotypical man has not always been this comfortable with his feminine side—his Moon. A man's Moon was once simply a projection of his other half, hidden beneath the dishes, diapers, and dinner preparations. He didn't identify with his Moon side because he didn't have to—she was embodied by his real-life domestic partner. Then, in the late Sixties and early Seventies, Uranus (the great awakener) and Pluto (planet of transformation) shifted into Libra, the zodiacal sign of equality and relationship. At first this wreaked havoc in relationships, spiking divorce rates and circulating the ill-conceived idea of "free love." Eventually, however, the slow rebalancing of gender roles in marriage and social institutions began. I was born in 1973, the year of the Roe v. Wade ruling. I thoroughly belong to this somewhat-confused generation.

Women went to work on a large scale in the late twentieth century, and with less time to cook, men entered the kitchen. As Neil Armstrong once said of our trip to the Moon, "One small step for a man; one giant leap for mankind." This was true in more ways than one. Men finally started exploring their inner lunar nature. Would he enjoy being a sous or dessert chef? Does he excel at creating ambience, writing gourmet menus, or organizing the meals for the week? When cooking, is he a conserver, more interested in what has worked in the past, or an innovator, open to discovering the common parsnip anew? Into the kitchen men went, developing expertise along the way.

It is oodles of fun for women to have a partner in the kitchen. Since cooking is a domestic, nurturing type of activity, a man's Moon sign can give you great insight into what kind of cook he'll be in the kitchen. My husband's Moon is in chatty, ambidextrous, sure-footed Gemini and I've got to hand it to him: he's inventive, always in the kitchen at dinnertime, and never at a loss for good conversation. There's food for thought and spontaneous surprises (like chocolate chili). When we're both tired of cooking, even I can appreciate falling back on an occasional quesadilla (Gemini Moon loves finger foods), temporarily abandoning the dirty dishes. It's a harmonious relationship … until I have to rally him to help clean up. Some gender differences may take centuries to change.

More than just fun, being with a man who can flex his domestic chops borders on erotic for some women. Shopping together, planning a menu, chopping vegetables, making a good meal—it's a wonderful way to spend time together, and it builds intimacy.

For my husband and I, cooking together is intimate foreplay for the main course of a lifetime: love.

Aries Moon Men: Aries is the archetype of leadership and the warrior, so help the evening along by admiring his deftness, speed, and control in the kitchen. Aries Moon men make great sous chefs and are excellent little choppers; he may enjoy the knives and cool kitchen utensils more than the cooking itself. Give him a plate of vegetables for the soup stock and he'll go to town. Despite his demonstrable take-charge attitude, he's sensitive—don't upset his confidence by threatening replacement with a food processor. Even if you helped, make him feel like he's made the best meal ever—trust me, he'll like the power.

Taurus Moon Men: Two categories here: "I'm relaxing, watching television, and will gladly eat what you set before me," or "I've prepared the most delectable gourmet cheese macaroni that smells like stinky feet—just for you, sweetie!" Of the loafers and the cookers, both Taurus husbands are eaters—he just loves, loves, loves good food and can have a hard time stopping himself from overeating. I knew a Taurus Moon man who was a far better cook than I, and being appreciated for his food was truly a source of self-esteem for him. A Taurus Moon man who enjoys cooking? I was happy to boost his morale one bite at a time.

Gemini Moon Men: At a couples dinner party, I asked my friend how she liked dinner. "Great. But did you notice how my Gemini Moon man didn't stop talking the whole time?" Oh, but didn't she notice how my husband, also a Gemini Moon, had his own show going? Clever, quick, creative, and downright ingenious when he wants to be, his main challenge in the kitchen is focus. He's got to stop talking long enough to put his beautiful hands to work, which puts a whole new spin on the phrase "eat your words." After hours of interesting conversational tidbits and four food projects going on in four different corners of the kitchen, I've tried and discovered: words can't fill a hungry belly.

Cancer Moon Men: Romantic, nurturing, and sensitive, these men know the way to a woman's heart is through hearth and home. He wants to make sure you're comfortable and cared for, so he feeds you. He loves to feed and provide for you. It makes him feel needed, and in turn, loved by you. He has an intuitive-spiritual-physical understanding about how spices and tastes can affect one's mood and happiness, elevating food from physical to spiritual nourishment. He's so tuned in to what you need that sometimes he wakes up having dreamt about what he wants to make you for dinner tonight. Ladies, you are so lucky to have this man in your life!

Leo Moon Men: *Gour-mens* is a term I've given Leo husbands: gourmet afficianados with a taste for the finest. Food is an event with a capital *E*, social and best shared at a five-star restaurant, over a five-course meal—which may be a problem if you don't like to make a fuss over your meals. These men want every meal to be a party/event, but when life doesn't oblige, superior organic food tides him over til the Friday night festivities. These men won't suffer imitations gladly; the occasional food snob may intimidate. With him, enjoy the fanfare of fine dining.

Virgo Moon Men: Efficient and organized, don't get in his way when he's cooking for you. There's an OOO (order of operations) in his head, and when you try to take a shortcut, he looks at you with a puzzled hurt-puppy look, like "why would you do that?" If you're cooking, assign him a challenging task you have no aptitude or patience for. He not only likes to feel useful, he enjoys mastery. Fair is forewarned: the servants of the zodiac, a Virgo Moon man can bite off more than he can chew. He might run the whole meal, soup to sweets, later expressing how he wishes you would've helped. Virgo husbands often enjoy doing dishes, which is weird, in a very good way.

Libra Moon Men: If you're in the kitchen, so is he. He wants to be with you. No, I didn't say he wants to cook, I said he

2011 ©. Elke Dennis Image from BigStockPhoto.com

wants to be with you. But this has nothing to do with food, this has to do with "us" time. *How can our relationship stay healthy if we don't do everything together? What, you want me to cook a pork chop? I'd rather stir a pot while falling gaga in love with you over boiling-over borscht.* The Libra Moon husband has a skill for creating romantic ambience. He loves to share. (Read: he will eat off your plate, so if you're food-territorial, be warned.) His speciality is togetherness, with a little lovin' on the side.

Scorpio Moon Men: Every activity holds potential for sexual intimacy with Scorpio Moon husband, most of all the sensual experience of cooking together. You may get sidetracked (wink, wink) in the kitchen. I'm not trying to stereotype your Scorpio man, but he is a Scorpio, and he is a man. There are certain things one can expect from him: He's an attentive eater. He's honest and sincere. He'll eat your food and say it's the best thing he's ever tasted, and he'll mean it. But you really want him to cook? Sure, he could do that. But why?

Sagittarius Moon Men: Adventurous eaters, these husbands are up for trying new foods. When it comes down to it, he's not really that picky. The kitchen is not his favorite place to be, which often translates as, "Whatever, if it's edible, I'll eat it." The trick is taking his humongous appetite for accumulating inner experiences into the kitchen with exotic cuisine and trips to special food destinations. The Archer is a perfect candidate for take-out meals—Thai, Mexican, Chinese, sushi. Due to his love of variety, these are the classic I-ate-the-leftovers-for-breakfast guys.

Capricorn Moon Men: Responsible, hard-working, and self-sufficient, the Capricorn husband likes to delegate roles and create procedures and timetables in the kitchen, because he finds order and structure nurturing. He has a set of internalized rules about how things should be done, giving you the opportunity to help him loosen up. If he's had to fend for himself (as many a Capricorn Moon has) he's likely picked up some mad skills, in which case he could be a SuperMoon, a domestic variation of SuperMan. He cuts a solitary figure, but deep down, he appreciates being attentively cared for, fed, and nurtured—a bonus if you enjoy playing mom.

Aquarius Moon Men: Aquarius Moons are the walking oxymorons: he can be very very conservative, or very very experimental. The latter guys aren't hard to figure out because he just keeps changing his diet with the times (raw food, macrobiotic diet, fruitarianism, etc.), which means weird food in the refrigerator. These originators are food techies, giving you a new way to peel an old potato (one Aquarius Moon man I know has developed a strangely efficient way of carving a cauliflower). Is he still eating the foods his mom used to make? The conservers could take a cue from the innovators. This Moon sign needs to break from the past, including unhealthy food conditioning.

Pisces Moon Men: There's no place like "om" for Pisces husbands. Eating and cooking together is about creating a shared atmosphere of timeless unity and love. These connoisseurs of consciousness will put on reggae music, pour the wine, light candles, and romance the mood to an ecstatic bliss state. It won't matter to you that the rice was a little burnt (because he lost all sense of time). These husbands are a bit disorganized in the kitchen and sometimes annoyingly messy to clean up after. But with him, you can taste the love … and that's why you married him.

About the Author
Jessica Shepherd is a counselor, astrologer, and teacher. Jessica has been exploring astrology since 1992, studying with Steven Forrest, Karen Hamaker Zondag, Stephanie Austin, and others. Jessica holds a bachelor's degree in business and art. Her writing has appeared in **Pregnancy & Newborn** *(USA),* **Well Being Astrology** *(Australia), and* **Constellation** *(USA) magazines, and online at Astrology.com, Sasstrology, Astrocenter, Constellation, and her own website blog, Moonkissd. She is the author of* **A Love Alchemist's Notebook: Magical Secrets for Drawing Your True Love into Your Life** *(Llewellyn, 2010). Jessica lives in Fairfax, CA, with her husband and stepdaughters in a little pink house. Her website is www .Moonkissd.com.*

Over the Moon: Achieving and Maintaining Healthy Weight

by Dallas Jennifer Cobb

Take a look at any magazine rack and you will confirm that we North Americans have an obsession with our weight and body image. Do you marvel at the shapely models and wonder how to look that way? Have you tried different diets only to drop down, then yo-yo up, eventually putting on even more weight?

I have tried many different diets, most with the yo-yo effect. But then I discovered that I could tap into the natural energies of the Moon to help me create needed change. I was able to achieve and maintain (for more than seven years now) what I consider to be a healthy weight for my body. Along the way, I have learned a lot about healthy hydration, nutrition, exercise, and attitude. And, best of all, I feel well and happy!

The information in this article can help you do it too. By using lunar energies to support your needed changes in diet, hydration, exercise habits, and attitude, you can put yourself "over the Moon," achieving your goals for weight loss and maintenance and building sustainable wellness.

What Is Wellness?

Because our health is an ever-changing and dynamic process, I like to think of "wellness" as the overall goal for lifestyle management. Sure, you want to lose weight, look toned and trim, and get strong, but to be "well" is the greater goal, one that encompasses all of these other factors.

Wellness is the active striving for improved quality of life through the gradual shifting of our behaviors and attitudes. Wellness can include improving nutrition, lessening stress levels, increasing physical activity, and improving feelings of contentment. Wellness also includes finding a balance within by caring for mind, body, and spirit and adopting ongoing physical, mental, and spiritual practices that maintain our well-being.

Wellness and Healthy Weight

A "well" human being has low levels of fat or adipose tissue deposited under the skin and surrounding the vital organs, and a high level of fat-free tissue such as muscle, bone, blood, and organs.

Wellness and healthy weight do not occur suddenly; they are the results of progress along the wellness continuum. Decide where you are on the continuum: are you ill, overweight, and sedentary? Do you have moderate health, are somewhat active, and a little overweight? Or are you well, active, and fit?

Take a moment and make note of where you are on the spectrum, then set a goal to move along the spectrum further toward optimum wellness. Set a small goal, a realistic goal, one that represents a step on the wellness continuum but not the final goal.

Wellness is about progress, not an all-or-nothing change.

Make your goal finite. Change the general "I will eat better," to the specific "I will eat more cleanly, adding one more fruit and/ or vegetable to my diet each day." Maybe your goal is to lessen the stress on your body. Make that goal finite through a specific action, such as reducing your consumption of addictive substances like alcohol, tobacco, soft drinks, or sugar, or making sure that you regularly sleep, rest, and recharge. If your goal is to increase the amount of exercise you get, make a finite plan that will work with your schedule. Maybe you can vow to walk for fifteen minutes each day at lunch. This will help you to get out and get active and help you to feel more at home in your body.

The Benefits of Activity

An active lifestyle will reduce your risk of dying prematurely by lowering the incidence of cardiovascular disease, obesity, high blood pressure, dangerous cholesterol levels, diabetes, and many other ailments.

Increased levels of activity can help you to favorably change your body composition, which also reduces the risk of cardiovascular disease, diabetes, and obesity. Increased activity helps to build muscles, improving physical appearance and tone. And, with increased muscle mass, your body will actually burn more calories at rest and during exercise to sustain those muscles, further reducing fat and increasing your resting metabolic rate.

Physical activity can make you look better, and that can make you feel better, raising self-esteem and feelings of well-being, improving mental and emotional health and your outlook on life.

An Active Lifestyle

An active lifestyle for achieving healthy weight is one that includes cardiovascular exercise, muscular conditioning, and flexibility training.

Cardiovascular activities primarily work your heart and lungs. They can be moderate-intensity or high-intensity activities, such as power walking, running, cycling, and swimming. Muscular conditioning is activity that builds muscle size and strength, such as weight lifting and resistance training. Flexibility training includes any activity that lengthens and realigns muscles after they are used. Flexibility training includes stretching, but is also a vital part of Pilates and yoga practices.

An active lifestyle can be as simple as taking a regular morning power walk followed by some weight resistance moves on the mat and a good stretch, or it could be gym-based and include a cardio workout on the treadmill, followed by a set of weight-lifting exercises, and a yoga class. Most importantly, an active lifestyle is one that fits your lifestyle—something you can commit to doing regularly.

While I love to go the my local YMCA and "run" on the elliptical trainer, use their machines for resistance training, and stretch it out in the luxurious steam room after, I also have a bare-bones routine that I can do anywhere. It includes thirty minutes of fast power walking, followed by a resistance set using my own body weight (pushups, squats, and lunges are three easy examples). I often use a resistance band or Theraband to work the muscles of my arms and shoulders. I follow my workout with a generous stretch that lengthens each of the muscles I have strengthened, returning them to optimum condition and preventing injury. The U.S. Department of Health and Human Services has established guidelines that adults should get at least 2 ½ hours of moderate-intensity exercise, or 1 ¼ hours of vigorous excercise, per week.

But enough talk about wellness and the benefits of activity—I don't need to convince you! What you really want to know is how to achieve and maintain a healthy weight, since that is your goal. With that in mind, let's see how the energy of the Moon can help you to achieve it.

Lunar Energies

As the celestial body closest to Earth, the Moon has a huge magnetic affect on water, specifically tides. Because the human body is almost two-thirds water, the Moon has a huge effect on us, too. Paying attention to lunar energy and cycles can help us to further focus our own energy, engaging it in order to achieve the goal of moving along the wellness continuum.

As the Moon moves through its different stages in a complete cycle, it possesses different energies. These energies can help you to set goals, eliminate bad habits, form healthy habits, and cultivate resolve. With some knowledge of lunar cycles and their specific energies, you can enjoy the support of the lunar energy when you make lifestyle changes that positively affect wellness.

The Lunar Cycle

While the Moon waxes and wanes in an endless cycle, we need to choose a point in the lunar cycle to start our gradual changes. So let's start at the time of a Full Moon.

Full Moon

When the Moon is full, it exerts a gravitational pull that affects water. Humans are affected by the increased internal pressure that is caused by gravitational pull on bodily fluids. Our internal water is literally pulled by the power of the Moon.

Pay attention to your body and how the Full Moon affects it. Notice how full and round you feel. And it's not just the physical feeling of your body that you need to be aware of, but how you feel emotionally or psychologically. The Full Moon often produces low self-esteem, poor mental health, and feelings of inadequacy.

With such powerful forces at work, how can we use the energy to propel positive change? Accept that the Moon's energy is influencing you and harness that energy to achieve your goal. During the Full Moon, practice proper hydration. Drink lots of water and eat high water-content foods. It is recommended that the average adult drink eight large glasses of water each day. Other fluids can count toward the desired amount, but try to keep your choices healthy: herbal tea, unsweetened juice, decaf coffee, etc.

Foods with a high water content are those that are juicy. They benefit you by providing nutrition that is easy to assimilate, as well as added hydration. The highest water-content foods are fruits, vegetables, and leafy greens, so these should constitute a large portion of your diet.

During the Full Moon, stay fluid physically and emotionally. Take time for solitary, reverential exercise. Enjoy a good stretch, take a yoga or Pilates class, or go for an evening stroll under the light of the Moon.

Waning Moon

During the waning Moon cycle, when the Moon is shrinking in size, focus on decrease—decrease the size of portions that you consume or the amount you eat overall. Psychologically, decrease your resistance to change by affirming what you want, stating it in the positive. *I am slim, fit, and healthy. I adapt easily and change.*

The waning Moon is also a time for focusing on your intent to decrease your physical size, let go, and detoxify. Your body, responding to the reduction in lunar gravitational pull, is more likely to respond now to gentle changes in diet and exercise.

Continue to stay well hydrated, drinking cleansing herbal and green teas. Continue to eat plenty of fruits and vegetables, supporting your body in the detoxification process. If you are up to it, a vigorous cardiovascular workout that makes you sweat will also help release toxins.

The waning Moon is the time to clean out your fridge, freezer, and cupboards. Use your focused intention and get rid of anything that is fattening, tempting, or downright bad for you. Clearing your kitchen of "dangerous" foods creates an atmosphere in which it is easier to do right, because you have no option of doing wrong. If you want a snack and all the cookies have been replaced by dried apple slices, you'll eat the apple slices.

Dark Moon

Now it's time to tap into the dark Moon energy of banishing and binding. Banish "bad" foods from your diet. Make a list of what you will no longer eat or drink and stick to it. My list includes anything deep fried, so-called fast food, carbonated drinks of any kind, empty carbohydrates, and candy. These are non-negotiable. I no longer have a choice to eat them or not—I have banished them. Make your own list of banished foods, adding one more during each dark Moon phase. Revisit your list each dark Moon to reaffirm that these foods are not options for you. After a while, you may find that the items on the list don't even sound appetizing to you.

Next, bind yourself to clean eating. Reward yourself with a feast of all of your favorite fruits—gorge on mango, papaya, watermelon, and cherries. Or maybe you want bind yourself to a structured exercise program. Sign up for a series of spin classes, join a walking club, or ask a friend to be your exercise buddy. Having an emotional bond with a person can help you get up and out to exercise, even on days when you don't really want to. The important part here is to make some sort of commitment to bind you to the new activity. You can't just skip a class you've already paid for, or bail on a friend who expects you for an exercise and gab session.

Emotionally, the dark Moon is a time of clarification. Without the gravitational effect of the Full Moon acting on us, we have a clear and calm sense of ourselves. Be clear. Write down a list of your successes to date, and affirm yourself. You have learned to hydrate, cleared your kitchen of dangerous food, begun to feed yourself healthy and satisfying foods, and undergone a bit of a detox. Good work.

And because the coming New Moon cycle is the best time to make resolutions and set up new routines, set some finite goals that you will "grow" as the Moon grows.

New Moon

What resolutions and routines do you want to consciously grow with the light of the Moon? Why not draw up an eating plan that works for you. Write it down, and then do the grocery shopping to support it. Make lists of all your favorite fruits and vegetables, and give yourself permission to buy them all. The waxing Moon is a time of increase, so focus on increasing your consumption of healthy foods, not on limiting your consumption of bad ones. Your kitchen should be clear of "dangerous" foods, now fill it with pleasurable foods, things you will enjoy eating that are good for you.

A whole-foods diet that combines a variety of foods in their natural state is the diet I usually recommend. Notice that I am not saying "be a vegetarian," or "don't eat this or that." Instead, I believe that we need to eat foods as close to their natural state as is possible. That means fresh fruits rather than canned and sweetened ones, steamed vegetables rather than French fries, and grilled fish instead of processed luncheon meats.

Also use the lunar energy of growth to increase the amounts and kinds of exercise you do. Try one new class, weight machine, or biking or running path. Try exercising on a different day or at a different time than you normally do. You may end up sticking with what you know, but your New Moon experiment might lead you to a favorite new routine. Like the light of the Moon, your discipline is growing, along with your resolve.

Full Cycle

When the Moon reaches full again, use the time of profound emotional energy to take stock of where you are, looking within for guidance rather than following outside influences. Notice what has worked well, and affirm it. Pay attention to what may have slipped, and decide whether it is something you want to focus on more closely in the next lunar cycle. Take time alone to acknowledge the accomplishments achieved throughout the lunar cycle, and let the Full Moon illuminate your successes. Celebrate what has prospered and is now abundant in your life.

While you privately celebrate the positive changes you have made, don't forget to set new goals for the next lunar cycle to keep you moving along the wellness continuum.

. . . .

Fortified with the knowledge of how lunar energies can support you in your endeavour to achieve and maintain a healthy weight, you can now get to work, moving one step at a time along the wellness continuum. By making gradual and lasting changes to nutrition, hydration, activity level, and attitude, you will not only achieve your desired weight, you will also lower your body fat ratio; reduce your risk of cardiovascular disease, diabetes, and hypertension; and radically change not just your body, but your life.

While there are no quick-fix solutions, with practice and commitment, you can become healthier, more fit, and happier. With each progressive cycle of the Moon, adjust, realign, and rededicate yourself to your goal, and soon you will find that you are well, healthy, and happy—so much so that you will be "over the Moon" with happiness.

About the Author

Life is what you make it, and **Dallas Jennifer Cobb** *has made a magical life in a waterfront village on the shores of great Lake Ontario. Forever scheming novel ways to pay the bills, she practices manifestation magic and wildlands witchcraft. She currently teaches Pilates, works in a library, and writes to finance long hours spent following her hearts' desire—time with family, in nature, and on the water. Contact her at jennifer.cobb@live.com.*

The Moon Deities of Ancient Mesoamerica

by Bruce Scofield

In ancient Mesoamerica—the land of the Maya, Toltecs, and Aztecs among others—many stories were told about the Moon and how it came to be. Some of these survive in oral tradition; others we know of through writings and inscriptions. Perhaps the most important source of ancient Mesoamerican mythology is the *Popol Vuh*, a document that contains the Maya account of creation. It was written down shortly after the Spanish Conquest but lay unread in personal collections or libraries until the twentieth century, when it was translated into English. In it is the mythic story of the Maya hero twins who defeat the lords of the underworld in a ritual ballgame. Their victory, however, was achieved by their own conquest of death itself through self-sacrifice and self-resurrection. The *Popol Vuh* recounts that after their triumph over death, they rose into the sky and became the Sun and Moon.

The *Popol Vuh* is the book of the Maya; other culture areas in Mesoamerica had somewhat different myths about the origin of the Moon that are found scattered about in fragments of documents. One common theme to all of Mesoamerica is the notion of the rabbit in the Moon. The surface of the Moon is not monotone—it has dark and light areas, some full of craters and others called *mare* that are relatively smooth. The contrasts between these features don't seem to take any particular shape, but in the West, the tradition is that one can see the face of a person—the "man in the Moon." But, like a Rorschach diagram, one can see other things as well and for the Mesoamericans, there's a rabbit in the Moon. It's possible that the idea of a rabbit originally came from Asia. Long ago, Buddhist myths included a rabbit in the Moon and the idea was adopted by the Chinese, who saw a "jade rabbit." This perception could have crossed over to Mesoamerica by land or sea in very ancient times, though there is no concrete evidence for it. The Aztecs preserved a story about the origin of the rabbit in the Moon as well. The folk story tells of the gods gathering and teasing the Moon. One flung a rabbit in its face and the impact bruised the face of the Moon, creating the dark areas, the mare.

Maya Moon Deity—Ixchel

Like the cultures of the ancient Mediterranean, the Maya saw the Moon as the embodiment of a goddess. In Classic Maya times (AD 300–800), the Maya Moon goddess was symbolized by the waxing crescent, represented as a fertile young woman, and was associated with childbirth. The waning Moon was connected with the grandmother—a symbol of waning fertility. It is possible that this older Moon goddess was also the same as Ixchel (ee-shell), "Lady Rainbow," a goddess with jaguar characteristics associated with healing and midwifery, as well as many things strictly feminine. Clearly, Ixchel's role in birthing suggests the connection with the cycles and phases of the Moon. In most human cultures, and of course in astrology, both fertility and gestation are subject to lunar rhythms. The sacred astrological calendar of 260 that was common to all ancient Mesoamerican cultures, the *tzolkin*, was thought to be the number of days in nine lunar months, and therefore the measure of gestation. The tzolkin divided by 9 gives a month of 28.9 days, a figure that lies between the sidereal period of the Moon of 27.3 days and the synodic month of 29.5 days.

Ixchel was portrayed as a scary goddess. She wore a serpent headress, had crossed bones on her skirt, and had claws instead of hands. Myths of Ixchel are scarce. One has her as the wife of the creator god Itzamna, with whom she had thirteen sons. Two of these sons then created the world. It was told that if humans upset Ixchel, she could get very grumpy and bring rainstorms. In some accounts, Ixchel is said to have invented weaving, was a patroness of divination and possibly the goddess of the sweatbath. In the Yucatan, women would travel long distances to Cozumel and Isla de Mujeres, today very popular tourist destinations, to seek her help with fertility problems. These two islands were once the location of many shrines and temples with images of Ixchel, but very little of these survive today. Women seeking help from Ixchel would paddle small canoes over the ocean waters to these island, exposing themselves to the dangers of the elements. Ixchel seems to have been a counterpart and predecessor to the earth goddess Toci of the Aztecs, the grandmother goddess. Toci (toe-see), known as "Mother of the Gods" and "Heart of the Earth," was the patroness of the sweatlodge and was associated with medicines and curing.

Aztec Moon Deity—Metzli/Tecciztecatl

Another Aztec goddess, Coyolxauhqui (koy-ole-shay-huh-kee), which means "golden bells," may have been a Moon goddess. She was a daughter of the horrifying Aztec mother goddess Coatlicue, but she led her siblings in an attack on their mother to end what they feared was a dangerous pregnancy. It gets even stranger. Huitzilopochtli, the principal Aztec god, who was in Coatlicue's womb, bursts out of the womb in full war gear launching an attack on his siblings, most of whom he killed. Coyolxauhqui he dismembered, but he threw her head into the sky to become the Moon and to comfort his mother, who could see her every night.

In Mesoamerican mythologies, the gods and goddesses take many forms. The Moon was not always female. Among the Aztecs, Metztli (mets-tull-ee) was a male god of the Moon, and by association, the night. He is generally assumed to be the same as Tecciztecatl (teh-chees-tay-caw-tull), who played a role in the creation of the Fifth Sun (see below). Tecciztecatl was a very ancient Moon god, the son of the water gods Tlaloc and Chalchiuhtlicue. His story is one of the best-known myths of the Toltecs and Aztecs and plays a major role in the creation of the present world, the Fifth Sun.

The story of Tecciztecatl begins at the end of the previous age, the Fourth Sun. The previous creations, called "Suns," are depicted in the central part of the famous Aztec calendar stone, the "piedra del sol." Each of these four creations had been brought into being and ruled by one of the great gods—Quetzalcoatl, Tezcatlipoca, Tlaloc, and Ehecatl—and in each creation, the ruling god bore the burden of being the physical Sun that brought life to the world. Each creation produced a world with humans, but each of the four came to an end because the gods were not satisfied with the people they had created. How to make humans properly was the great problem of the gods and after four tries, they were discouraged. Then Quetzalcoatl, along with his twin Xolotl, boldly descended to the underworld, where they tricked the god of death and retrieved the sacred bones of the ancestors. Back in the world, Quetzalcoatl ground up the bones and mixed them with corn and his own blood, a recipe that finally made acceptable human beings. But there remained the task of being the Sun. Quetzalcoatl had already carried this burden in a previous creation and couldn't do it again. He called the gods to a meeting at Teotihuacan, the great ancient city of Mexico, to settle the matter. After meeting, it was decided that the future and possibly last creation, which now has proper humans, will have to come about as the result of a ritual sacrifice. Two gods are chosen for this cosmic transformation: Tecciztecatl and Nanauatl (nah-nay-hoo-a-tull).

First the gods make a big fire, which burns for four days to reach a sufficient level of heat. Tecciztecatl was a rich and haughty god. He attempted to jump into the fire and make his sacrifice, but he became fearful and failed. Four more times he tried but still failed because the heat of the fire was so strong. By now the other gods were getting very frustrated with the lack of progress on this fifth creation, and so they asked for the poor and diseased Nanauatl to be the first sacrifice. Nanauatl closed his eyes to control his fear and jumped into the flames on his first try. When Tecciztecatl saw that Nanauatl had jumped, he felt shame and jumped in after him. Nothing happened right away, but eventually two large orbs appeared in the sky, the embodiments of

Nanauatl and Tecciztecatl. But the gods were troubled because the fearful Tecciztecatl was glowing exactly the same as Nanauatl. They perceived this as unjust and decided something had to be done about it—so one of the gods took a rabbit and threw it at the orb that was Tecciztecatl. This caused a loss of brilliance in the orb, and the rabbit left a mark on face of the disk. So Nanauatl became the Sun and Tecciztecatl became the Moon, and the Moon still has the mark of a rabbit on it.

But the story doesn't end there. Because the Sun still didn't move, the creation appeared to be a failure. The gods next decided that a larger sacrifice was needed—they all needed to die so that the Sun and Moon could move and humans could live. The great wind god Ehecatl then sacrificed all the gods, and made the Sun and Moon begin to move with a powerful wind. This story was told to remind humans that they need to repay the gods with their own sacrifices. This legend is interesting in that it locates the gods outside of the earth; they have no power in this world and exist somewhere else. To see them, one must use a magic mirror of polished obsidian. Only the presence of Ehecatl, the wind god, can be felt by the people of this world.

Mesoamerican Calendars

There was a sacred astrological calendar of Mesoamerica. It was, and still is, used like an almanac as a source for information on good and bad days, and for personal readings. There are twenty day-signs in this calendar that are much like the signs of the zodiac. One of them, the eighth sign, is Tochli, symbolized in the Aztec version of the calendar by a rabbit and ruled by the goddess Mayahuel, a goddess with four hundred breasts. She was also the goddess of the maguey plant from which the powerful alcoholic beverage pulque was made.

The astrological calendar has lunar periods built into its core structure. The 260 days of this calendar are divided into thirteen twenty-day periods (twenty day-signs) and also twenty thirteen-day periods (day numbers 1–13). Why thirteen? The *trecenca*, as the thirteen-day weeks are known in Spanish, probably reflect the astronomical fact that the Moon travels in one day the same distance that the Sun does in thirteen days: 13 degrees. In one day, the Moon travels about 13 degrees along the zodiac, but it takes the Sun thirteen days to cover the same distance. There is another 13:1 Moon/Sun ratio in astronomy—there are roughly thirteen lunar cycles in one solar cycle, that is, thirteen lunar months in one year.

We don't know for sure, but these correspondences were very likely noticed by ancient Mesoamerican astrologers, and they built it into their unique kind of astrology. The day sign and number were used as a means of locating personality types and each of them was like a zodiac sign. Each day of the 260-day year is numbered, beginning with 1 and going through 13, then repeating. Each day is also assigned one of twenty signs, which also run in a repeated pattern. Thus, each day has a unique number-sign combination. The trecenas each begin on a 1 day, and they are named for the number-sign that begins the period: 1 Crocodile, 1 Jaguar, 1 Deer, etc. The trecena that your birth date falls in is considered your "sign." It appears to be that these signs are descriptive of our lunar persona, the side of us that is feminine, reactive, and feeling.

The Pyramid of the Moon

Perhaps the greatest city of ancient Mesoamerica was Teotihuacan, the Aztecs' name for the "place where the gods come to earth." Here are three great pyramids, one for the Sun, one for Quetzalcoatl, and one for the Moon. The Moon pyramid is the second largest of the three. The pyramid of the Moon faces the immense Plaza of the Moon, from which extends the long Avenue of the Dead. This pyramid was built sometime between AD 200

and 450 but it covers a structure that is older than 200 BC. At about 150 feet, it is not as tall as the nearby pyramid of the Sun, but it is just as high because it was built on higher ground. It is also far more complex and elegant architecturally than the pyramid of the Sun. The association with the Moon has to do with the pyramid once being capped by a temple for the ancient goddess Chalchiuhtlicue, a goddess of water and probably of the Moon as well. Archeological investigations have found that the pyramid has undergone at least six reconstructions, and each new addition was larger and covered the previous structure. A tomb dedicated to Chalchiuhtlicue was discovered in 2007 that dated to the fourth stage of construction. It contained a human male sacrifice and skeletons of a wolf, jaguars, serpents, birds, and many other relics, including greenstone and obsidian figurines, ceremonial knives, and spear points. If you ever visit Teotihuacan, one of the greatest attractions in all of Mexico, be sure to climb the pyramid of the Moon and take in the incredible view of what was once the world's biggest city in a dry basin surrounded by mountains.

For Further Reading

Burland, C. A. *The Gods of Mexico*. New York: G.P. Putnam's Sons, 1967.

Duran, Fray Diego. *The Book of the Gods and the Rites and the Ancient Calendar.* Trans. and ed. by F. Horcasitas and D. Heyden. Norman, OK: University of Oklahoma Press, 1971.

Markman, Roberta H., and Peter T. Markman. *The Flayed God*. San Francisco: Harper Collins, 1992.

Miller, Mary and Karl Taube. *The Gods and Symbols of Ancient Mexico and the Maya*. London: Thames and Hudson, 1993.

Sahagun, Fray Bernardino de. *Florentine Codex: General History of the the Things of New Spain,* Books 4 and 5. Trans. C. E. Dibble and A. J. O. Anderson. Ogden, UT: University of Utah Press, 1957.

Scofield, Bruce, and Angela Cordova. *The Aztec Circle of Destiny*. St. Paul, MN: Llewellyn Publications, 1988.

Scofield, Bruce. *Signs of Time—An Introduction to Mesoamerican Astrology*. Amherst, MA: One Reed Publications, 1994.

About the Author

Bruce Scofield is a practicing astrologer who has maintained a private practice as an astrological consultant and conference speaker for over forty years. He is the author of seven books and hundreds of articles on astrology. He has served on the education committee of the National Council for Geocosmic Research since 1979 and was that organization's national education director between 1998 and 2003. He holds a master's degree in history and a Ph.D. in geosciences, and currently teaches at Kepler College and at the University of Massachusetts. Bruce Scofield and Barry Orr maintain a website, www.onereed.com, that contains articles and an online calculation program on Mesoamerican (Maya and Aztec) astrology.

2011 © Miroslav Ferkuniak. Image from BigStockPhoto.com

Mother Moon:
Parenting with Astrology

by Amy Herring

> *Making the decision to have a child is momentous. It is to decide*
> *forever to have your heart go walking around outside your body.*
> —Elizabeth Stone

The Moon in one's chart has traditionally been said to represent the mother, and the Sun (or sometimes Saturn) represents the father. That may have been true when the roles of mother and father were traditionally and rigidly carried out, where the mother is the nurturing, overbearing one and the father is the distant disciplinarian. However, in modern astrology, it can be much more effective to think of the Moon as representative of our primary nurturers, be they male or female.

The Moon's parenting role in your chart goes beyond even representing the primary nurturer, however. To look at the personality and disposition of our primary nurturer, it's best to go to the source and simply look at Mom or Dad's chart! What the Moon in your chart reveals is not just your own nurturing style but *how you actually received or did not receive your parents' love and care.* Our natal Moon reflects us both as child and as parent, since we are both. It shows us how the messages of love, trust, and shelter landed in our hearts (or didn't, as the case may be). One person's show of love can be another person's feeling of smothering or neglect, for example, simply because of vastly different styles in emotional communication and what sorts of things build or break down trust for each individual.

The Moon's role in parenting is a two-way street. In a parent's chart, it represents our instinctual nurturing style, the ways we demonstrate love and affection for our child, and how we protect them, as well as what we feel we most need to protect them from. In a child's chart, the Moon represents the most direct ways they can receive the message that they are loved, safe, and accepted.

Mother Moon Signs

The following describes how you can nurture your child best according to their Moon sign through some basic, bottom-line statements that get right to the heart of your child's most fundamental needs. What builds or breaks their trust? What makes them feel happy or hurt? How do they handle their own feeling and the feeling of others? What is their instinctual defense when they are feeling hurt or scared? These things are primarily Moon questions.

If your child's Moon is in **Aries**, they like to live big and feel big. They are learning about initiative independence, namely in their ability to explore and conquer the world around them! Some children tend to exhibit fearless, daredevil qualities, while other children hold back—this typical Aries quality is very dependent on the rest of the chart, but the truth in either case is that Aries

Moon children need to test themselves and the world around them. Therefore, it's important for an Aries Moon child not to be overprotected to the point where they can't trust their instincts.

Like all fire signs, they tend to be rather playful and may enjoy good-natured teasing and physical play—anything from play wrestling with their parents or siblings to organized sports. Physical expression is also a great way for them to work out their feelings, especially when they're stuck and having difficulty expressing the more sensitive emotions. Their blood runs hot, figuratively speaking, so they can be easy to rile up but can also easily release energy. It's not good for them to stay pent up for too long. Watch out for hurt or fearful feelings leaking out in other ways, such as irritability or combativeness; these can be a sign they are having difficulty expressing the real problem.

If your child's Moon is in **Taurus**, he or she is going to be most comforted by a sense of stability and routine. They like to know what to expect so they can count on it. They can do well with change provided that they know what's coming and can be given ample time to get accustomed to the new idea, otherwise they are likely to get cranky because they're feeling afraid.

Taurus Moons don't like to be rushed, whether it's dealing with change or simply getting out the door in the mornings. The more they are rushed, the more likely they are to drag their feet. They can be a master of passive resistance; their stubbornness knows no bounds and is their primary defense when they are feeling hurt or scared. Gentle and persistent encouragement can go a long way when they are being introduced to a new idea, whether it's new food, a new school, or a new home.

A Taurus Moon child tends to have a fairly even temperament and can be quite content most of the time. These are the babies that sleep through the night early on and don't make much fuss (unless other factors in the chart say otherwise). They can be quite cuddly and sweet and love lots of lazy time with their families.

If your child's Moon is in **Gemini**, they will want stimulation and change, yet routine is still reassuring for any child so that they can feel they have some control over their world. Therefore, the stimulation and change that Gemini loves may need to come not in the form of a chaotic schedule but in a variety of things to engage their attention. They love a good puzzle, whether it's an actual board puzzle, a video game, or even taking apart mechanical devices. They love to take things apart and find out how they work. Gemini Moons are born with natural curiosity that will continue far into adulthood, and if properly fed, grow into a life-long love of learning.

Typically, a Gemini Moon likes to chatter to those they feel comfortable with; it's a good way for a Gemini Moon to bond and feel like they are being heard, as though what they say—and more importantly, what they think—matters to those they love. Listening and asking questions with sincere interest is a great way to gain a Gemini Moon child's trust. They will probably ask more than their fair share of questions because they are on a quest for information, and this can be especially true when they are feeling vulnerable, since knowledge helps them feel secure.

If your child's Moon is in **Cancer**, you have a tender, kind, and sensitive soul in your family who will feel nurtured by the full traditional mommy treatment: hugs and kisses when they scrape their knee, warm blankies, and after-school snacks. Being hugged, touched, and held by someone they trust is some of the deepest comfort.

They tend to be protective of themselves and when they've been hurt, they typically need to retreat. At the same time, they also need to know that they are not being ignored or abandoned by you when they do. Their tender natures can make it difficult for them to bounce back quickly from emotional wounding. It can be difficult for them to talk about their feelings, even though they have a lot of them, so they may have a tendency to sulk or give the silent treatment as a way to cope until they feel it's safe to come out and express their feelings.

Cancer Moon children are very loving and are drawn instinctively to creatures that seem to need tender loving care. They love to take care of others, whether it's the family pet, younger siblings, or a stuffed animal. Unlike fire sign Moons, Cancer does not typically like teasing or sarcasm; they have gentle natures, so sincerity and kindness are how they build trust for others.

If your child's Moon is in **Leo**, they have a creative and expressive heart, and they want to show it to you. They love to perform when they feel like they have an audience they can trust to appreciate them, whether they're hamming it up with their jokes or showing you their artwork. Nurturing their creativity by demonstrating your interest and praise is a great way to build trust with a Leo Moon child. They can be hurt easily when they are ignored or shamed for wanting so much attention.

Teaching a Leo Moon child to have confidence and self-appreciation while maintaining humility and an awareness of others is challenging. They tend to get caught up in the drama of their emotional experience and can lose perspective of their effect on those around them. Leo is the archetype of the king or queen, and you will see it early on in your prince or princess. They don't appreciate being treated like a child who is not as important as the adults. They can be very demanding if they feel they are not getting the attention or consideration they deserve and can also be territorial of what they feel is theirs (the king must have his kingdom to rule!)

If your child's Moon is in **Virgo**, they are nurtured not by unlimited freedom, but by rules, limits, and clear boundaries and expectations, so they can feel as if they know how to succeed in meeting those expectations. Your Virgo Moon child may enjoy things like chore sticker charts or other ways of measuring the accomplishment of their goals.

A Virgo Moon child has a deep need to feel useful and will often thrive when they are presented with opportunities to be helpful. They will go the extra mile for someone they love. They tend to like to keep themselves busy, so creative projects, especially when they can make something tangible and practical like jewelry, sewing, or mechanics can be very rewarding for them.

Virgo Moon children are very sensitive to criticism because they are deeply motivated by getting things right, so patience and sincere compassion go a long way. When they get upset at something they perceive as a failure, they can feel nurtured by a parent's acknowledgement of what was done incorrectly without making it about a personal flaw in themselves. This way the Virgo Moon child can learn to try again without feeling ashamed about not getting something right. They can sometimes be reluctant to try new things out of a fear of not doing it right.

If your child's Moon is in **Libra**, they need emotional equilibrium in their home and their inner life without a lot of unresolved stress or fighting. Their temperament tends to be rather even and genial, so they can get along well with others and in fact often prefer to have a playmate rather than playing alone. A Libra Moon child has a strong sense of fairness. They are master negotiators and tend to respond well to the "if/then" parenting technique (*if* you clean your room, *then* you can watch your show on TV). Don't be surprised if they beat you at your own game, though, and start finding loopholes in the negotiated deals they agreed to a moment ago!

Libra Moons are natural peacemakers—wanting everyone to "just get along"—so much that they can have a hard time revealing their own feelings of anger or sadness, especially if they are afraid of not being liked or loved because of those feelings. They sometimes hold their feelings in too long as a result, so good examples of respectful and loving conflict resolution in the home are important.

If your child's Moon is in **Scorpio**, they can seem rather intense and extreme in their moods. There is an emotional depth to them that can be difficult to handle at a young age, for both you and them. They dive deeply into their emotions, and whatever they are feeling can be magnified and consuming.

A Scorpio Moon child will have a sort of sixth sense about things and can recognize when there's more going on than meets the eye, even if they don't quite know what the real story is. This quality tends to make them rather good at and interested in mysteries, whether they are of the Sherlock Holmes fictional variety or researching odd subjects on the Internet. They have a tenacity that makes them obsessed with having an answer once their interest has been piqued.

One of the surprising ways to nurture a Scorpio Moon is to mitigate the urge to protect them by withholding information from them. Because they are already more observant to the undercurrents of the interactions between people, they will appreciate you being as honest as you can about what they observe, therefore validating what they perceive. Their trust is most easily broken by lies, even well-intentioned ones. Yet, you will need to walk the fine line between truth-telling and not going too far past their natural innocent state as a child and what they can handle.

If your child's Moon is in **Sagittarius**, they need lots of space and freedom to play and run, because they are off and running to explore the world. They have a natural enthusiasm and optimism, and they tend to bounce back easily when life trips them up. They can be quite restless and always in search of their next great adventure. As a result, they don't tend to respond well to overprotectiveness or encouragements of caution and restraint. Teaching them to think before they leap is a challenge because of their inherent optimism that "things will work out." They tend to live in the euphoria of what they are experiencing at any moment and don't always think ahead in logical steps.

A Sagittarius Moon child will tend to trust others who have a smile on their face more than a frown. They tend to like to keep things light. They may have a harder time understanding when others feel low since they bounce back more easily than others do. They don't often act very seriously, so getting them to settle down or confront them about a problem can be a challenge.

If your child's Moon is in **Capricorn**, they may be a child but their eyes reveal a wise, old soul. They are inherently a little more reserved and mature than most children may seem, with a serious disposition. They have a great deal of independence and enjoy being self-sufficient, often happy to play contentedly on their own and do simple things for themselves when they are able.

A Capricorn Moon child tends to be very responsible and can be vulnerable to taking things too seriously and making themselves responsible for too much at an early age. While allowing them their independence is nurturing for them, they will need more guidance than they appear to need or want. As independent as they seem, their trust is damaged when they feel like they don't

have an adult to count on or look up to in their life, which can be a challenge since they are already so naturally mature.

While all children cry sometimes, a Capricorn Moon child doesn't tend to get very emotional in general and prefers to remain in control of themselves. Emotions can be very unnerving and make them feel out of control, so they may try to withhold how they're feeling or just push past it quickly. They can benefit from the example of being compassionate and soft with one's self, taking the time to deal with feelings and not be embarrassed.

If your child's Moon is in **Aquarius**, prepare to be surprised regularly. One of the things an Aquarius Moon child is learning is to appreciate their individuality. However, this is not an easy lesson, especially when other children can be so critical of differences and adults are always trying to (in good will) train children in the appropriate ways of being and behaving. Emphasizing the value of uniqueness and being true to yourself can be very nurturing for this child, especially if you live by example.

To develop individuality, they need to be able to emotionally "hold their own," so they tend to have quite a contradictory nature, both internally with themselves and in their interactions with others, especially authority figures or those who would tell them what to do or how to behave. Aquarian Moons are delightfully surprising and refreshing in this respect, although it can be a bit exasperating as a parent! Their emotional reactions to things tend to be more objective, seeming to be processed as thoughts rather than feelings, and observations rather than emotional experiences. They don't tend to be very mushy or demonstrative with their feelings.

If your child's Moon is in **Pisces**, they have a big heart and a big imagination. Creative and fantasy play such as dress up and costumes or reading can be favorite pastimes. When they play, they often get lost in their own little world for hours. *Lost* can be the operative word here, because it can be very difficult to keep a Pisces Moon child on your level, where schedules and commitments are more solid things than the fluctuations of their moods. They may tend to daydream and dawdle a lot.

Pisces Moon children are quite sensitive and gentle at heart. This child's style is not combative or confrontational, so they don't respond well to being bombarded by the Harsh Truth of Life and will need to be gently but firmly made to understand some of the realities of living in a world with commitments and consequences. Their sensitivity also makes them very empathetic, easily tuning into the emotions of the people around them and responding to them, sometimes drawing emotions of others onto themselves (such as can be seen when a crying baby sets other babies to crying). If a Pisces Moon child gets too wrapped up in what they are feeling, they need help to diffuse the emotion and settle themselves before they can easily talk about what happened or what they need.

About the Author
See page 314 for Amy Herring's complete bio.

Relationships and Your Natal Lunar Phase

by April Elliott Kent

When I began studying astrology, I imagined that sexy Venus and passionate Mars held the secrets to understanding love. After all, most youthful dreams of future soul mates feature torrid tangos of passion and enthrallment. The notion of ending up in a relationship like Mom and Dad's—so little kissing, so much bill-paying!—tends to fill idealistic young hearts with horror. And yet, more often than not, when we finally settle down into a committed partnership, we find ourselves reenacting much of what we saw our parents doing in their relationship.

Decades later, a career spent studying the astrology of relationships (not to mention seventeen years of marriage) has taught me that there are really two different narratives that underscore every romantic partnership. One, driven by the passionate eroticism of sexual chemistry, certainly does seem to be reflected in the astrology of Venus and Mars. But the other, a quieter tale of compatible temperaments and united purpose, seems better illustrated by the astrological connection between the Sun and Moon.

Of course, there is no one-size-fits-all definition of an ideal partnership. Some couples thrive on friction, while others crave ease. Some like to flirt, others prefer to fight. The lunar phase at your birth, representing the relationship between the Sun (masculine) and the Moon (feminine), describes the partnership style that comes naturally to you. The rapport between the Sun and Moon in your birth chart is a dance of the lights, illuminating the personal relationship fairy tale that lives in your subconscious, a story drawn from observing your parents, reading books, and absorbing messages from television shows and movies. Understanding your natal lunar phase can help you understand why you keep having the same kind of relationships again and again—and how to make relationship choices that are truly satisfying.

How to Find the Lunar Phase at Your Birth

Finding the Moon's current phase is easy: just look up in the sky! Locating your natal lunar phase, however, is a little more complicated. Fortunately, many computerized birth charts include your natal lunar phase. (If you'd like to access a free online resource to get this information, follow the instructions at the end of this article.)

If you have a copy of your birth chart but it doesn't show your natal lunar phase, here's a relatively easy way to find it. First, find the sign opposite your Sun sign. Now, move around the circle counterclockwise until you reach your natal Moon. If the Moon lies between the opposition point and the Sun, then you were born between the Full Moon and New Moon. If your finger has to pass over your Sun (moving counterclockwise) before it reaches the Moon, you were born between the New Moon and the Full

Moon. Combine this information with the natal aspect (if any) between your Sun and Moon to find your natal Lunar Phase in the table below. For example, if you were born between the New and Full Moons and there is a trine aspect between the Sun and Moon in your birth chart, you were born during the first quarter Moon. Remember that the movement around the chart is counterclockwise.

Phase	Begins When the Moon Is...	Sun-Moon Aspects (Degrees)
New Moon	0° ahead of Sun	conjunction (0), semisextile (30)
Crescent Moon	45° ahead of Sun	semisquare (45), sextile (60)
Second quarter Moon	90° ahead of Sun	square (90), trine (120)
Gibbous Moon	135° ahead of Sun	sesqui-square (135), quincunx (150)
Full Moon	180° ahead of Sun	opposition (180)
Disseminating Moon	225° ahead of Sun (*135° behind Sun*)	quincunx (150), sesqui-square (135), trine (120)
Fourth quarter Moon	270° ahead of Sun (*90° behind Sun*)	square (90), sextile (60)
Balsamic Moon	315° ahead of Sun (*45° behind Sun*)	semisquare (45), semisextile (30)

New Moon (Moon 0 degrees ahead of Sun)

Born at the New Moon, your ideal relationship is one in which each partner is completely in the other's corner—in which each supports the other's goals unconditionally and will move heaven and Earth to see that they are reached. If the Sun and Moon are 30–45 degrees apart or in different signs, your interests and temperaments will probably be quite different, but you still need to feel that you and your partner are one another's greatest boosters.

Boasting one of Hollywood's most enduring marriages (to actress Joanne Woodward), actor Paul Newman was born at the New Moon. "Joanne has always given me unconditional support in all my choices and endeavors," Newman was quoted as saying, "and that includes my race car driving, which she deplores. To me, that's love." Likewise, First Lady Nancy Reagan, born just after a New Moon in Cancer, was fiercely protective of her husband, President Ronald Reagan, both during his political career and during his long illness from Alzheimer's disease.

If you were born at the New Moon, you will need to guard against the extremes of codependency in relationships, or avoiding relationships altogether! What you seek is the elusive, happy medium: a relationship in which each person is whole and independent, yet completely devoted to (and respectful of) the other.

Crescent Moon (Moon 45 degrees ahead of Sun)

Born at the Crescent Moon, relationships feel most natural to you when they're challenging and stimulating. If your Sun and Moon are close to the 45 degree semisquare that begins this phase, the friction of living alongside another person—like the irritant that stimulates a mollusk to produce a pearl—forces you to strive for achievement and self-improvement. If you were born near the waxing sextile (60 degrees), you like relationships with those who are enough like you in temperament for you to feel comfortable, but just different enough to keep you interested.

Both types of Crescent Moon phase people seem to thrive on togetherness. Chef Julia Child, born at the waxing semisquare, was described as being determined to maintain, "that lovely intertwining of life, mind, and soul that a good marriage is." "We are a team," she often said of her husband. "We do everything together."

Paul McCartney, born at the waxing sextile, had a long and famously close relationship with his wife, Linda. As McCartney told *People* magazine, "The only eleven days we ever did not spend the night together was when I got put in jail in Japan for pot. That's quite amazing."

Second Quarter Moon (Moon 90 degrees ahead of Sun)

Born at the second quarter Moon, you're direct, action-oriented, and at your best with a partner who approaches life in the same way. If you were born close to the waxing Sun/Moon square (90 degree), you gravitate toward partners who are temperamentally quite different from you, or who move at a different pace. The resulting friction provides a powerful catalyst for achievement (and sometimes for arguments).

Elizabeth Edwards, late estranged wife of former U.S. vice presidential hopeful John Edwards, was born at the waxing square. A woman of formidable intellect and determination, she was a trusted political advisor to her husband, perhaps because she was known to disagree with her husband publicly if she felt strongly on an issue.

If you were born near the waxing Sun/Moon trine (120 degrees), you prefer a partner who is as dynamic as you are and who moves at your speed. You'll dash through life together as though it were a relay race, passing the baton back and forth and spurring each other on to great achievement. Bandleader and television pioneer Desi Arnaz was born with a waxing Sun/Moon trine, and while their marriage had its problems, his business partnership with wife Lucille Ball changed the face of television.

Gibbous Moon (Moon 135 degrees ahead of Sun)

Those born during the Gibbous Moon phase don't expect relationships to be easy. If your Sun and Moon are close to the 135 degree sesquisquadrate aspect, one of the most important relationship lessons you'll learn is how to recognize the moment when persisting with a difficult relationship has become the equivalent of flogging a dead horse.

If you're born with the Sun and Moon close to the 150 degree quincunx, compromise and adjustment present critical challenges in your relationships. Prince Charles, born at the waxing Sun/

Moon quincunx, reportedly married Princess Diana as a compromise. He had reached "marrying age," and her background and appearance made her an appropriate choice. But the temperaments of a middle-aged man and a bride just out of her teens were ultimately too different to make the marriage a success.

Eventually Prince Charles was free to marry his old flame, Camilla Parker-Bowles. Even then, however, compromises and adjustments had to be made. Upon the death of Pope John Paul II, their ceremony had to be rescheduled to avoid a conflict with the funeral. The groom's parents did not attend the civil ceremony, possibly because of the sensitivity of the Queen's position as Supreme Governor of the Church of England. And the bride has chosen to be addressed as Duchess of Cornwall rather than Princess of Wales, a title closely associated with Charles' first wife.

Full Moon (Moon 180 ahead of Sun)

If you were born during the Full Moon phase, relationships are more than important to you—they're an essential part of how you learn about yourself. Your desire to find balance in all relationships can propel you—with varying degrees of success—into partnerships with those of opposite temperament, or who seem like surprising choices of the "odd couple" variety. Opposites attract and can certainly be complementary; but because you're extremely sensitive to the moods of others and often unconsciously adopt them, it's important that you surround yourself with close partners whose best traits reinforce your own.

For some Full Moon phase people, there may be a sense of being "on stage" in your relationships, of playing a role; in the case of entertainers, this is sometimes literally the case. Roseanne Barr, born during the Full Moon phase, parlayed her real life as a housewife into a stand-up comedy routine and enormously popular television series. That marriage didn't last, but her role as a "Domestic Goddess" certainly did!

Full Moon people may also serve as a sort of mirror that reflects the true nature or condition of their partner, or even of their partner's family. Diana, Princess of Wales was also born at the Full Moon. In her marriage to Prince Charles, Diana performed the role of princess to near perfection, looking the part at state occasions and producing two sons—"an heir and a spare"—to the throne. But she claimed she was hurt by her husband's infidelity, and when neglected, a Full Moon person can turn rebellious. Diana's modern expecations and defiant nature turned into a public-relations nightmare for the royal family. Even her untimely death compelled Buckingham Palace to defend itself against public disapproval over its handling of the situation.

Disseminating (Moon 225 degrees ahead of Sun)

The Disseminating phase is similar to the Gibbous: both include the sesquiquadrate and quincunx aspects between the Sun and Moon, but the Disseminating phase also includes a waning trine. If you're born with the Sun/Moon quincunx during this phase, you may feel wary of or even trapped in relationships, especially when you're young. The Disseminating phase symbolizes the urge to spread one's words and ideas far and wide, and that can cause problems in conventional relationships. In fact, for some—like many-partnered Warren Beatty, born at the waning sesqui-square—this can be a Goldilocks and the Three Bears lunar phase, as you cycle through a succession of partners who seem promising but end up being not quite right. Of course, the flaws or weaknesses we perceive in our partners usually reveal more about us than about them.

If you're born close to the waning trine, you may find it easier to eventually settle down in a contented, comfortable partnership—sometimes (like much-married actress Elizabeth Taylor) more than one! For some born with this aspect, simply finding a partner can feel a bit like the relief of putting salve on an itchy rash. But if you've come to terms with your own questing nature and chosen wisely, it can also be the relief of discovering the *right* partner—one who finds the world as fascinating as you do, and wants to spend life exploring it with you.

Fourth Quarter Moon (Moon 270 degrees ahead of Sun)

Born at the fourth quarter phase, you need a partner who supports your enormous ambition and can offer understanding, patience, and practical skills to help you. Yours is a restless, driven soul, and it takes the right kind of person to live comfortably with someone who is always somewhat dissatisfied with the status quo. Eleanor Roosevelt, born at the waning square (90 degrees), is best remembered as the formidable wife of one of America's greatest presidents. In her own right, however, she was an independent and politically adept author, speaker, and crusader for human and civil rights.

If you were born closer to the Sun/Moon sextile (60 degrees), there is a greater emphasis on conversation, ideas, and friendship with your partner. You seek, above all, a partner who can make you laugh—and who "gets" you. Oscar-winner Meryl Streep, born close to a waning sextile, has been happily married to sculptor Don Gummer since 1978. Of her marriage, she has said, "My husband understands the compulsion to create things. With somebody who had a regular job, I think it might have been harder to translate those creative impulses and the need to satisfy them ..."

Balsamic Phase (Moon 315 degrees ahead of Sun)

The Balsamic lunar phase is the Moon's dark time. It is symbolic of our need for rest and our connection to the psychic and spiritual realms. For those born during the Balsamic phase, relationships may feel karmically charged; a series of relationships, or even just one that is characterized by emotional drama and artistic expression, may be a way of tying up karmic loose ends. And because the Balsamic phase can be connected to illness, health issues may also play an important role in your relationships.

Painter Frida Kahlo was born during the Balsamic phase. Chronic pain and other health problems were a motif that ran throughout her life and art. She married painter Diego Rivera—twice—in passionate but tumultuous unions marked by both partners' infidelity. Yet Kahlo and Rivera also inspired and supported one another, producing some of their most acclaimed works while together.

Born at the waning semisextile, Betty Ford enjoyed a long and generally happy marriage to President Gerald Ford. Along the way, however, she suffered a nervous breakdown, an addiction to pills and alcohol, and a highly public struggle with breast cancer. She's perhaps best remembered for her frank public revelations, supported by her husband, about her recovery from addiction, which prompted her to co-found the famous Betty Ford Center for alcohol and drug rehabilitation.

Conclusion

The lunar phases are a dance of light, the Sun and Moon's elaborate *pas de deux* of anima and animus. Each of us is an amalgam of both proactive (Sun) and reactive (Moon) energy, and our closest relationships reflect both sides of our natures. The soli-lunar ballet calls us to the barre from the moment of birth, outlining the steps we need to learn and suggesting the shape and movements of our ideal dance partner.

Your lunar phase relationship style may be an easy waltz, a complicated reel, or a jubilant fox-trot. Whatever style is right for you, I wish you joy and fortune in finding a partner who can match your steps and, above all, help you enjoy the dance.

To Obtain Your Natal Lunar Phase

Visit http://www.astro.com/cgi/genchart.cgi?&lang=&gm=a2 and select Other Charts > Lunar Phases Fertility Calendar from the dropdown menu. Click the "Click here to show the chart" button. Enter your birth data as a guest or create a registered profile for future visits, then press "Continue."

The Lunar Phases Fertility Calendar appears. The natal Phase of the Moon is shown to the right of the birth time. Phase of the Moon 297.53, for example, means the Moon is 297.53 degrees ahead of the Sun, which is a last quarter Moon.

All celebrity birth data from Astrodatabank: http://www.astro.com/astro-databank.

About the Author

April Elliott Kent, a professional astrologer since 1990, graduated from San Diego State University with a degree in Communication. Her book Star Guide to Weddings *was published by Llewellyn in 2008. April's astrological writing has also appeared in* The Mountain Astrologer *(USA) magazine, the online journals MoonCircles and Beliefnet, and Llewellyn's Moon Sign Book (2005–2011). April, who was born at the last quarter Moon phase with a Sun-Moon sextile, lives in San Diego with her husband and their two cats. Her website is http://www.bigskyastrology.com.*